BEDTIME STORIES

ADVENTURES IN THE LAND OF
SINGLE-FATHERHOOD

TREY ELLIS

MODERN TIMES

Library of Congress Cataloging-in-Publication Data

Ellis, Trey.
    Bedtime stories : adventures in the land of single-fatherhood / Trey Ellis.
      p.   cm.
    ISBN-13 978-1-59486-529-9 hardcover
    ISBN-10 1-59486-529-9 hardcover
    1. Ellis, Trey. 2. Novelists, American—20th century—Biography.
3. Novelists, American—21st century—Biography. 4. Single fathers—Biography. I. Title.
    PS3555.L617Z46 2008
    813'.54—dc22
    [B]
                                                     2007047038

Distributed to the trade by Macmillan

2   4   6   8   10   9   7   5   3   1   hardcover

To Chet and Ava, the centers of my world[1]

---

[1] And no, I still won't get us a pet. I already have a puppy and a kitten.

Acknowledgments

For all the pushes in the right directions and the helping hands without which we would never have made it, I need to thank Lucia, Nora, Shirley, Mary Anne, Andy, Mike, Sheila, Bruce, Helen, Steve, Dominique, Kasi, Vondie, Howard, Caroline, Yule, Ursula, Tony, Helen, Sam, Eleanor, Billy, Lewis, Jennifer, Jesse, Brett, and Paul. I'd also like to thank Dan Jones and my agent, Lisa Bankoff, for believing in the worth of our story from the beginning. Finally, I will be forever grateful to my editor, Leigh Haber, not only for her tireless support of this tale but also her patience and prowess in improving its shape.

PROLOGUE

SURE, I GOT SOME pity right after she left us, but not nearly as much as I deserved. You'd have thought that all those moms at my daughter's preschool would have been lining up with casseroles for a newly single dad like me, but no. After I put Ava and her baby brother, Chet, to bed, more often than not I ended up either microwaving a Healthy Choice hospital-quality frozen dinner or nuking whatever was left from what Lucia, Chet's nanny, had fixed him for lunch that day, washing it all down with a few juice boxes (they're so small!) on the couch in front of HBO. *Taxicab Confessions* is one of my favorite shows, with cameras hidden all over the back of a taxi giving us a glimpse into the real lives of late-night drunken tourists. I often fantasize about having cameras installed all over my home so people can see how I live, see what an attentive father I am. Over the course of the season, viewers would also discover the other hurdles I've vaulted: my cranky kidneys, the deaths of my parents . . . It would become the breakout reality show of the season. In my fantasy, e-mailed (re)marriage proposals would soon be spamming my in-box.

BEDTIME STORIES: "DADDY! DADDY! COME QUICK!" (SEASON PREMIERE)

"Daddy! Daddy! Come quick!"

As fast as a fireman, and not yet fully conscious since it is 4:15 in the morning, I trip toward my kids' room while trying to hop into the legs of my sweatpants. Their bathroom light is on, and inside it looks like Aerosmith just stayed there: wet, unspooled toilet paper hanging from the medicine cabinet, an entire bottle of deliriously overpriced Mustela baby shampoo puddled on the toilet seat cover. My (almost) two-year-old son is standing in the middle of the wreckage looking confusedly at me. I only learn later, after interrogation, that his sister had to pee in the night and forgot to shut the bathroom door with the childproof plastic bulb over the knob. She then went back to bed, only to be awakened a little later by her brother's celebration. Why Chet was out of bed at four in the morning I don't know and never will. He still holds the pot of hair gel that he generously applied to all parts of his face and much of his hair. Devo had less product in their hair. Trying to wipe away the goop only applied it more evenly, so I gave him a warm bath, and by a little after five I was back in my bed, ready to be up again at seven to get Ava to preschool.

BEDTIME STORIES: CHET LEAVES A PRESENT (EPISODE FIVE)

I wake up to discover both kids naked and scampering happily around their room. They look like rare, almost mythical forest mammals that I feel privileged to be glimpsing in the wild. At first the vision compels me to smile. Then I start to wonder what has become of Chet's diaper and notice two little brown stains on his tiny bed. Not too disgusting. I've seen worse. A quick swipe with a wipe, a spritz with the Spray 'n Wash, and I pitch the sheets into the dirty clothes. The diaper itself I discover under his bed, miraculously immaculate.

I give the kids a bath, fearlessly washing, conditioning, and detangling Ava's dramatic mass of hair like a junior José Eber. Their naked splashings, Ava's queries—Daddy, why can't I marry Chetty when I grow up?—all make me feel like the luckiest parent in the whole wide world. Those boring, ordinary, two-parent households have to share indelible moments like this. I get to greedily hoard them for myself without having to compromise with a signifi-cant other who might feel that maybe kids shouldn't be encouraged to see who can burp the loudest or play Wiffle ball in the middle of the living room. In my house I am the tsar. Trey the Terrible.

I am smiling at these happy thoughts as I walk back into their bedroom. Suddenly I stop. Just next to my foot, on the carpet between an overturned baby stroller and a naked, headless black Ken doll with amazingly ripped abs, looms a mountain of turd nearly as large as my son.

I pull Chet out of the bathtub and bring him to the cairn of shit. I don't think he ever looked cuter.

Do not take your diaper off. Do not leave piles of crap all over the . . .

It is getting too complicated, so I midcourse correct to get back on message. Do not take your diaper off.

I haven't had a dog since I was five, but I have seen people training them, so I model my tone of voice on theirs.

Chet just smiles and nods, his thumb as always plugged into his mouth, his index finger hooking his nose.

"Mommy-Daddy, Mommy-Daddy."

That's what he called me when he first started talking, a little over a year after she left.

I love it. I loved it in the moment and I love the anecdote it instantly became. I imagine, thanks to my show, that all the world has witnessed me heroically cleaning up the crap and spraying carpet cleaner on the carpet; that all the world has observed that I haven't strangled my son, raised my voice, or even just slapped him around a little. I imagine I would be a shoo-in for Father of the Year. Being black wouldn't hurt my chances either, since American men of my race are more renowned for our absence than our presence.

I even fantasize an elaborate and televised ceremony, warm and funny speeches, my (feigned) embarrassment at all the attention. I imagine my kids at my side, spit-shined and radiating the pure joy of the well-parented child. Bill Clinton on behalf of the Children's Defense Fund gives me the award, as golden and as weighty as an Oscar.

Five years later I'm still waiting for that award. Instead, most nights, after giving the kids a bath, brushing their teeth, telling them a story, and singing them a song, a loneliness so great it threatened to swallow me whole would swell inside me. An episode of *24* or *The Sopranos* later, before going to bed myself, I would return to their room, reorient Ava on her bed, and pick Chet up off the carpet. He was too feral for a crib but flopped around too much to remain in his toddler bed, even with a guardrail, so I had moved his mattress to the floor. More nights than not I'd find him sleeping facedown on the carpet, sometimes as much as five feet from where I'd first laid him. I'd carefully work my arms under his warm, chubby body, and he'd squirm, groan, and smack his lips yet rarely wake up as I gently placed him back on his bed.

Sometimes I myself would lie down on the carpet, breathing in the warm silence of their room, so tempted to sleep there until they woke me in the morning.

The conversations are as I remembered them, as are the humiliations, the victories, and the diaper pail changes. Some of the names have been changed, but some haven't.

Mine is a true story, recounted as honestly as I dared.

1

I MET ANNA at a black bohemian soiree up in Harlem. Just
a few weeks before, I had been dizzyingly in love with a white, six-
foot-tall, Yale comparative literature PhD candidate and runway
model named Sally. We had friends in common, and she later confessed that as soon as she saw my hands, she knew that she wanted
them on her body. For a month Sally and I were intensely together;
then I went off on a long-planned trip to Europe, and when I came
back, she was back together with her old boyfriend, a former University of Michigan tailback. Since I was six I had grown up being
the only black kid in white neighborhoods, yet Sally was my first
white girlfriend. Actually, she was also only my third girlfriend
ever, even though I was twenty-five years old. I had been so pain-
fully nerdy all the way up through college that I had rarely mus-
tered the courage to let a woman know how I felt about her.

I had grown into a young novelist with a fantastic apartment on the Upper West Side that I had inherited three years

before when my dad died. Still, when Sally broke my heart, I instantly soured on the city and became itching to scram. Since I was dividing my writing time between novels and screenplays anyway, I decided to migrate to Santa Monica for the winter to allow my heart to heal.

In early January, a week before I was set to leave New York, my friend Greg Tate, writer, genius, and king of black bohemia, was throwing a big holiday party. I assumed I'd know everyone there, but just in case there was a girl I hadn't already asked out, I decided to dress up. The year was 1988, and I am horrified to inform you that dressing up for me back at that time consisted of putting on a houndstooth WilliWear jacket with Frankenstein-sized shoulder pads, black cowboy boots, and puffy, pleated black pants.

Moments after entering the party, my heart stopped. Not only I but all the guys in the room were whispering to their boys, *Where'd she come from?* Joan, a friend of mine, knowing my weakness for the fantastically beautiful, sidled up to me, but before she could even finish asking, Have you checked out that Lisa Bonet–type over ther—?

I assured her that this new girl was all that I would be thinking of that night.

In one evening I was determined to make up for my dreary adolescence, not to mention Sally's icy rejection, by getting this movie star's phone number.

I took a deep breath and was swaggering over to ask her to dance when suddenly one of her girlfriends intercepted me.

I hear you're from Hamden! I'm from Hamden too!

Hamden, Connecticut, is a suburb of New Haven and had been my home until my mother died when I was sixteen and my dad moved us to Manhattan. I knew this girl before me was my future wife's friend so I couldn't blow her off. (I actually called Anna my future wife in my head that night—but then again, I had said the same thing about a woman I'd glimpsed on the number-one train taking the subway earlier that evening.)

I watched with horror as an acquaintance of mine, the now-legendary saxophone player Steve Coleman, swooped Anna right onto the dance floor. I wanted to weep but forced myself to just nod and smile as Anna's friend went on and on about Dixwell Avenue and Hamden High School and did I know Cindy Covington, who apparently was on the track team. Anna and Steve danced through song after song, as my mood continued to sink. I was just about to give up and go home—I had packing to do anyway—when I saw Steve leave her to go get them drinks. My moral compass prevented me from taking advantage of the fact that my friend was at the bar—that would have been just wrong—but that didn't stop some young pretty boy who leaped right in and asked her to dance. When Steve returned to the dance floor, he tried not to look crushed as he held out her drink. She took it from him, but then turned right back to the new guy she was dancing with. Steve wilted and retreated.

Oh God, she's a cold-blooded killer, I remember thinking. Just my type. The good news was that I didn't know and instantly disliked this new guy she was dancing with, so I hung around the sidelines waiting for the song to end like a shark on a reef.

Finally, in the tiny gap of silence between Prince and James Brown, I asked her to dance and she said yes. My dancing is not nearly as bad as my basketball playing, but they are both definitely subpar for a brother, so after just one song, I lured her off the dance floor with the offer of another drink. Having learned from Steve's mistake, I insisted that she come with me to get it. Then for the next two hours I had her pinned in the hallway as I motor-mouthed my entire life history, name-dropping despicably, Eddie Murphy this, Spike Lee that, in general making a total ass of myself. I had rarely been in the same room with someone so beautiful, let alone one who was actually listening to me. When I finally let her get a word in, she told me that after graduating Wellesley, she had worked in Spain for two years and had just returned. A smart girl, a world traveler, and gorgeous. My head whirled. I had lived in Florence after graduation and had rarely met another black person who was as international as I liked to think I was. She said she might be going to Brazil next to teach English, and I lied that I might be going to Brazil too—who knew?—anything to see her again. But before long, reality started settling on me. I'd never see her again, but I also knew that I'd never forget her.

I'd like to kiss you.

Anna blushed sweetly and nodded yes. She was the lady, I was the tramp. I leaned down and gave her the chastest, driest little kiss.

That wasn't good enough; I have to have another, I told her.

Who was this suave Casanova in the boxy suit and cowboy boots? Nerdy Trey was dead and gone.

And I kissed her again, this time only a little better.

Her Wellesley girlfriends were itching to go home; Anna was the only one who had found somebody. I gave her my number and she left. I didn't dare ask for hers because the nerd in me was still skeptical that she would have given it up. As soon as the girls had left the party, my friends encircled me as if I'd just won a prizefight.

Two days later I drove across the country as planned, with Ben, one of my two best friends since the sixth grade, ready to see if I could live in Los Angeles. But I obsessed about Anna daily and cursed myself for not asking for her number. Three months later I was getting ready to drive back to New York when the friend subletting my place in New York called to tell me that some girl named Anna had left her number for me.

My heart rattled inside of me.

Give me the number; give it to me right now.

I was drunk, my friend said. I can't read my handwriting; the last number's either a nine or maybe a seven.

If it's the wrong number, I will literally tear you to pieces and feed you to rats.

I slammed down the phone and immediately dialed. A man answered.

Hello, sir, I said in my best Eddie Haskell voice. Is Anna there?

When she got on the phone, my heart seemed to splash life into every dry creek and box canyon in my body. It turned out she had just been in LA herself, had just gotten back, but was on her way to a little town in northern Japan to teach English for a year. Brazil hadn't worked out. I told her I was driving back to New York the next day and begged to see her before she left. She said she had to leave as soon as her visa came and that could be any day.

I drove vast stretches of the Southwest at 110 miles per hour. When I got back to Manhattan, she hadn't left yet so we met for dinner with two of her friends. I wanted her to myself so I could let her know how much I'd been thinking about her since those first two dry little kisses. Desperate to make my feelings known, I slipped my finger near her hand at the table's edge, and she curled hers around mine like a baby and then slipped our hands to her knee so no one would notice. When I saw she was blushing, I had to remind myself to breathe again.

The next night we had our first proper date, and somehow we started talking about birthdays. She went first.

I was born October 14.

Yeah, right.

What do you mean?

When I saw she was serious, I instantly got dizzy.

I was born October 14.

Stop lying!

I scrambled to dig my wallet out of my front pocket and shoved my driver's license at her.

Now let me see yours.

I don't have one.

She hadn't needed one in college or later in Madrid.

I teased her that I didn't believe her, but I was secretly surer than ever that I had finally found the person I'd spend the rest of my life with. While waiting for our tiramisu, I imagined putting our two kids to bed, a boy and a girl, and them clamoring for me to tell them yet again the story of how we'd first met.

Oh, Trey, not that old chestnut, Anna would complain, but she would smile and secretly enjoy the retelling as much as the kids did.

As perhaps you can tell by now, I am almost psychotically romantic and in fact had had this same fantasy about the three previous loves of my life.

Every day she called the Japanese consulate, and every day they said her visa would come any day now. We lived each day as if it would be our last together, and most days of the week she would stay over, only occasionally returning to her father's place in Jersey.

A week into our romance, we had just made love when she blurted out, I love y—. She bit her tongue before she could finish the sentence, but her eyes burned into mine to gauge my response.

I love you too.

I said it without hesitation. I'd wanted to say it after our first dinner.

By the time she left, three weeks later, I was already looking into getting a ticket to go visit. For two months in the summer, I wrote her almost every day and called her once a week. She was miserable in the little town of Fukushima, in the middle of nowhere, a few hours north of Tokyo by *shinkansen*, Japan's bullet trains. I was polishing my second novel and writing a script for Columbia Pictures, so I packed up my laptop so I could keep working in between making love.

You're flying around the world to live with a woman you've only known for three weeks? asked every single one of my friends.

I just smiled and nodded. They didn't know what my heart knew.

I had planned on staying one month, but that turned into four. Fukushima was our extended honeymoon, the first of our many adventures around the globe. In December we returned briefly to New York and then packed again to move out to a frumpy pink and turquoise apartment building on Venice Beach. We thought we'd stay through the winter and see how it went.

That was sixteen years ago.

• • •

FOUR YEARS AFTER WE FIRST MET, on Christmas Eve at her parents' house, when I was thirty and she was twenty-seven, I trembled as I poured two glasses of champagne. I toasted to our love and she started to drink. I stopped her hand.

D-d-do you like the glass?

It's nice, yeah, bunny.

Then, finally, she noticed the pear-shaped diamond ring nestled in the bottom of the champagne flute.

We were married in our new four-bedroom home overlooking the Pacific in Santa Monica Canyon. I was writing lots of movies, she was getting her PhD in history at UCLA. My dad had taught me some tricks for traveling on the cheap, and I would rent out our house so we could spend months in Paris, on Martha's Vineyard, and on the Greek island of Santorini. We'd drop in on Madrid and Rio, Amsterdam and Saint Barth's. For our honeymoon we toured Provence for a week, then settled just outside of Saint-Tropez for three.

While on Santorini, I was writing a script in the mornings, but in the afternoons, Anna got it in her head to borrow my laptop to try to write a novel. When we returned to Santa Monica, she would study history all day and then continue working on her novel until five in the morning. Two years later, when she finished her book, I warned her that publishing was a tricky business. Even if she was lucky enough to sell it, I told her, she should brace herself for the pitifully low advance. I was paid $5,000 by Random House's Vintage Contemporaries for my first novel, *Platitudes*.

She sent her manuscript to my agent on a Wednesday, and by Monday they had an offer for $100,000. She dropped out of UCLA just short of getting her PhD.

I thought about the horrible luck of my adolescence and then looked around at where I was now. Somehow I had found a brilliant, talented woman who loved me so much she cried when I was called out of town for longer than a weekend, a woman so beautiful she was routinely stopped in the street by admiring women and men and, on the night we went to the Emmys (I'd been nominated for writing the HBO film *The Tuskegee Airmen*), by that guy Mr. Blackwell, who said that of all the movie stars and models in the auditorium, she was the most radiant. We held hands in the house, for chrissakes. We were insufferably blissful.

But not always. Between five and seven days before her period, she would alternate between sobbing that she had to get away, anywhere, and be by herself for a few months and curling up at my feet and just lovingly mooning at me while I wrote. I used to call the latter state *Lovey-Dovey Overdrive,* and it was during one of these times that she wrote this song:

> *We live in paradise,*
> *Me and my hubby, Trey,*
> *We live in paradise,*
> *That is the Ellis way,*
> *We play, play, play all day,*
> *We kiss, kiss, kiss all night,*
> *And if we have a [insert problem here]*
> *We know that it's all right,*
> *Because we live in paradise,*
> *We live in paradise,*
> *We live in paradise,*
> *We do . . .*

We threw great parties, and often. Anna would cook a
deep pot of gumbo or the Brazilian stew *feijoada,* and dozens of
friends would descend upon us. We were the charmed hub of a
fascinating social network of young black and white writers and
filmmakers. We were convinced we were on our way to becoming the greatest literary union since Dashiell Hammett and Lillian Hellman.

During our first seven years together, I was the more
spiritual. My grandparents began as Baptists back in Dayton,
Ohio, when my father, then a teenager, started going to the more
bourgeois black Episcopalian church. Eventually he convinced
them to switch, but for years the extent of my religious education from my parents was listening to the soundtrack of *Jesus
Christ Superstar* on Sundays. Then suddenly, when I was fourteen, my parents got it into their heads that I should be confirmed as an Episcopalian. This was in the seventies, mind you,
and I fervently believed in Jesus and love and peace and even
went to New York City to see *Godspell.* Yet I refused to be confirmed. I saw organized religion as the opiate of the masses. I
agreed with Lao Tzu, although I wouldn't read him until years
later, that ritual is but the husk of true religion. My parents were
pissed. Finally we hammered out a deal. I was addicted to thrill
sports, and if I promised to get confirmed, they would let me
take rock-climbing lessons.

You see, my dad was a child psychiatrist and my mom a
child psychologist during the 1970s, so they never absolutely
forbade me from doing anything. How I avoided heroin, EST, or
the Reverend Sun Myung Moon is anyone's guess. My folks
were permissive and politically correct and yet I never did drugs,
I despised drinking, and I never got into any real trouble. Until

I was sixteen, I prayed every night in my own black pseudo-hippie countercultural way, until the day my father returned home gasping that he and the police had found my mother dead in our car in Yale's Paine Whitney gym parking lot. She had shot herself in the heart.

I had already been accepted to boarding school—before her death, my parents were divorcing and I was sick of my old school; however, after her death, getting far away meant even more to me. My best friend, Ben, was transferring with me to Andover; yet besides him, there would be nobody else to radiate their pity. I was just learning about stoicism and tragic heroes in English class, and even before my mother died, I knew that that was what I wanted to be when I grew up.

Three years later I was a freshman at Stanford taking a journal-writing course based in Hindu and Buddhist meditation. Zen instantly spoke to me, and I continue to meditate to this day (less consistently now that my kids pounce on my back the moment I try to sit still, but I try).

Anna, on the other hand, had no interest in spirituality. Her father had become born again, and her brother was a follower of Siddha Yoga. She was determined to avoid religious extremism of any stripe.

Then one day she ventured into our lovely backyard, recently landscaped with stepping-stones and moss, the air sprinkled with curious butterflies and hummingbirds, and there God spoke to her.

When she told me, smiling that luminous smile of hers, she quickly explained that, no, she wasn't a born again. I sighed and she laughed. Then she said that she had never known for sure whether there was a divinity beyond our own. Now she was positive. She went out and bought every book on spirituality she could get her hands on and, amazingly, she had never seen *Jesus Christ Superstar*. I bought her the video, and she played it at least daily for the next two years. She stumbled across something called rebirthing, where someone guides you to breathe rapidly with your eyes closed and you put yourself into a trippy, ethereal state. She loved it so much that she enrolled in the teacher training course.

The change was shocking at first, but I loved her so much I had no choice but to go along for the ride. We decided to have a child, and I crossed my fingers that the responsibility would ground, at least a little bit, her burgeoning New Age flightiness.

In just three months, Anna was pregnant with a boy, which made our picture-perfect life feel even more so. Then one night she started spotting and cramping. She was crying as I held her, sure that she was miscarrying. I assured her that everything would be all right. The next day at the gynecologist's, they confirmed that she had miscarried and immediately performed a D&C to remove what was left of the pregnancy. Anna howled and her heartache broke my own heart. This was the only bad thing that had ever happened to us.

Four months later, we began trying again; and two months after that, Ava began to grow. Anna wanted to birth Ava naturally, so she braved the first six hours of contractions. Finally, however, the fetal heart monitor started beeping quickly, telling us little Ava was showing signs of distress. The doctor called in an anesthesiologist to jab Anna in the back with a huge needle. She was now numb from the waist down, and soon Ava popped out.

Anna and I instantly cried out, burst into tears, and hugged each other so tightly. It was easily the most amazing, holy, and otherworldly moment of my entire life. The nurse handed me a pair of surgical scissors, and I carefully cut through the chewy umbilical cord. To this day I brag to my kids that although their mother birthed them, it was I who made their belly buttons.

Anna was determined to be a super mother, but the epidural didn't heal right so the level of spinal fluid dropped, causing a horrific, wincing and perpetual headache. Breast-feeding went wrong from the very beginning. Anna developed an abscess in her left breast but still tried her best to soldier on. She cried for hours. Her mother had come from Atlanta, and the two of us tried our best to help her; however, Anna's disappointment at this first stage of motherhood fogged our house with sadness.

Two months later, when she finally abandoned breast-feeding, our house once again became happy, and we settled into enjoying our magical little baby girl. Our friends wagged their fingers and warned that our jet-setting days were behind us; now we'd be miserable and grounded just like everybody else. Determined to prove them all wrong, it wasn't long before we wrapped up little Ava and carted her off to Ramatuelle, the medieval village just outside of Saint-Tropez that we frequented before she was born.

Back in the States, we each continued to crave our freedom. Since we were both working artists, and I an enlightened dad raised in the seventies, we decided to divide child-care duties right down the middle, scrupulously so. I watched Ava every morning, giving her a bottle in the beginning, and then, when she had graduated to solid food, she'd have breakfast nestled under my arm while Anna slept. Lucia, the nanny, arrived at ten and stayed until two, when Anna took over. Then, in the evenings, Anna and I would alternate putting Ava to bed. All day Saturday was Anna's responsibility and all day Sunday was mine. I was pretty goddamn smug about our politically correct division of labor until I realized that I was seeing less and less of my wife. On Saturdays, I tried to stay close so we could do some sort of family outing together, but on Sundays, Anna would skitter off like a rabbit in the woods. Some Sundays it was her ecstatic dance class, and others she said she simply had to be alone in nature.

A few months later, while I was in my home office slogging through the first draft of an already overdue script, I heard her across the hall in her room, the door closed, cackling to herself. To add insult to my injury, I could hear that she was typing her new novel almost bionically fast.

I knocked on her door and she said to come on in. Her eyes were glistening and her fixed smile troubled me. I could smell the pot in the air, but that wasn't unusual. Then she showed me what she had written and my heart stopped. *Fjeikcim mmmieim jmdskaij jkjakop aalkkmmie jajjdakj jjiejfj jieeiieieij jijvmiiuthaian ksjj iej jjj jaiewpppwojgj jjskakkoaiijfai jjisdija jaijfai wpq[[[weomvmi aijfiemviia* . . . For more than one hundred pages. Since my sophomore year in college, I smoked pot myself sometimes, most of my friends did too, yet I'd never heard of a reaction like this. With my mom and my dad gone, all I had left in this world was this woman and our little girl. If I lost Anna to madness, I knew that I could not survive. Our Dashiell and Lillian lifestyle was rapidly devolving into that of F. Scott and Zelda.

At UCLA she had studied the First Great Awakening, the outbreak of religious piety in the American colonies right before the Revolution. She told me that *this* was her Great Awakening, the first step in changing from a run-of-the-mill buppie into a conscious, spiritual being, and that she'd never felt more fulfilled in all her life. She even went down to the main branch of the LA public library with a printout of what she'd written, trying to discover what language her spirit guide was using to communicate with her. I didn't know what to do. I was convinced that she was self-medicating for postpartum depression and started looking into different treatment programs. Luckily, a few days later, she started writing in English again, and I thought the crisis had passed. In fact, great times returned. Sure, I had a kooky wife and she a straitlaced husband, but wasn't that how it was supposed to be? Major Nelson had his Jeannie to dream of; Darrin was bewitched by his Samantha.

• • •

ONE DAY ABOUT A YEAR LATER, I noticed that my feet had swollen. After a few days, I finally called up a doctor friend of mine (now family, but in college Karol was the first woman I ever loved). She ordered me to go to the emergency room immediately. I gave a urine sample that turned out to be awash with protein. A biopsy later confirmed that I had focal segmental glomerulosclerosis, FSGS, the most pernicious autoimmune disease of the kidneys. After I was released from the hospital a week later, I started taking thirty pills a day, and still the lower half of my body was flooded with an extra twenty pounds of fluid. Every morning I had to tug on and then unroll up my legs thigh-high, old-lady-looking compression stockings just so I could stand up. If I didn't wear them, after about three minutes my ankles would disappear and my toes would start throbbing. Sweatpants were about the only pants that would fit over my bloated thighs, and my dick looked like a water balloon. When I should have been trying to write, I would often pull open the waistband of my sweats and just stare at the deformity until abject panic overflowed into my throat. The immunosuppressants I gobbled three times a day made me so susceptible to the tiniest bug that every few weeks I would find myself convulsing face-first over the toilet bowl, only to have to jump to my feet to try to get my ass around to the bowl before another unspeakably messy explosion from my ass. The majority of FSGS sufferers, like basketball players Sean Elliot and Alonzo Mourning, end up getting a kidney transplant (they actually add a third instead of taking out the other two—who knew?), but they still have to take mountains of meds for the rest of their lives. My doctor and I wanted me to fight to keep mine and wait for a cure.

My medicines have changed a bit during the eight years since I was diagnosed. After five years I got off steroids, thank God. Even just two milligrams sometimes sent me into what is clinically described as *steroid psychosis*. I would call it simply drunk. Writing, until it passed, was impossible. I don't know how Faulkner, Hemingway, and Bukowski did it.

Medication	Purpose	Dosage	Frequency
Azathioprine	Suppresses immune system	50 mg	Twice a day
Cyclosporine	Suppresses immune system	100 mg	Twice a day
Atorvastatin	Reduces cholesterol	20 mg	Once a day
Amlodipine	Lowers blood pressure	5 mg	Once a day
Lisinopril	Lowers blood pressure	40 mg	Twice a day
Metoprolol	Lowers blood pressure	25 mg	Once a day
Fludrocortisone	Controls blood potassium level	0.1 mg	Once a day
Folic acid	Treats anemia	1 mg	Once a day
Aspirin	Thins the blood	81 mg	Once a day
Niferex	Provides iron	150 mg	Once a day
Omega-3 fish oil	Promotes cardiovascular health	2000 mg	Twice a day
L-arginine	Synthesizes nitric oxide	8000 mg	Once a day
Epoetin alfa	Treats anemia	20,000 IU	Inject every ten days

Throughout all of this, Anna was amazingly supportive. She held me when I cried, and lit candles and saged the house to bring white light to help protect me. There was no cure for what I had (there still isn't), so I was open to anything. In fact, her loving treatments were the only things that made me feel a little better.

About a year and a half later, the swelling mysteriously disappeared. It wasn't quite remission in that I still had (and have) to take the same pounds of pills, the same injections; however, my energy came back, so I no longer almost passed out just standing up. I returned to yoga classes and the gym and to wearing a belt instead of only drawstring pants.

I thought the most difficult chapter of my life was behind me. Instead, as soon as I stopped needing her constant comforting, we started living increasingly separate lives. The center of hers became that ecstatic dance class every Sunday morning. Once she got me to go, and as I walked in, I saw a hundred of them, from now-old original-issue hippies to young wannabes, all twirling, undulating, and hooting. I had been open to many New Age practices that I otherwise would have ridiculed—rebirthing, for instance, was trippy yet amazing—but flailing my arms next to overweight, tie-dyed grandmas named Serenity was a path I just could not bring myself to head down.

Then one night she went without me to a party for some of her dance friends, wearing red-sequined devil horns and the red Kenzo shearling coat I had bought her one summer in Saint-Tropez (the most expensive article of clothing I have ever bought anyone). The next morning I could tell something had changed. Ava was by now two and a half and Anna and I were in her room, cooing over her as she napped, when Anna told me that at the party the night before, she had made out with a raw vegan, a white guy who'd changed his name to some Indian jumble of vowels, and now she was convinced that he was her soul mate. I had to force myself to keep breathing. I went downstairs and lay down on the scratchy sisal carpeting. Suddenly my entire body started trembling—my legs, my arms, my chest all quivered as if somebody had put a quarter in the slot of some cheap motel's Magic Fingers bed massager. Anna came down and held me and told me that she still loved me too but that the *new* her needed to be free to love the world, not just her husband.

I don't remember how I survived the rest of that day and that night, but I do remember driving to Denny's sometime before the next dawn and ordering a Grand Slam Breakfast that I forked but did not eat.

Before Ava was born, I'd spent a year manning a hotline at a suicide prevention center, and in the next few weeks I found myself so devastated that I often contemplated using a technique a very depressed old woman had once described to me—ducttaping a plastic bag over your head. For weeks I couldn't write, I couldn't do anything except drive up and down Wilshire Boulevard wondering how and whether I was going to survive. But eventually I always came home and ended up just playing with Ava. I knew that I could never rob from her what my mom had robbed from me.

Anna insisted that she still wanted to make our marriage work so she found us a New Age couples' counseling team who were students of a technique that I had actually turned her on to, based on a series of books advocating absolute and complete honesty. It was exactly what both of us needed to try to clear the undergrowth of mistrust that had been growing between us. I had been trying to morph her into Shirley Jones on *The Partridge Family,* while she had wanted me to shape-shift into Lenny Kravitz.

She swore the fucking soul mate was now just a friend, and I gradually began to hope that we could rebuild our life together. Our relationship seemed so solid that we both thought it would be a good idea for me to go off on a weekend yoga retreat in Santa Barbara. Though Anna had started taking classes months before me, I soon became addicted, first to build endurance for surfing; then yoga became my major regular exercise. When my kidneys quit on me, I had to stop for a year, but now that I was feeling so much better, this upcoming retreat would be definitive proof of my getting my life back.

The night before I left, Anna told me that I could make love with someone there if I found a true heart connection. Even though a yoga class, especially in Santa Monica, is stocked with some of the most beautiful working and nonworking actresses in the nation, and their gyrations have certainly been a factor in the zeal with which I have perfected my *asanas,* I told her that she was being absurd.

Her free love pass did not come totally out of the blue. As residents of Southern California, we were practically ordered by the state to practice Tantric sex, and I had discovered this lovely Italian *tantrika* on the Internet who came over once and gave us both an extremely hands-on, simultaneous lesson. Furthermore, I had not been a saint during our twelve years together. I was no stranger to Internet porn and had slept with two Heidi Fleiss–type girls at my bachelor party in Las Vegas. When I had confessed to her these misdeeds years before, even before couples' counseling, my friends thought that Anna and I, two nutcases under one roof, deserved each other. Maybe they were right. Though she always said she loved my (retroactive) honesty, as I look back on it now, I know that she never fully trusted me again and that at least part of the reason for her making out with the white boy with the Indian name was old-fashioned payback.

As luck would have it, when I got to the retreat, I found myself surrounded by gorgeous *yoginis* (including my tent mates, an almost six-foot-tall blonde Swede and a then-unknown Naomi Watts). Nevertheless, I didn't try anything with anybody. I didn't want to. Our marriage was already so fragile that I knew that it would not withstand a fling, no matter how much New Age tolerance Anna spouted.

More important than sharing a hot tub with a naked Naomi Watts (believe it or not) was the retreat's signaling my return to full health. Sure, I was still gobbling handfuls of pills three times a day, but there I was, twice a day, sweating my ass off in the most strenuous classes of my life. In *Blazing Saddles,* when Alex Karras knocked out a horse with a single punch, he said, "I strong like bull." That's how I felt. So, as I drove home from Santa Barbara, burning up the Pacific Coast Highway with the top down and my Mustang's engine growling contentedly, I was sure that we had turned another corner, that our once-fairy-tale lifestyle was returning to us.

I must have been going at least seventy-five when a cramp mysteriously knotted my gut. I squeezed the steering wheel and concentrated on not crashing, but the pain forced tears from my eyes. I could actually see the contractions in my belly, like just before that thing in *Alien* bursts out of its human host. The knotting spread down my legs to my driving foot, and I had to force myself to calm down and coast to the road's shoulder.

As the other cars screamed past, I actually pushed on my cramped body to make it unfold. The yogic bliss that had filled me that whole weekend had instantly been replaced with breathless terror. The shimmering Pacific at my back must have been gorgeous, but I didn't notice it. When I had first gotten ill, I was terrified that I would die early, as my parents had, leaving me to finish raising myself. When I got better, I took it to mean that I had returned to perfect health and would live another fifty, maybe sixty years. This mysterious episode, however, brought the terror flooding back, not so much for myself, but for my little girl. Finally I got back in the car and drove home.

When I arrived in Santa Monica, Anna's eyes were shimmering. She sat me down and breathlessly told me about the incredible adventures she had had while I was gone. She showed me her new butterfly tattoo, then went on to tell me how one night she had made out with dozens of different guys all over the Westside of LA. With each and every one, she insisted, she had had the type of heart connection she had wished for me on my retreat. I was sure she was just kidding. She is a great storyteller, and I thought this was some sort of prank.

Now, however, as it started to sink in that she was telling the truth, that the tattoo was as real as the men she had made out with, I began to realize in short little steps over the course of perhaps a minute that everything, everything, everything was about to change.

Nevertheless, for the next several months we threw

ourselves back into couples' counseling. We even drove up to
Santa Barbara for an intensive weekend seminar taught by Gay
and Kathlyn Hendricks, the inventors of the relationship technique our counselors were trained in. By Sunday Anna and I
ended up crying in each other's arms, vowing our undying, ever-
expanding love for each other. I concluded that I was wrong and
our once-storybook romance was not terminal after all.

Ava was now three years old. Anna and I had been
together ten years and had already weathered a lifetime's marital conflict. We thought we'd come out on the other side with a
marriage that was tempered and now invincible. So we decided
to have another child. Surely having two kids would ground her
through her wilder New Age episodes, and for the first few
months after Chet was born, everything did seem perfect again.
Thanks to hypnobirthing, he shot out without anesthesia and
we got her a breast-feeding coach his first day. Then, when Chet
was about six months old, I noticed that Anna seemed again
consumed by sadness. I assumed it was postpartum again and
would disappear with time, but this time it only got worse. For
weeks her eyes would skitter away whenever I tried to find
them with my own. The emptiness in her eyes told me that she
had spent herself crying, though she rarely let me see the tears. I
had had built for her an opulent walk-in closet with shoe racks
to the ceiling and silently sliding built-in drawers. Now that Ava
had commandeered Anna's office, she had loaded her movie-star
closet floor with pillows, laid her laptop on the floor, and would
shut herself inside to write for hours. I would ask her how it was
going, what she was writing, but she would only answer in non-
answers. Daily I dwelled on my mother's death. One day Anna
asked me to fix something on her computer, and I took advan-

BEDTIME STORIES • 23

tage of the opportunity to spy on her diary. In it she talked about how trapped and overpoweringly depressed she felt, how suicide wouldn't be the end of the world. I confronted her and she agreed to see a therapist.

She was almost immediately better. She started talking to me again, told me about her new book, a roman à clef about her voyage to enlightenment. Her character was married to a boojy film director named Lloyd. I begged her to change his name—I mean *Lloyd?*—*geez!*—but she insisted. Still, I was positively giddy that we were talking again and making love again and seeing our friends again. What an adventurous marriage we had! So full and dramatic. So extraordinary. Oh, the stories we'd have to tell our kids![1]

I redoubled (or requadrupled at this point) my efforts to bail out our sinking ship. To give her even more freedom, we invited a young Santa Monica College student to live downstairs in the guest bedroom in exchange for babysitting at night and helping with the kids on the weekends. She was a friend of our regular weekday nanny, Lucia. I was also between writing gigs, so giving her free board was much cheaper than shelling out $10 an hour every time we wanted to see *Die Hard VIII: The Resurrection* or *Spiderman IX: Revenge of the Larvae.*

On Saturdays, my day off, instead of leaving, I would glue myself to my little family, drive us all out to Malibu to wander a beach. I remember once that Rick James was shouting on the stereo and I checked out our giggling kids in the rearview mirror. When Rick James sang, "Give it to me baby," Ava kept singing instead, "Give it to *the* baby." Anna and I shared a look, one of the

---

[1]When they were much, much, much older.

tenderest we'd had in months. My heart ballooned. We both loved our kids so much that I just knew that they would be the bridge that reconnected us stronger than fucking ever. Just a few more afternoons like this and surely we were going to make it after all.

We were making love, the kids were most excellent, so the night Anna insisted on stripping at the amateur night of a place called 4Play, I absolutely positively refused to panic. Anyway, I knew by now the futility of trying to stop her, and she very reasonably told me, Trey, you like to jump out of airplanes. This is my thrill. Look, I didn't have to be the reincarnation of Dr. Freud to surmise that at least part of Anna's new compulsion was avenging herself against her very jealous husband for his fucking two high-class hookers at his bachelor party eight years earlier. So I steeled myself to not only accept it but to support her. I'd be damned if I'd let her paint me into a corny, conservative corner. I was determined to convince her that I was not the paternalistic lout of her imagination. For god's sake, my name was not Lloyd!

Her best girlfriends came with us to the club that night, by now used to her eccentricities. She was the only real amateur on the tiny brass-railed stage; the other dancers were stiletto-slinging, pneumatic pros. When it was Anna's turn, I squeezed the arms of my chair but pasted on a store-bought smile. She was wearing that expensive red Kenzo coat I'd bought her in Saint-Tropez and red lingerie that I'd bought her just for the occasion. She dropped everything before a dozen or so regular Joes, and she giggled sweetly more than shimmied. It actually was pretty damn brave of her, and I'd bet the onetime fantasy of many if not most women. When she got offstage, I gave her roses and a big kiss.

Oh, how smug I was. Her friends just shook their heads

and tried their best to smile with her, but me? I was an evolved man in an evolved relationship. Nobody had to understand us as long as we understood each other.

I can't remember if it was immediately after we'd made love or put the kids to bed, but I remember how close I felt to her, how healed I felt when she called me into the kitchen and insisted I not only take a lover but also tell her all about it—anything, she said, to shake up our boring lives.

Okay, not what I'd expected to hear, but it could have been worse. She wasn't talking about (a) killing herself, or (b) fucking somebody else. In our counseling to create a transparent marriage, I had once told her that I found one of my yoga teachers extremely sexy; and a few months before this current request, while we were lying in bed in the dark, Anna had told me that she had run into the yogini at her ecstatic dance class and had informed her about my crush.

I couldn't see her face in the dark, so I couldn't quite tell what sort of trap she was laying. I knew a normal wife would never ever do such a thing, but for years now, I knew that normalcy was nothing I had to worry about. This teacher looked like a young Julie Christie. Perhaps having a crazy wife had its advantages? I forced my voice to sound as if I were discussing the trade deficit.

Oh really? Wasn't she shocked?

Yes, at first, but then I told her that she was a beautiful woman and it was only natural and if she felt a heart connection with you, then you two should make love.

Hmmm.

That was all that I could say in my attempt to feign disinterest. My penis, however, was a lie detector tenting the sheets.

Wh-what did she say? My voice cracked for the first time in twenty-five years.

Oh, she said . . . she said . . . I don't quite remember, something about . . .

That was all Anna could get out before she began giggling. I rolled on top of her, kissing her quiet.

This time, however, the request's being real deflated me completely. My guy friends were thrilled for me. At least, they said, if things don't work out with Anna, you'll already be on your way in a new relationship. I understood their callous logic, of course; it had occurred to me myself. Still, that was a door that I was not at all prepared to open. I was convinced that the very instant the head of my penis inched past the opening of another woman's vagina, the glass house of my marriage would instantly and noisily shatter. Further complicating the telenovela that had become my life, Beatriz, the student we had downstairs, moved in with her boyfriend and her sister, Angela, having just arrived from Uruguay, took her place. She was nineteen and found an American boyfriend in less time than most people need to find a used car. Whereas her sister left her room downstairs as often as a mole, this new girl loved to wander through the rest of the house. While Anna was off dancing or rebirthing or eating raw food, Angela would find me watching *The Sopranos* in the living room, and she would complain about her current boyfriend's hair trigger in bed. Somehow we got to talking about Tantric sex . . . all right, I brought it up. She seemed fascinated, so when she went down to bed, I went up to mine, pulled one of my various, illustrated Tantric books off my nightstand, and delivered it down to her room. When she opened the door again, my mouth was sand. Could it be that I was actually turning into *that guy*? The universally reviled and mocked creepy married old guy? As Groucho Marx used to say, indignantly, *I resemble that remark.*

Coming to my senses, I shoved the book at her and fled, taking two flights of stairs, two steps at a time. The woman I was in love with, the one I had planned to and promised to grow old with, said I never ever made her horny; yet here was this obscenely young, cliché-ridden young, Trey-what-the-hell-is-the-matter-with-you-young Uruguayana (who looked like a young Jane Fonda by the way) asking me for sex tips. Luckily, the next day I told my friend Keith my dilemma, and he told me something that was so concise and so true that it seems like it should have been translated from the original Latin: You don't shit where you eat.

For months Anna kept asking me if I'd found somebody, and when I'd say no, she'd just roll her eyes with disgust. She said if I really cared about saving our marriage, I'd take a god-damn chance. Around Christmastime she finally told me what she had been itching to tell me and what had been so clear to everyone else but me for years: that she wanted to sleep with other people, to have a totally open marriage or no marriage at all. I told her that if she wanted to take a female lover (and not even allow me to watch), I could stomach that because I knew that eventually she would come back to me. But, and here I drew a last-ditch line in the sand, she would have to choose between me being the only man in her life and her being with every other man in the world but me. I was about eighty percent sure that she would come to her senses. After all, we were made for each other. Hell, we even have the same birthday.

She just looked at me with a smile of sweet pity and told me that we would always be friends.

Nothing in my life has ever so emptied me. I would drive

and cry, and the tears would streak back toward my ears and feel cool in the breeze. Even though she had decided to leave me, I moved out. I was the man, and wasn't that what men were supposed to do? The kids need the mother more. The father scavenges for every other weekend.

Chet was just six months old so he couldn't understand the sea change, but Ava was going on four. Anna and I were both committed to shielding her from as much pain as possible. We weren't fighting or even nasty to each other, so the most profound changes in Ava's world would only come at nighttime, after she and her brother were asleep. The down-to-the-minute division of labor that Anna had insisted upon when we were married now served us well. I had been so proud of how enlightened we had been, splitting parenting duties right down to the hour, but now I realized that our impending divorce was actually years in the making.

So while her little brother was napping, we explained simply that we would be living in separate places but everything else would be as it always was. I would be there in the mornings, then Lucia would come and Ava would go to her magical preschool, and then Mommy would play with her in the afternoons and Daddy and Mommy would take turns putting her and her brother to bed. She just looked at us like What's the big deal? Why were we acting so weird? It almost hurt me more that she couldn't yet understand. How could a family that was just starting out already be falling apart?

For a week I slept on different friends' floors and then got up at six in the morning to get back to the house by seven, when the kids woke up. That was the part of our routine that I knew had to change. I thought it was crazy that Anna wouldn't get up with them while I was out of the house, but she insisted that the kids were so used to me in the mornings that it would upset them too much to change now. I was too disarticulated to protest. Everything in my life, it seemed, was collapsing simultaneously. I hadn't had a writing assignment in over a year and was $100,000 in debt; the credit cards were all frozen and full, so I couldn't even charge a hotel room. To make things worse, horrible songs with lyrics like "You left me just when I needed you most" and "If you leave me now, you take away the biggest part of me" played over and over in my head.

I have always been a big fan of self-pity. Even when most everything in my life is going pretty well, I am expert in discovering something to lament. Now that a true catastrophic emergency was upon me, I positively gorged on self-pity, gobbling huge mouthfuls like a lion on the carcass of a gazelle.

I remember very clearly the night I was trying to sleep on a foam remnant on the floor of my friends' apartment in a rough section of Venice. A police helicopter was circling the neighborhood, its angry floodlights burning the curtains and the backyard. I looked at my 1965 stainless-steel Rolex that used to make me feel like Steve McQueen and wondered where the nearest all-night pawn shop might be. I thought about the giddy summers Anna and I had spent around Saint-Tropez ever since our honeymoon there eight years before. For some reason I thought about why I had picked Saint-Tropez for our honeymoon in the first place. I had always planned on honeymooning on Santorini, Greece, after seeing the movie *Summer Lovers* about an American couple who honeymoon there and wind up in a playful threesome with a French woman. I couldn't wait, however, and Anna and I lived on Santorini for six weeks soon after we met.[2] My next choice was the fault of George Burns, Art Carney, and Lee Strasberg. Back in 1979, when I was seventeen, I saw their movie *Going in Style,* about a band of geriatric bank robbers. Their grand dream was to steal enough money to make it to the south of France before they died. Throughout the film their giddy refrain is "Saint-Tropez, where the women don't wear no tops!" What kind of man takes his newly minted wife to a place swimming with other women's breasts? No wonder she left you, you broke, vain, superficial piece of shit.

So this is the bottom, I said to myself. I always wondered what it would feel like.

The next day I received a check for $120 for I don't remember what, and it was drawn on the same bank that I used, so, like a day laborer, I delighted in getting the cash on the spot. The money, and the prodding of my friends, convinced me to go back to Anna and demand that she be the one brushing her teeth in the sinks of her friends. She was the one who craved freedom. I just craved my kids. My dad had raised me after my mother died, so I knew single-fatherhood was possible. Of course, he shepherded a teenager, not a toddler and an infant, both still in diapers.

A few days later, I remembered that out of the blue, years ago, American Express had offered me a second line of credit (at a rate of interest that would have discomfited Tony Soprano). I just then remembered that when I had accepted their terms—just in case—I had told myself to forget about it, to break glass only

---

[2]Just the two of us, by the way.

in case of a true emergency. Although in general I am quite expert at overreacting, the circumstances at the time seemed to have easily qualified.

This newest line of credit would give me perhaps another month and a half of liquidity. In my mind, I grasped it the way Popeye grabs that last can of spinach. This was all I needed, this tiniest air pocket in my capsized and rapidly sinking *Titanic*. In my version, against all odds, the hero lives.

I paid for a little studio Anna had found for herself in Venice. She would still have a key to the house because she would still be coming over every afternoon to look after the kids, but that delicious king-size bed was now mine mine mine.

I also asked Angela, the young live-in, to leave. In my state, it was just too tantalizing to have her wandering my halls in just an oversize T-shirt.

It's so hard trying to remember what it was like those first nights changing Chet's diaper alone, pulling on Ava's pajamas alone, and singing them the theme song to *The Mary Tyler Moore Show* alone.

Truthfully, I had felt alone for at least the last three years, since soon after Ava was born. I think I must have felt some sort of relief that our physical reality was finally catching up with its psychological twin. I was an often-depressed, cartoonishly nerdy kid who didn't get halfway cool till after college, and I think much of me never really settled in to my obnoxiously giddy early years with Anna. The easy money, the travel, her beauty that stopped my heart daily, and the babies that reminded me of minor deities, it was all too much to take in. I was being repaid way too much for just losing my parents. Looking back on those years now, I feel that a part of me must have always been waiting for the old melancholy me to retake the hill. It felt so familiar, so comfortable having Michel Legrand and his orchestra forever following behind me violining the self-pitying minor chords of "Theme from Summer of '42."

I've always felt more Charlie Brown, more Woody Allen, than James Bond.

2

CHET, AT JUST EIGHT MONTHS OLD, was in the ninety-ninth percentile for weight and height. You couldn't gaze at his round, smiling Buddha nature without smiling yourself. Now, four years later, you still can't. He was an ever-giggling, superfat, hormone-enhanced butterball, so fat that he scared some people—you could see it in their faces—as if when he finally decided to walk, they expected him to lay waste to whole cities. He was so fat he made you hungry just looking at him.

Ava had been a fat baby herself, but as soon as she began to walk, she lost the weight; and by the time her mother left, when Ava was three and a half, she was generally considered a breathtaking miniature person. She looked as much like her mother as a child can resemble an adult, and whenever that fact made me sad, I would condemn myself for putting such a heavy load on such a little girl, and that would make me sadder still.

Our morning routine hadn't changed a bit. When the

digital clock in their room flashed 7:00, Ava would wobble into my bedroom and poke me until I opened my eyes. I would change her first and then haul Chet out of his crib and change his diaper too. Most of Ava's friends had already been potty trained for more than a year, but my little beauty was on strike.

It was odd. When she turned two, her favorite book was *Once Upon a Potty,* so we bought her one and waited. She even went through a phase when she insisted on trying to put on her own diaper (and she succeeded, sort of). However, now, at three and a half, she preferred to lie on her back and have me perform her toilet as if she were the reincarnation of Marie Antoinette.

Reasoning with her seemed futile, and yet I tried.

Honey, if you feel it coming, why don't we just set you on the potty and let it fall into the water?

I don't want to.

Just like in the book. See. Look at the picture. Bye-bye, poo-poo.

I don't want to.

Instead, she would disappear into another room and return with a sideways look that said, Are you gonna make a big deal out of this or are you just going to suck it up and wipe my ass?

Anna and I were raising our kids according to the Resources for Infant Educarers method, where you don't pressure them, you listen to them and respect their present needs. RIE's not as cultish as it sounds, and I am convinced that it has helped my kids become as amazingly self-possessed as they are. Still, if a leprechaun had ever materialized in the kids' room to grant me three wishes, wish number one would have been that Ava would learn to take a crap on her own. Having to change two little ones, especially when they're not too little, was getting to me. My life was being consumed by waste management. I was emptying the diaper pail so often that I swear neighboring parents must have been illegally dumping their old diapers in my house.

Every time I felt newly inspired to nudge Ava into bodily waste self-sufficiency, something else always came up. By "something," I really mean that my marriage was disintegrating, and I didn't want little Ava to associate the trauma of wiping her own butt with the dissolution of her parents' marriage. She had been doing so well so far, braving this petrifying new chapter, that I couldn't bring myself to add my timetable to her stress. Looking back I still think it was the right decision, however it added mightily to my stress load. Because of what she's been through, I have a hard time denying her anything. Because Ava is as in love with me as teenaged girls in the sixties were in love with the Beatles, it is so easy for me to allow guilt and pity to influence my parenting decisions toward overindulgence and materialism.

But I'm getting ahead of myself. Downstairs, I'd fix Ava and myself bowls of Cracklin' Oat Bran (I'm just realizing while writing this that perhaps my choice of breakfast cereal contributed to my family's fecal overabundance), and for Chet I'd open a jar of organic beets (a great diaper-product color enhancer) and pop open a can of formula.

Lucia, the nanny, would arrive and make lunch for Ava and take Chet out of my arms so I could drive Ava to preschool. Then I would hurry back home and shut myself in my room to write and worry about money (not necessarily in that order). Anna, who had suddenly decided to change her name to Carmen, would reenter our world in the afternoons.

Of course it was beyond strange to keep seeing the wife you were losing every weekday afternoon and Saturday in the house you once shared. I don't think that's what therapists mean when they talk about a clean break. However, our goal was to disturb Ava as little as possible. She and her brother were in bed by seven, so the fact that her parents were no longer sleeping in the same bed after she'd gone to sleep didn't have to negatively impact her life.

A few months earlier my friend Yule was dating a divor-cée with young kids, and their solution was to keep the house as a sort of Switzerland for the kids while the parents rotated in and out every two weeks. This meant it was the parents who had to lug around the backpacks with extra clothes, shuttling between their new bachelor pads and the home they had built together. I first heard about their arrangement when my marriage was intact, and it had seemed like just some more Left Coast lunacy. However, I now understood the logic—and not just for the sake of the kids. Like us, their house was their only real asset and the market was still skyrocketing. Buying out the other parent was prohibitive, but selling right now seemed a shame. *Carmen* thought that this was the magical solution that would usher in our new-millennial marriage dissolution. I hadn't seen her this excited, this happy in years.

Don't worry, Trey, I won't leave condoms around, she assured me.

I didn't want to share the house with her. My wants were simpler. I simply wanted to curl up under the comforter and not wake up until after this nightmare was over.

• • •

DURING THIS PERIOD of mourning my marriage, Sundays were always my longest days. The kids and I were completely on our own. I needed to prove to myself that I could take them to the beach alone, so one day I decided to just do it. Before the kids were born, after putting in my four hours writing a new script or a book, I would often stuff a novel and a towel in the rear basket of my beach cruiser and coast down Entrada Drive all the way to the beach. If I had a little more time I would slide my longboard into the back of the Explorer and drive up the coast to where Sunset Boulevard meets the Pacific Coast Highway and surf till it got dark. For years, right before going to sleep, Anna would ask me, What did you do today, bunny? And I would catalog my various adventures, so satisfied with the variety of my days.

That was then . . .

Now, just maneuvering all three of us from the house to the beach took a logistical genius. My '73 Mustang's trunk is as shallow as a roasting pan and mainly occupied by the spare tire. I managed to shove the diaper bag back there, but the stroller wouldn't fit, so it had to ride next to me like a passenger. Chet and Ava had to be lashed into their car seats in the back. I had traded in a new Mustang convertible for this '73 Mach I muscle car back when Ava was on the way, because I had thought that I would have to grow up and get a family car. I found the Mach I on the Internet, paid $4,000 for it, and planned to sell it the day Ava was born. Instead, I became addicted to restoring it to precisely what it would have looked like back in '73 and I was eleven years old. When I wasn't surfing, Anna/Carmen drove the Explorer. When she left she took the SUV with her.

At the beach parking lot, I coaxed Chet's stroller out of the bucket seat like those metal puzzle rings magicians have to twist exactly so to disentangle them. Then I tried to yoke the diaper bag to little Ava by its strap, but it was longer than she was, so instead I had her carry a plastic bucket. I added the dia-per bag to the bag of beach toys and the kite shaped like a P-51 Mustang that were already hanging from my neck and then tried to drag Chetty in his stroller backward through the sand. Remember, Chet was as big and as heavy as a medicine ball, so the stroller sank wheel-deep in the loose sand and stopped. I felt like my great-great-grandpa back in Selma, Alabama, before the Civil War, trying to plow a field.

The beach is a hundred yards wide here, but I really wanted to get us near the water. I just couldn't figure out how to get us all there by myself. The only solution that came to me was to wait until Pamela Anderson bounced by and offered to give me a hand. Not likely, to be sure, but also not entirely out of the realm of possibility. *Baywatch* had been filmed on that very beach.

Finally I carried Chet in my arms, loaded his car seat with the diaper bag, the toy bag, and the kite, and dragged that lighter load to the water's edge. When I couldn't find the sun-screen at the bottom of the beach toy bag, my heart shrank, my breath left me, and I very nearly threw myself down on the sand to wail. Then I found it and rubbed down the kids, reminding myself to avoid putting it near their eyes this time. The last time, the sting had made Ava cry. The last time, Carmen (née Anna) had whipped out a Mustela wipe and quickly cleaned her eye. It was always surprising how great she was at stuff like that.

Seconds after unpacking, I found myself talking aloud in an almost demented way. Forced phrases burst from me like: *There! Now isn't this nice! Aren't we having the best time!* I had never once used that damn kite, though we'd had it for months. It looked cool, and this afternoon Ava begged me to make it fly, but no matter what I did, I couldn't get it to rise for more than an instant before it nose-dived into the sand. It is at times like that, when the metaphor is inescapable, that being a writer is the world's cruelest curse.

• • •

THOUGH IT WAS NEVER ENOUGH, I did get some sympathy from my friends immediately after she left. Actually, my relationship with being the center of attention is complicated. I simultaneously crave fame and shun it. I am both preternaturally vain and rather withdrawn. When my mom died when I was in the tenth grade, I could still feel the pity beamed at me from everybody at my little school. The naked attention embarrassed me; so much of me just wanted them all to just leave me alone. I was already just one of about five black kids in a school of several hundred and was already sick of always sticking out.

On the other hand, I have always been terrified of being ordinary and on occasion indulged the thought that maybe uppercase Tragedies such as Death and Divorce were some sort of cosmic proof of my Specialness.

Of course my divorce also catapulted me back to the feelings I still carried around about my own parents' shitty marriage. I already fancied myself sort of a combination of Holden Caulfield meets Hamlet meets *The Cosby Show*. Before my mom died, my parents had told me that they were separating. That part did not come as a shock. During the final five or six years before she died, whenever they were in the same room together, they were either silent or hostile. Dad found any excuse he could to be away on business. Mom, at thirty-two, had enrolled at Yale law school and buried herself in her studies. Her plan was to move to DC after graduation and practice law there. She also had promised to buy me a Hobie catamaran and a hang glider. I was fifteen. So I believed her.

This current hurt cut in an even deeper, more soul-ripping way. I think when you're young, catastrophes just overwhelm you and you shut down; but as a parent, I didn't have the luxury of being able to, say, sneak off to Club Med Fiji to bartend for a decade or two until I healed. I was chained to my earthly duties of raising two phenomenal little heroes. After all, it was in my blood. My dad had stepped up to the plate after my mother died, and raised me. After spending my young lifetime wishing he would hang around the house more, after Mom died, my dad, in fact, became my best friend in the world.

Two weeks after the beach ordeal, I was ready for another test so I drove the kids three hours down to Legoland, which would like you to believe that it is Disneyland with Legos, when in fact it was little more than a semi-interactive garden with plastic statues.

At the end of the long day, driving us back home to Santa Monica would take about three hours, so just outside of San Clemente, I stopped at a diner for dinner. San Clemente being the home of the Nixon library, I was hoping for wacky Tricky Dick references in the menu. (Agent Orange Juice, anyone?) Instead, Ava and I ordered hamburgers and I got Chet a hot dog. I always order him a hot dog when we're out, even though it always makes my heart race. I had seen a news report that said a hot dog's diameter is precisely that of a small child's throat, and from that day on, I couldn't help but think of them not as nitrate-filled, Cuisinarted spare pig parts, but as evil kiddie plugs. All of that explains why I snatched Chet's plate away from the teen waitress and swiftly severed it lengthwise, the knife noisy against the plate, well before it neared my son's outstretched fingers.

After dinner I wanted to pee before getting back on the road. Of course I'd take Chet in there with me, but since Ava was the perfect little lady in her booster seat and I only have two hands, I thought the teenaged waitress seemed perfectly capable of watching her for the fifty seconds it would take me to take a whiz.

When I tried to explain all of this to our server, she looked at me as if I'd just asked her to star in barnyard porn.

So I snatched up Chet into my arms and herded Ava ahead of us into the narrow men's room. While holding Chet in my left arm, I managed to unzip my fly, but what about the up-zip? I had never noticed that you need two hands to zip up a zipper until it was, tragically, too late. Still, hoping for a miracle, I tried and tried and tried. I squeezed my knees together, hoping to create enough downward tension on the teeth. No go.

Stinks in here, Daddy. Let's go.

In a minute, sweetheart.

I looked at myself in the mirror and smiled.

Welcome to your new world.

What, Daddy?

Nothing, princess.

I left the bathroom with fat Chet slung low over my crotch like novelty underwear—you know, like an elephant's face with a long, curving trunk.

Back on the road, the kids were asleep before we'd passed the next on-ramp. If it wouldn't have gotten us killed, I could have lost myself for hours staring at them in the rearview mirror. They were both deflated in their car seats, their heads almost touching, as my Mustang angrily gobbled the road.

• • •

SEMI-TOUGH WAS ONE of my favorite films as a kid, so when my agent called to tell me that Miramax was doing a remake and he had gotten them interested in me to write it, I knew immediately that this project would lift me out of my creative, financial, and emotional ghettos. I watched the movie again and for weeks thought of nothing but how I would turn in a first draft that would have the studio exec, upon reading my words, tumble out of his Aeron chair and weep with joy. At first some people might turn their noses up at yet another soulless Hollywood remake, but thanks to my acerbic, deliciously devilish wit, I would create the funniest sports satire since *Slap Shot* (an even better film than the original *Semi-Tough*).

Landing any screenwriting gig, at least at my midlist level, entails not one meeting with the big boss, but several meetings as you work your way upstream from pool to pool like a salmon desperate to spawn. My first meeting was with a junior executive at the Four Seasons Hotel in Beverly Hills. I armored myself with my vintage Rolex, which I'd begun to wear again. It was no longer mocking me. Now it was my accomplice in conning this exec who had flown in from New York to meet me. I had to make her think that I didn't need this gig; that I was doing her a favor by putting all the rest of my exciting projects on hold because I was so passionate about this one. The reality, of course, was that I had to economize, so instead of spending something like $10 to valet (I always,

always tip the guys because they're brown, I'm black, and we have to stick together), I had discovered that you can self-park for free around the back.

In the hotel bar, with Death Row Record's Suge Knight leading a meeting in one corner and Liam Neeson, or maybe just his stunt double, by the piano, I did what I like doing least in Hollywood: I pitched. As I performed my five-minute, one-man-show version of *Semi-Tough, the Remake,* my hands flew at odd angles, I affected a menagerie of different voices, and my eyebrows danced on my head like drunken caterpillars. If you have ever wondered why most American movies are so crappy, predictable, and bland, it's because too often the personal, solitary, interior act of writing a compelling story is commissioned to the person who gives the best five-minute public performance. It makes about as much sense as hiring a chef based on how well he chews.

That said, I killed in the room.

The exec was laughing when I wanted her to laugh, hanging on my every word. As I headed back down the elevator to the garage, I found myself humming Gene Autry's "Back in the Saddle Again." It was all gonna work out. I'd be able to keep the house and pay Carmen, over time, what she would have earned had we put our house on the market.

That house. We had moved in eight years before, after looking all over Santa Monica and Venice for over a year. Our by now cynical realtor had shown it to us one morning, and we signed the papers by the end of the day. Santa Monica Canyon was and still is considered the most desirable neighborhood in all of LA, but the house had languished on the market for six months, so the price just kept falling. Though it was big, with four bedrooms and an ocean view, it hadn't been renovated since the

Bicentennial, when it was built. Pink with turquoise trim and jammed into the side of a hill, it looked like a miniature, independently owned and operated Best Western. Inside, the shag carpet was a whitish meadow of nylon, and the mirrors were smoked and marbleized like Caesars Palace in the seventies. All of our friends were horrified when they saw what we had bought.

Anna never interested herself in architecture or design, but I'd flirted with the idea of becoming an architect when I was in boarding school, and this house was as close as I was going to get. The carpet was the first thing to go. I immediately flooded the entire house in an ocean of golden sisal. I had the beige walls painted light yellow. The outside was trickier. I had studied in Florence and was obsessed with finding the perfect burnt sienna color for the stucco. The first pass turned out more Day-Glo than Tuscan. The Halloween House, we called it. Our new neighbors were understandably troubled. We eventually toned it down; however, still, months later, a neighbor told me this with a smile: I like the color. I don't care what everyone else says.

During those first months in the house, instead of writing, I drove to building supply companies and helped the guy renovating our kitchen load bags of plaster and thinset mortar. After-hours, the landscaper and I drove around and stole jigsawed chunks of broken concrete from construction sites to make the stairs up our steep hillside. I helped pour the concrete for the bench at the top of the hill, a blue bench, like the blue bus benches around Santa Monica, but this one had a view of the ocean and palm trees and Malibu.

Our once-kitsch, very Brady home was transformed into an exultant, Italianate beach house. Unfortunately, however, by the time I signed the last check, the total cost of the renovation had ballooned to just a little less than Bush II would later spend on the war in Iraq. In a strange bit of luck, just weeks after finishing the work, on the morning of January 17, 1994, a magnitude 6.7 earthquake dribbled our king-size bed around the room. The picture window cracked, and the two-hundred-year-old Japanese *tansu* chest crashed to the sisal. We were lucky. The really big mansion just down the road and once owned by Lon Chaney fell off the hillside onto the Pacific Coast Highway. Our resulting FEMA loan not only helped us rebuild, it carried us financially until I landed another paying gig.

So now, eight years later, I did not want to be forced out of my home and onto the streets by a combination of work drying up and my marriage drying up. I would write the remake of *Semi-Tough,* collect my awards and riches, and the kids and I would look back at these few tough months and laugh.

My agent confirmed that the meeting had gone well and said that now I just had to convince her boss and the job would be mine. He was flying in from New York in the next few weeks, and they would set up the meeting soon. Days passed. Okay, he's not coming out as soon as he thought, but he's so excited he wants to hear the pitch over the phone. I had never pitched over the phone but was not opposed to the idea. I figured I might even feel less like a professional plate-spinner in a gorilla suit than I do during face-to-face pitches.

It's great to meet you, Trey, even if it's just on the phone.

You too. How's New York? I grew up on the Upper West Side.

Really? I grew up in Santa Monica.

We've stolen each other's lives.

He laughs. I laugh. The first female exec I met with

laughs as well. Then, in the dead space that follows, I know it's time to dive in. I spin the tale of the funniest, raunchiest, wittiest goddamn football movie you've ever seen. As I babbled, I flattened my ear against the phone, trying to divine if on the other end of the wires they were smiling or rolling their eyes at each other and pretending to shove their fingers down their throats. But I was doing just fine, I could tell. They were laughing right where I wanted them to laugh.

I hung up happy. What a world. You talk to some guy on the phone for half an hour, and he decides to either pay you nothing or $250,000.

I don't know about you, but when I feel sure that great riches are about to come my way, my imagination dances off on an orgy of preshopping—especially if immediately before this I wasn't going to the movies or even to Starbucks because money was so tight. I needed a new computer; that was for sure. And it's tax deductible. Also, my surfboard was full of dings. Didn't I deserve a new one to celebrate this momentous life change?

A few days later, my agent called.

Well, I heard back from Miramax.

I took in air all the way to my toes. He didn't sound too enthusiastic, but then again he never does.

They like you a lot. They liked your take. But they liked somebody else's better.

Jesus Christ! Don't they realize that my wife just walked out with my heart and great, jagged chunks of my soul? She used to make up songs about how crazy in love with me she was, follow me around the house and moon as if I'd hypnotized her, weep when I went out of town even for just a night, call me her goddamn samurai love bunny! Don't they realize that she's not

even the first woman I've loved to walk out on me? That my
mother killed herself when I was an already seriously screwed-up
sixteen-year-old? Don't they realize that my kidney disease could
be fatal, almost always leads to a transplant, has me gobbling
twenty-three pills a day and poking a needle into my leg once a
week with a substance genetically engineered on the backs of
laboratory mice? Don't they realize that my dad . . . my dad practically died in my arms? Fuck. Don't they realize that I'm good at
what I do? Don't they realize that while for some writers landing
the assignment would mean the difference between a Beemer and
Jag, for me and my kids, right now, it means the difference
between staying and selling?

Oh well. Their loss. I practically sang this to my agent
over the phone to show him how nonwhiny this writer could be.
But I quickly hung up before my true feelings seeped through the
cracks. An old blues song burst out in my skull: "If it wasn't for
bad luck, I wouldn't have no luck at all."

On the other hand, I was so damn tired of hanging on by
a thread; of possessing a brain whose every cranny was con-
taminated by an obsession over debt. The next day, while I was
on the phone with my latest lender trying to figure out the last
possible day I could pay the previous month's mortgage before
they ratted me out to the credit Nazis, while simultaneously on
the Internet trying to launder money from what was left of my
business account to my personal account, Ava was wrestling
with her little brother in their room across the hall. They were
shrieking and giggling with a vibrant happiness that I don't
know I've ever felt.

Please! Ava! I am on the phone!

The silence in the other room was immediate. My stomach

somersaulted into my throat. I pressed my thumb over the cordless phone's mouthpiece and inched into their room. Chet was
crawling around on the floor like a stocky brown bulldog. Ava
was sitting in her little rocker pretending to read the potty book.
As soon as I was off the phone, I picked her up.

I'm sorry, baby. I didn't mean to snap.

That's okay.

Who knows how much she knew about what was going
on. I thought about the Father's Day present she had just given
me. In her preschool they had spelled out *DAD* in chocolate.
She'd dictated a note to Miss Beth, her teacher, who was so
attentive and angelic that I thought that even if Carmen and I
turned out to be crappy parents, Ava might just turn out all
right anyway. The note said, *To Daddy. I like him very much
and I love him.*

In writing this book, I often consult my journal from back
then. Here's what I wrote when Ava was just six months old:

> Ava had her first meal yesterday and I fed it to her. I feel so
> tied to her, creating her belly button (I am the one who
> expertly cut the cord) and now feeding her her first meal
> (sweet potatoes). She loved them and now whenever she
> eats anything she will think of me.

Somebody please tell me why, for a while there, I obsessed
more over retaining that damn ocean view than over protecting
the childhood of my perfect children? Though everyone else
does it, I can't blame it all on LA. I'm a Zen Buddhist, for chrissakes. When would I ever fucking realize that *desires are inex-
haustible.* And yet, with my screenwriting career already on the
skids, I also knew that if everybody *knew* it was on the skids, I'd

have an even harder time getting a job. Hollywood only wants to hire you if everybody else wants to hire you too.

To be fair, about my house mania, I had just lost my wife. My motto is, if you can help it, take one loss at a time.

I raced over to my realtor friend's house and told him I was finally ready to put my place up for sale. He gave me a list of things to do to enhance its curb appeal, and that afternoon I set about doing them with a maniacal intensity. I touched up the paint on all the walls myself, strategically rearranged the rugs to cover all the water stains on the damn sisal, repainted the front steps, and added sand to the paint so no one would slip if it ever rained. Including all the money I originally endowed in remodeling the place, now eight years after I'd bought it, the realtor expected me to double my money. Contrary to what you always hear about California divorces, Carmen wouldn't get half. Since I had put down the entire down payment (every penny from the sale of my dad's apartment back in New York), all of that would come back to me before I split the rest with Carmen. Our $100,000 of debt would be split in half as well.

I don't think I have mentioned yet that Carmen had graciously declined any alimony. She knew that in the past few years I had earned about as much as a public school teacher's assistant. At the divorce mediator's (dramatically faster and cheaper than two divorce attorneys), I had agreed to pay one hundred percent of the kids' costs, and she would take away only her proceeds from the house.

So it turns out the kids and I wouldn't be living in a dented, used RV parked on some side street as I had feared (and perhaps secretly hoped for the great story it would make when we got rich again). I immediately started looking online for our new home and realized that every day I was feeling lighter and lighter, almost giddy. I was truly starting over again, both emotionally and financially.

One night after Internet house hunting well into the night, I jumped up from the computer and decided to wander through every room. The kids' room across the hall was the first stop, and as always at this hour the air they breathed was thick with peace. The bathroom outside their room was a children's store of lotions and toys and a bulletin board now empty. I had dramatically removed all the photos to a drawer within a half hour after that first night she had moved out. Our bedroom was now my bedroom, so I didn't need to dwell there, so I walked downstairs in the dark to the kitchen whose tile pattern I'd designed and whose sea mat ceiling we put in to remind us of the late summer and early fall we had spent in Santorini, Greece. The living room's forty-foot-high ceiling had twenty-five-foot-high bookshelves that I'd helped design and one of those library ladders with the sideways wheels. I then went down the stairs past the front door to the door off the garage and poked my head into the almost subterranean guest bedroom for perhaps only the twentieth time since living there. Snooping around this room was always a bit thrilling because it had never felt like it was actually mine. Being built into the hillside, it always smelled damp and was reserved for guests and then the nannies when they started living in. It had a crazy little shower hidden under the front stairs that I had used only once in eight years—the day we got married. That day I had ceded our bedroom to the bride and her friends. We didn't call them bridesmaids because we didn't make them dress like sherbet. Anna, the black female judge—who was around the age my mom would have been—and I all stood at the top of the stairs we had just put in on the hillside behind our house. Below us was everybody we had ever known, grinning up at us as if we were about to bring peace to the planet.

But enough about that day. Even marriages that end begin with beauty.

Where was I? Oh yes, the guest room. Most recently, Michele, our friend who'd just moved back from London, had lived there until she found her own place. She had volunteered to watch the kids sometimes, which made it easier for me to fire Angela, the Uruguayan Barbarella whose young beauty had so tempted me to even further complicate my already disastrously complicated life.

Then, back upstairs, back in familiar territory, I looked out the window into the side garden at the banana tree, with its weighty hairdo of actual bananas dangling into the yard. They were still green, hard—there was no way they'd ripen before the house was sold. Past the banana tree shimmered the Pacific, that is, when the neighbors trimmed back their hyperactive ficus. In fact, to boost the sale price, I made a note to call them.

It was when my eyes lit on the sandbox that my heart tightened. For Ava's coming, we had painted her room the per-fect shade of lavender, hunted at flea markets for the perfect painted dresser, ordered the ridiculously expensive wicker glider from some guy in San Diego who'd made one for Demi Moore's kids. Before Chet arrived, we had gotten him nothing but a few new onesies. But when Anna was in her eighth month with Chet, I suddenly decided to exhaustively research sand-boxes. Nice wooden ones cost as much as a round-trip ticket to France. Dinky plastic ones shaped like a turtle that Toys "R" Us had could barely hold two kids, and after a single season in the sun, they looked fit only for a home that can be towed by a truck. No, for my son I had to create the sandbox equivalent of a Bentley.

I sketched out the eight-foot-square box and drove straight to Fisher Lumber. I had them cut planks of Douglas fir, bought metal L brackets, and rushed home. I screwed the box together until I realized that the side yard sloped more than I thought, so I had to stop to dig out a level area for my master-piece. Hours later I was back at Fisher Lumber buying more wood to buttress the side of the hill and heavier brackets to replace the ones that had bent and broken. Then I went back a third, or maybe a fifth, time to buy more primer and then more paint and then more sand. Did I say more sand? I'm talking twelve fifty-pound bags. They weighed so much that I had to ferry them home in my SUV in shifts. All of my friends were, conveniently, at work during the day during the middle of the week, so alone and one by one, I waddled each bag up to the side fence, worked the bag onto my shoulder, and, using my legs, pushed myself up to standing, and then with my arms tipped each dead baby hippo over the fence.

The next morning I was paralyzed by back pain but hap-pily manly.

Now I know that you must be asking yourself, But what about the cat pee? Sandboxes quickly become litter boxes for every stray cat in the state. For days and sleepless nights, I obsessed over a stylish solution. When it finally hit me, I gasped and wanted to call Smith & Hawken. I was a genius. I bought a hunk of bamboo fencing for about five bucks and turned it into a curtain by nailing one edge to the sandbox and tying a rope handle to the other. Whenever Chet and his friends wanted to push Tonka trucks through the sand, I just had to push back the stylish, rustic curtain.

Rarely have I been so proud. I had made the sandbox Frank Gehry would have made if he had ever made a sandbox. I imagined *Architectural Digest* and *Dwell* squabbling over the rights to photograph it first.

Now, unless the new owners had kids younger than six, my masterpiece would be demolished before they'd even unpacked.

Or maybe, as the house slowly rotted on the market, another job would fall on me from Hollywood Heaven. The three of us would stay put, and Chet could end up actually playing in the sand for more hours than it took me to make the damn thing. Then I'd make us one humongous, celebratory banana split from our own backyard bananas.

The house sold four days after listing it. I was suddenly flush again financially but still heartbroken and now homeless. We needed at least two bedrooms and a home office. I found three rentals on the Internet, the first one a block off the boardwalk in Venice. From the picture online, it looked like a child's rendering of a space station from the seventies. It wasn't quite geodesic but seemed geodesic-adjacent. And dirty. But it was also almost three thousand square feet, twice as large as the other houses in my price range.

When I drove over to see the house, I was surprised to find it on a wide street with many charming old Venetian cottages. And then in the middle of the block there was a large, pink stucco wall in the process of being strangled by some sort of angry, hyperactive, flowerless vine. The bottom of the wooden gate was rotted and jagged, the warped wood up top bellied like a sail. Inside the gate, the courtyard was a little bigger than a parking space. There was a jacaranda tree in the middle with a rusted birdcage jammed around the trunk. It must have been fitted around the trunk decades ago because now the tree was growing right through the rusted wires. The house itself was pink stucco with a blue curved roof and uneven blue and red tiles wandering up one side of the door, glass brick up the other. The place was so butt ugly I just had to see the inside.

Inside, past a normal enough entryway, the house opened up into a two-story atrium lined with a chain-link balcony. Mad Max's Thunderdome immediately came to mind. The exposed wooden planks of the ceiling curved like the inside of an arc. The owner told me that Frank Gehry was supposed to have designed it, but something had happened and it ended up being his young apprentice Fred Fisher's first commission back in 1978. It was perhaps the ugliest, most cluttered, and most obviously dilapidated home I had ever seen. My old house was so lovely; everybody said so as soon as they stepped inside. The yellow, the ocean, the garden with hummingbirds buzzing and red-tailed hawks circling overhead. This house was all angles, gray tile, and black grout.

I was trying to back out of the dump and make it in time to check out the other houses on my list when the owner convinced me to go upstairs and check out the master bath.

I'd never seen a urinal inside a private home.

I was told that the original owner liked to play with water. There was a shower outside and a shower on the roof.

I told him I'll take it.

How could I resist? What more does a divorcing man need to rebuild his life than his own private urinal?

I closed the bathroom door and unzipped my pants.

• • •

I GAVE AWAY AS MUCH stuff as I could, determined to start my life anew. Back in Manhattan one summer during college I had worked as a furniture mover for Nice Jewish Boy with Truck, so I knew how much movers overcharge. Instead I borrowed a friend's Ford F-150 and moved the small and medium-size pieces myself, with just a few (whining) friends.

Three years earlier I had splurged on a Tempur-Pedic bed, you know, the ones made of that Swedish astronaut memory foam. For a year before I had finally invested in one, I had been waking up with my back on fire with pain, and the mattress had cured me. I thought hard about giving it away. What symbol in a house is more charged than the conjugal bed? Ava and Chet were both not only conceived on that mattress, they'd begun their labor into this world on it as well. Anna and I had lain on it, face to face, almost touching, the night she decided she was going to leave. I wondered who could tell me how long memory foam would remember?

For about a week, I divided my time between both houses, still sleeping in Santa Monica but spending my days unpacking and childproofing the new house. At the new house there were great, child-size gaps in the interior balcony that I had to fit with Plexiglass and stairs everywhere that had to be gated. I loved the work. Manly, yet domestic, I felt like a red-tailed hawk preparing his nest. I was contentedly laboring away when Anna called and announced that her sublet was up and could she crash with us for a few days?

Even though she was the one who left me, I was worried about how she would manage in the world without me there anymore to take care of her. And the kids and I were still in the old house which, technically, was still Carmen's as well.

Sure, I said.

I've got a party tonight, she said, so I won't get in until late.

A few days before, Anna had asked me for the number of a physician friend of ours. When I asked her what was wrong, she said she thought she had a urinary tract infection. And Lucia, the nanny, a few weeks earlier had been amazed that I hadn't noticed the big hickey on Anna's neck.

Why the fuck would I want to notice something like that?

• • •

I WAS SPENDING MY LAST FEW DAYS in the old house. Ever since I'd decided to sell, I'd been sleeping the sleep of the peaceful. Yet one night something woke me a little after three, and I stepped down the stairs, one at a time for once. There she was, curled up on the big couch in the living room, her hands under her head like an angel praying. I couldn't take my eyes off of her. I cried at least once a day while packing the photo albums (I couldn't help myself and had to flip through all of them before caging them in boxes). Yet after twelve years of watching her sleep, this last time I didn't feel sad. I just felt. I felt a lot. But I couldn't call it sadness. I picked up an orange crocheted afghan her mom had made but Anna hadn't wanted to take with her and floated it down over her shoulders. Then I hiked back up the stairs to sleep in our king-size wicker sleigh bed for the very last time. Tomorrow the Disabled American Veterans were coming to take it away.

The miracle mattress, however, was coming with me.

3

EVERY MOMENT SPENT UNPACKING in the new house, every moment spent driving to and from the hardware store for more drywall anchors to resecure the closet shelves where they had ripped out of the fragile walls, every moment spent overloading a Bed Bath & Beyond shopping cart with bedding, trash cans, a twelve-piece knife set, shower mats, shower curtains, shower caddies, and a Magic Marker that insisted it truly was (making any scratch on any piece of wood disappear), every moment spent clapping my hands together in fake enthusiasm and chirping to Ava, I know! Let's see who can stuff the most old newspaper (that had been used to pack the dishes) into the trash bag!—every moment spent righting our capsized ship felt like a scene from an overly earnest Lifetime movie. Chet only had to touch me with his little fat feet, and tears would jump out of my eyes. Ava only had to tug her little brother's pants over his jumbo diaper, and my heart would ooze lava to the driest and most hidden corners of my chest.

We were on our way. In a leaky ship, as I soon would learn when the winter rains came, but it was our ship. Only ours.

I decided to train myself to start calling Anna Carmen. I decided that it would actually be easier for my heart. My Anna had disappeared in some mysterious accident—flying an ultralight solo across the Sahara or eaten by the locals during an expedition in the Purari Delta in New Guinea. This Carmen person, with her dreadlock hair extensions and some sort of mystical, fist-size rock tied around her neck, was maybe my late wife's kooky sister.

This Carmen person had a new special friend named Doug. The first time Ava had mentioned him, I think I pretended not to hear; but over the next week, she said *Mommy's friend Doug* enough times to render impossible any plausible deniability. As part of the Dissolution of Marriage contract, we had vowed not to introduce significant others to the kids until we knew the new person for six months. I took a deep breath and reminded her of that fact when she came over because it was her night to put the kids to bed. In my house. I had given her a key. Yet another reason for Lucia to yell at me.

They don't see us do anything, Trey. Besides, Doug is a shaman. A guru.

Lucia had met Doug when Carmen was dropping off the kids one day. She described him as looking like a homeless person or a not-very-successful pot dealer.

Carmen told me that if I didn't want them around him or her *enlightened*[1] friends, then maybe I should feed the kids

---

[1] Emphasis mine.

over here. Her place was too small for Ava's playdates anyway, she said.

And just like that, she was half-moved back in with us. She would come over in the afternoons and explode my large but seventies-era kitchen with not just organic, but raw vegan everything: chopped cashews soaking in water to make *cheese,* soaked flaxseed *crackers,* shredded zucchini *angel hair pasta.* I felt almost as sorry for the food processor as I did for myself.

Lucia was livid.

You let her run back in here and run all over you, she said. She's out there every night doing anything she wants while you're stuck here. She's got two places now, this house and her sex studio.

In fact, that was exactly what Carmen had been angling for. She didn't really see us as divorced as much as expanded. She floated the idea of a weekly tribal feast, where we would all eat together, Lucia too, one big anthropological case study. She said the kids needed it. Maybe it would have been good for them, but it would have been terrible for my own health. My heart already felt as if it were dissolving in a rusty can filled with battery acid. If I were to croak, who would be there to pay for the pillowcase-size bags of cashews to soak?

I had discovered that Carmen had been telling Ava that she still lived with us while I had been gently, gently trying to accustom our princess to our new situation.

Mommy will be right here. She lives just down the street, I used to tell Ava.

Mommy lives here, I heard Carmen once say to our daughter. I just also have a place down the street.

I never, ever corrected her. Ava would end up repeating

this or something similar to it for another year and a half.

Of course I should have been stronger. Of course I should have stood up to her from the beginning. Everyone was telling me to. I told myself that I always let Carmen have her way because of the kids. I was dedicated to protecting them from her eccentricities. And the less things changed, the easier it would be for them.

Now I know that some of that was true, but what was also true was that I was too wounded, too fucked up to fight back. I blamed myself for her drifting out into a sea of New-Age-raw-vegan-rebirthing-Pleiadian-shamanistic-indigo-childishness. I never blamed her and still don't. It is only recently, however, that I can blame the real villain in this story—the river of time that simply floated us down ever-separating distributaries.

I finally met Doug one day in my tiny cement front yard. He was with Carmen pushing Ava in the tire swing hanging from our crazy tree with the birdcage imprisoning the trunk. The swing was the first thing I had installed in the new house, hoping it would distract Ava from the ruin of the rest of the house. Now there she was laughing like a bird. The way she laughs with me. I closed the gate behind me, and he straightened up and shot out his hand. His hair was short. He looked like a normal enough white guy. Not too homeless-looking at all. Sure he wore a plaid blanket wrapped around his waist as a skirt, and he had the same kind of chunky rock lashed around his neck as Carmen did. But this was Venice. No tourist would have stopped to take his picture.

I found out later through Lucia that Carmen had made him cut off his beard and his matted, white-boy dreads.

It was so odd, how I did not feel even a pinch of jealousy.

They looked so good together, down to their matching rocks. She had begun her great New Age awakening six years earlier, when she was twenty-nine. I rolled with the tarot readings and the incessant *Jesus Christ Superstar* CD playing. That soundtrack became important to me too. When I first got so sick, I was legitimately concerned that I would die before seeing Ava learn to walk. During the worst of my circus-freakishly swollen legs, feet, and cock, Anna could sense the edge I was about to sail over, so she would come into my office, hold me, and soothe me with her rendition of "Everything's Alright."

However, just before my kidneys rebelled, one of our best friends asked me whether, if I had just met this New Age Anna, I still would have married her.

I hate hypotheticals and answered him with the sadness in my eyes. Yet back then I was nevertheless determined to stay married to her—to stay married to her until she or I died, because that's exactly the kind of thing the character called Trey that lived in my brain would have done.

• • •

DOUG AND CARMEN CLOSED the gate, and I carried Chet up the stairs while Ava puppied between my legs. I looked around this shabby old hippie house, better suited to a couple with rocks around their necks than a buppie who still missed his sisal, and decided that I needed to get out more. I called Lucia that night and asked her to put up an ad at Santa Monica College for a babysitter for nights and some weekends in exchange for the big room behind the kitchen. I even flirted with the idea of inviting Angela the Uruguayana back.

A few days later young women began calling about the job. The first of these was Linda, who had nannied for four years for a young girl. Our interview was for six, but I was running late from yoga (in Southern California, regular yoga practice is mandated by the state), so I didn't arrive until 6:10, sweaty and spent. Carmen and the kids were sitting on my living room couch with a young Latina dressed like a banker in training. Apologizing, I hurried past everyone to take a shower. From the first glimpse of her, I would have to say that she was gorgeous, and as long as she didn't have a criminal record for child abuse, I knew that she would soon be living in the house with the kids and me.

It had not been my intent to include Carmen in these deliberations, but when I'd told her I was going to hire a new sitter, she insisted on being the second judge. As I hurried back down the stairs after showering, still fingering water from my ears, I heard Carmen tell her, Yes, it is lovely here. We have so much space and light.

We?

I found Chet in Linda's lap, grinning like a drunk, and Ava giggling as Linda wormed a finger along my little girl's belly. Linda was as perky as a cheerleader for a winning team. Everything, it seemed, made her smile.

I was just telling your wife that you have a lovely home, sang Linda.

Thank you. The kids and I are still getting used to it, but we like it.

I so wanted to remind them all, *ex*-wife, but little Ava looked so happy.

Linda, may I ask how old are you?

Old now, she replied. I just turned twenty-four. I have another year at SMC, and then I hope to transfer to a four-year school.

Her happiness hypnotized me. The shrunken parts inside of me immediately started swelling back to life. And I'm not talking about what you think I'm talking about. She brought the sunshine inside with her, and my kids deserved that. With me, lately, it was mostly cloudy, except when I faked the sunshine because I knew my kids so craved it.

She moved in that weekend. Her boyfriend helped drag in two suitcases and several trash bags full of clothes. While Chet crawled, Ava giggled and bounced around and around Linda's new room. Linda handed her a sweater to put on a shelf, and Ava rose to her full (tiny) height and cradled it like an Oscar. I could have kissed Linda for bringing such a smile out of my little girl.

But I didn't.

Let's talk about Jay, her boyfriend.

Most notable about him to me was his age—just about exactly my own. I shook his hand while pretending not to notice the eyebrows of Linda's thong as she loaded the lower shelves with sweaters. While Jay and I chatted about cars, we weren't really chatting about cars at all. Every year I give a screenwriting lesson in subtext. Our conversation could be a stellar example for my students.

I saw your Mustang in the carport. Is that a '70?

(Don't even think about messing with my girl.)

'73.

(Do you think she's flashing her thong at me on purpose?)

I've got a '69 Camaro. Red on white. 350 ponies. ZZ4 V8.

(Did you hear me? I said, Don't even think about messing with my girl.)

Cool. I love them. I know there's supposed to be this crazy competition between Ford and GM, but when it comes to vintage cars, I think we're all in the same boat.

(Don't worry. A good friend of mine told me, Don't shit where you eat. But what if she finds me irresistible? What if she sleepwalks in the nude? I'm a brittle, fragile man and, dude, your girlfriend is walking sunshine.)

When he left, he gave her a sloppy, noisy kiss at the door, which sent Ava disappearing behind my leg. Linda clapped her hands together.

Well, now that he's gone, let's play!

She carried Chet to the top of the carpeted stairs, sat him on her lap, and whee-ed them all the way down, bump, bump, bump. And before Ava could protest that she wasn't included, Linda had jerked her up by her arms, swung her like a monkey, and slid down with her too. When Linda saw my look, she said:

Oh, is this all right? Do you mind?

Mind? I wanted to weep. The kids and I might just possibly make it after all with this very cute Flying Nun filling the kids with the wonder that I wasn't yet capable of giving them again.

The next day, Sunday morning, Ava didn't wake me at seven with, Daddy, Chet's diaper leaked all over his crib and he's got brown on the side of his mouth! Oooh! Ooooh! She woke Linda. By the time I came down at 8:30, I was drunk on whatever the opposite of sleep deprivation is. I fitted the car seats into the back of Linda's car, and she drove off with the kids, some jangly pop song loud on her radio. I was writing when they came back.

Daddy! Close your eyes!

Yeah, Daddy! Close your eyes!!!

That was Linda yelling first. I don't know if I liked her calling me Daddy. But I closed my eyes and I heard them rumble up the stairs.

Ta-daaa!

Linda and Ava were wearing matching red T-shirts and powder blue sweatpants.

Old Navy, Daddy.

They were on sale, Linda explained. I wanted to get them presents. She then held up a tiny little football jersey for Chet.

Wow! Thank you! I said. But of course I'll pay you back.

It's just Old Navy. It's not like Prada or anything.

I made myself look away from her absurdly big brown eyes.

On Monday morning Lucia arrived as Linda was coming out of her room behind the kitchen in her robe, on her way upstairs to use the shower she shared with the kids. I introduced them while Lucia was making Ava's lunch for preschool. Linda was circling her index finger around Chet's belly button, making him cackle maniacally as she sang:

Los pollitos dicen, Pio! Pio! Pio!, quando tienen hambre, quando tienen frio.

Lucia then told Linda, in Spanish, not to let me run all over her.

Como Lucia runs over *mi*, I said, making them laugh together in exactly the same way. Then Linda noticed the clock on the oven and sprang up the stairs with a squeal. Lucia immediately opened her eyes wide at me.

I know. She's great.

(I whispered that so the kids wouldn't hear.)

Why don't you marry her?

Don't think it hasn't crossed my mind.

Aye, Trey! Cabron.

• • •

AT THE END OF THE DAY, I was bathing the kids, unloading much of a bottle of conditioner onto Ava's scalp so I could run the padded brush through her hair without making her cry. The explosion on top of her head is her most dramatic feature. When it's clean and out, she looks like a miniature Macy Gray, a mini-supermodel–rock star. She looks like her mother. Carmen or Lucia usually wrestled with it, but I was slowly learning. In attempting a braid, I could only get through a turn or two before the hair rioted, so I'd just seal off the relatively controlled part with a barrette and let the rest pouf out like fireworks. Almost always the braid would be high and outside, but Ava was sweet enough not to complain. Instead, while looking at herself in the mirror, she would tilt her head over her shoulder to center the poof and say, It's good, Daddy.

Back when Carmen and I were still together, Ava often asked me why she didn't have straight hair like all her friends. The first time it happened, I lifted her up to my height. Carmen and I had dreaded this day. We had read her *Happy to Be Nappy* and *Nappy Hair,* but how could that counterbalance being the only brown-skinned person in her preschool? I explained to her, as many times as she needed to hear it, that girls with straight hair pay thousands of dollars to make their hair curly, and girls with curly hair pay thousands to make theirs straight. The trick is to love yourself for the way you are (and spend all that money you save on chocolate).

I hadn't heard her complain about her hair in months, not even after coming back from a week at her grandmother's outside of Atlanta. Within seconds of arriving in Social Circle, Georgia, Carmen's mother always ensnared Ava's wild hair into fine, tight plaits right out of *Roots*. The moment she was back with me, I sat her in front of the TV and unknotted her.

After I had dried Ava off from the bath, using it as an excuse to hug her and lay her over my knees and noisily kiss the back of her neck, I pumped some Lubriderm, cold and white, into my hand and spread it down her tiny face. Just as I started to rub it in, she stopped me.

Don't rub it in.

Her eyes sparkled, making my heart sparkle too.

Why not, ladybug?

I want to have skin like my friends.

I pulled Chet out of the tub and just threw a towel over him. I needed to concentrate on his big sister. And yet at the same time, I didn't want her to feel the panic that was racing through all my wiring. She looked so happily matter-of-fact as she waited for my response.

Um, ladybug. You are the most beautiful color in the world. Everybody else wants to look like you.

It's true. She is caramel.

But I was white when I was little.

That's true too. For her first few months, she'd been as pale as a Swede.

Some golden brown children take a little while for their color to come in. Like toast.

Mommy-Daddy.

Chet had tried to crawl out of his bath towel but had only succeeded in burying his head in the tangle. I lifted him up, careful of my back, and dried him.

I didn't know what else to say to Ava. I had grown up in white neighborhoods as well, yet in a very different time. In the seventies, I was chased through Italian-American sections of East Haven by bodybuilding goombahs shouting, *Go back to the Congo!* Kids shouted, *Nigger!* out their school bus windows. We'd moved from Detroit to Ypsilanti, Michigan, in 1968, when I was six and then to Hamden, Connecticut, outside of New Haven, in 1972. Detroit was the only time I hadn't been a minority until Ujamaa, my tenure in Stanford's black-themed dormitory twelve years later. As I grew up, my parents were so desperate for me to have a black friend that in junior high my mom drove me an hour to meet some strange black kid whom they knew through friends of friends of friends. We didn't call them playdates back then; they didn't have a name. Regardless, the kid and I couldn't be bothered with each other. We both thought it queer that our parents had gone through such hoops to set us up.

My kids were now dry, and I still didn't know what else to say to Ava, so I put them to bed (I think I ended that night with a creaky but oddly soulful rendition of James Taylor's "Sweet Baby

James") and went down to my default dinner: a bag or two of the prewashed carrots Lucia always popped into Ava's lunch and a few jagged slabs of supermarket rotisserie chicken. Instead of swiping a couple of juice boxes from my kids, this night I rubbed my hands with glee in anticipation of the treat that awaited me. Tonight I didn't despair that this burnt orange piece of crap refrigerator with the jagged broken plastic shelves and jangly handles was an insult to all of refrigeratordom. I didn't despair because I had bought a six-pack of Pepsi the other day, something I do only a very few times a year because as soon as it's in the house, I end up sucking them all down like crack.

I laid out my bachelor's feast on the table in front of the TV and loaded a DVD of the documentary *Dogtown and Z-Boys*. I turned out the lights so it would seem more like the movies and I'd snuck in food. Just as I pressed play, Linda walked in.

Hel-lo, she said, as if singing a song. Whatcha watching?

I told her.

Cool.

She dropped to the couch, caving us into each other.

Oops, she said. And then, Pepsi! Can I have one?

A great excuse for me to rebound off the couch.

Sit, silly. I'll get it.

It occurred to me that back in '78, when this house was full of promise, the carpet was a recognizable color, and my side-by-side refrigerator was a symbol of status, Linda was just being born.

Not long into the film, I forgot about Linda. The documentary spoke about the very place where I happened to be watching it, Venice Beach in the seventies, where skate-youth culture was born. Growing up in Ypsilanti, Michigan, and then Hamden, Connecticut, I realized that it was this image of California—headbands, sunglasses, and terry-cloth tube tops—that had so infected me at such a young age. The result was a several decades long fever for everything Californian. I remember when I went in for my consultation with my college counselor at Andover and she asked me where I wanted to go to college. She knew I'd have my pick. I was a nerdy, studious, pimply little grade-grubbing black kid with killer SATs.

California, I told her.

California is not a school, she sneered. It is a state.

If I had been cooler, I would have replied, It's a state of mind, babe, slapped on some Ray-Bans, and skated off.

Back on the couch, Linda fidgeted.

You're really into this, aren't you? she asked.

I remember watching these guys on TV and then begging my parents for my own skateboard with polyurethane wheels and sealed bearings.

Well, boss, enjoy your trip down memory lane.

She pushed off from the couch and took all the dishes to the kitchen with her on her way upstairs to the bathroom. A few minutes later, she clattered down the stairs holding her clothes, one towel around her body and another around her hair.

Good . . . *night?* My voice cracked for maybe the first time in two decades. I winced, but it was too dark in the TV room for her to have seen me.

Sweet dreams, she said. Dream about me.

I stopped the DVD to collect my thoughts. The direction

that our nascent relationship was going was leading me straight toward a tawdry, scandal-ridden hell. I had hired her so that I could get out and begin living like the newly single man that I now was. Yes, there were issues. I didn't really drink, hated bars, and the last time I'd been on the prowl Phil Collins was topping the charts.

All right, that wasn't completely true. I had gone out once a few months ago, right as Anna was leaving me. My friend Yule had dragged me to The Brig, our local meat market. It was a Friday night, and when the big, black bouncer eyed my driver's license, I joked that I was almost old enough to be legal two times over. His only response was to tug his huge head toward the door. Inside, as I watched a carpet of twenty- and thirtysomethings shout at each other and spill beer on each other in an attempt to have sex with each other, my stomach convulsed. Out of the hundreds of sweaty yuppie girls in this room, I was positive that not one of them could I ever love. I could have collapsed to the floor in a sobbing heap—if it hadn't been so crowded that my arms were pinned to my sides.

I've gotta get out of here, I told Yule.

We just got here.

I am about to throw up in my mouth.

I turned to shoulder my way back out the front door. A blonde woman, and just about the only woman there my age, blocked my way and wasn't moving. Who knows what she might have looked like if she hadn't been so damn drunk, but as it was, all her facial muscles were so relaxed by alcohol that she looked as if she were melting.

You are fine!

Excuse me? My words served two purposes. I didn't understand what she had just said, and I wanted to get around her quickly.

You are fine! I saw you as soon as you came in, and I said to myself, He is fine!

I looked at her more closely this time. Was she just messing with me?

Uh . . . thank you. Wow. Thanks.

Circling each other, we traded places so I was now nearer the exit.

Um. 'Bye.

As the cool and the quiet of the outside hit me, I cackled.

She called me *fine*! I am knocking on forty and had never been called *fine* by anybody, not once in my life. Perhaps she was some sort of drunken angel, come to earth to help me through.

• • •

ALL OF MY FRIENDS HAD advice for the best way for me to meet women, but actually one guy, who was not a particularly good friend, gave me the best hint. He asked me if there were any women that I knew when I was married who, if I hadn't been married at the time, I would have asked out.

He was right. No matter how in love you are with your wife at the time, there are always women, were your wife to be, say, flattened by a tour bus, that you would ask to help console you. The problem is that since you never have to actually test the theory that they are interested in you, you can happily delude yourself into thinking that you are the most desirable man in the tristate area.

The first woman that came to mind was Anna's former best friend, Stacey. She was inseparable from us for a few years. We three lived together in Mallorca one summer and then in Paris and then Ramatuelle the next. She's a witty Yalie writer, gorgeous, Korean-American. If I could have convinced Anna and Stacey (and the United States government) that I just had to go back to my West African polygamous roots and take a second wife, I would have seriously considered it. However, after that summer in France, the women stopped talking to each other, and Stacey moved to San Francisco, met a caring man, and had two babies.

However, a few days later, while I was driving home, top down, distant sailboats in the ocean taunting me with their windy freedom, I suddenly blurted out, *Sabina!*

How could I have forgotten about her? She was a Pakistani model-turned-actress raised in Glasgow. She was part of the outer ring of our circle of friends. Admittedly, I have terrible intuition about such things, but I'd always felt there was a bit of a charge in the room whenever Sabina and I were together. I think Anna felt it too because she used to tease me about her. Unfortunately, I hadn't seen Sabina in three or four years, didn't even know if she was still in LA.

As soon as I got home, I scavenged my oldest address books and finally found her number and tried calling. I held the phone away from my ear, prepared to hear the annoying three rising notes and then a chilly recorded announcement of disconnection.

Hello?

Sabina! Wow. I . . . I didn't expect you to answer.

You called my phone. Who is thi—Trey?

Uh, yes. I was just thinking about you and thought I'd call. A lot has been going on around here. Anna and I are getting a divorce.

I'm sorry to hear that.

Don't be. It's been a few months already, and we're both doing fine. The kids, too.

In the silence, I tried to think of an elegant segue to the business at hand.

How about dinner? I mean, would you like to go out to dinner this week?

In this next silence, I made faces and tried to pull my hair, but it was too short.

I don't think so. You're still married.

Only legally. Otherwise I wouldn't have called you.

The Dissolution of Marriage paperwork had only been filed a week before and would take another six months to finalize.

When I heard Ava crying downstairs because Chet had hit her with something, I knew exactly what I had to do. It was Wednesday, so Anna/Carmen was downstairs looking after the kids until 5:30.

Look, I'll put Anna on the phone if you don't believe me. Don't go away. Promise?

I . . .

I ran down the stairs to where Ava was puppeting two Barbie dolls, a brown one and a pink one, while Chet chewed on the corner of a board book. At first I didn't see Carmen anywhere, but then I looked around a corner and saw her folded into an armchair, her eyes closed, her wrists lightly rest-ing on her knees, her thumb and forefinger two circles offered to the sky.

Um . . . Carmen . . . ? Carmen . . . ? I need to ask a favor.

She opened one eye and then the other.

Sabina! You still there? I shouted into the cordless phone. Hold on one more second.

Can you come upstairs with me?

Away from the kids, I pressed my thumb over the phone's mouthpiece.

Remember Sabina? I um . . . we have been talking about going out, but since, technically, you and I are still married, she is a little wary.

Carmen smiled a smile I hadn't seen in years. She smiled the kind of smile that once made my heart explode with love and gratitude at my great luck in having found her.

Of course, said Carmen. I always thought you two would make a cute couple.

She took the phone and walked into the other room.

My heart seemed to be ricocheting around the walls of my throat.

Endless minutes later, Carmen bounced in, handed me back the phone, and vanished.

You've got balls, Ellis. I'll have to give you that.

Her Paki-Glaswegian accent, the flirty-angry way she called me by my last name, reached right through my chest and seized my heart with two hot hands. When I hung up, I realized Carmen was right outside the door.

So . . . ? Did she say yes?

I wanted to tell her to mind her own business, but I was

so excited, I just had to tell someone—even my future ex-wife who happened to be screwing a white Rasta shaman named Doug.

Yes, she did. What did you tell her?

I told her you and I would always love each other, but we were committed to sharing each other with the world.

I didn't want to argue semantics because the kids were downstairs.

Besides, I had to get back to work. I was way behind on a spec script I was writing about a brilliant, surfing scientist who, after his wife is killed in a car accident, exiles himself to a deserted island in the South Pacific—until the CIA tracks him down, kidnaps him, and trains him to be a spy. Neither my agent nor my manager had called in months about new assignments so I was counting on this script to reinvent myself in the eyes of Hollywood. The New York novelist and writer of quirky, highbrow historical screenplays had died with his marriage. The newly single Trey Ellis would be paying for his kids' private schools by transforming dumb, bloated action movies into smart, bloated action movies. The kind of American movies I myself am a sucker for and race out to see.

Writing the script did double duty as great escapist therapy. August Welch, my protagonist, was me, only instead of wiping my son's ass on top of the dryer and finally throwing out all the parenting books and bribing his big sister with an entire raspberry chocolate mousse cake if she would start crapping in the toilet already, I was racing a 1963 Ferrari 250 GTO Scaglietti through medieval Italian towns while the bad guy shrieked after me in a brand-new Lamborghini Murciélago. The August me was still bitter and wounded after the suspicious and sudden death of my wife, but I was slowly beginning to learn how to love again thanks to my CIA handler, a seasoned superspy who bore an uncanny resemblance to Angelina Jolie.

I had three whole days before my first date in twelve years to fret, fantasize, and fret some more. The last time I had seen Sabina was maybe three years earlier. Sure, she looked great then, but what if, oh, I don't know, what if she was getting a chemical peel and they left the acid on too long so now she looked like the little sister of the Crypt Keeper? Why else would a successful international model/actress (a) not only be free on a Saturday night but (b) say yes to going out with a broke guy with two kids and a not-yet-ex-wife who still spent most of her day in his house.

In those days I was in such a perpetual state of tenderness, the slightest breeze would make me cry. What if I got my hopes up for Sabina and then discovered she was riddled with cancer or secretly a man or, perhaps more realistically, liked me well enough until getting to know me and then abruptly stopped returning my calls?

How would my heart handle another trauma?

Not at all well.

I had to interrupt my morbid reverie to bathe the kids. I couldn't remember when Ava had last had her hair washed, so I rolled up my sleeves.

I remembered how my scalp had hurt when my father dragged a pick through my naps, every *ow!* punctuated by his saying either *Oh, it doesn't hurt that bad* or *Good. If you would take better care of it, your hair wouldn't get so nappy.* I was determined to do better. So while Chet piled bubbles onto the headless neck of one of Ava's black Kens, I poured pitcherfuls of

water over my daughter's head and worked almost a quarter of
a bottle of Johnson & Johnson into her forest. Then, after rinsing, I spread almost a half pint of conditioner on the front,
middle, and back of her head. Chet's few puffs of crazy old man
hair got the shampoo left over on my hands and then, if he was
lucky, a button of conditioner. If he had any idea how many of
her leftovers I've forced on him and if he were old enough to use
a phone, he would have dialed social services. When Ava was
his age, she'd gotten creamy massages every night like a Kobe
steer. Every movement or threatened movement was recorded
on film or video and in a flowery journal her mother and I were
keeping for her. Chet, on the other hand, was lucky if I remembered to feed him. Then again, he was the exact dimensions of
a Sumo wrestler in miniature, so even if I forgot his organic
macaroni and cheese for a few days, I'm sure he'd have still
done just fine.

Determined not to make Ava's ponytail lopsided this time,
I brushed back her hair and wound a pink stretchy band around
and around. The bun was not nearly as tight as when the women
in her life did it, and after a few tries and much muttering under
my breath, I resigned myself to yet another asymmetrical failure.
I dried my hands and stood up when I made myself stop. I straightened my back and rededicated myself to finally getting it right.
After three more tries, however, I only succeeded in tangling the
stretchy band so deeply into her hair that to get it out I had to cut
it out with a child's toenail clipper.

To make it up to her, I pulled Ava out of the tub first, the
way she liked, captured her in a towel, and kissed her cheeks until
she giggled and nosed me away. I then buttered her with lotion,
and she put on her own pajamas while I hoisted Chet out of the

tub. I didn't want to nag her, didn't want to give her a complex, but I couldn't help myself when I picked up *Once Upon a Potty* and laid on the floor to read to them. I was getting increasingly desperate. Even the promised chocolate raspberry mousse cake bounty had, so far, had no effect.

Not that book again, Daddy.

You love that book.

Her look told me that she wasn't buying it, but I started reading anyway.

Hello, I am Prudence's mother, and I would like to tell you about her new potty.

Ava huffed like a teenager while Chet crawled over my legs like an iguana.

Chetty, stop. Listen to the story.

When Ava had been his age and I had read her a book, she would burrow into my lap and hang on my every word. Chet saw books and everything else as a potential meal. He was like a lion cub, tripping around the old gray carpet on his outsized paws.

After the story, I clapped my hands together twice— *Clap! Clap!*—like a pasha, and Ava leaped off my lap and dived into her toddler bed. I hoisted Chet over the rail and into his crib. I had already lowered it to the lowest rung, but still when he stood, he seemed dangerously close to effecting an escape. I figured I had about a month before I would absolutely have to buy Ava a bigger kid's bed and move Chet into the toddler.

Like every night, I extemporized a final good-night story, this one about a little girl named Ava and a little boy named Chet who rose up in the air, flew over the mountains, flew over the deserts, flew over the forests, flew all the way to their grand-mother's house in Social Circle, Georgia, where she (Carmen's mother) was out front sweeping when she saw them and invited them in for snicker doodles and milk. Then she sent them back home over the forests, the deserts, and the mountains until they dropped back into their beds so tired that their eyes were already closed before they landed. Then I sang them my version of Israel Kamakawiwo'ole's (Bruddah IZ's) version of "Somewhere Over the Rainbow/It's a Wonderful World" as I backed out of the room.

I don't remember what I had for dinner. A frozen chicken potpie? A wing and some slices of breast from a supermarket roast chicken and a little bag of carrots? Then, after a frustrated evening spent channel surfing (this was pre-TiVo), I checked on the kids, as I did every night, to make sure they were still breathing. Then I pushed the button to lock my bedroom door for yet another date with Playboy TV.

Then I stopped.

I thought about Sabina and our promising future. I didn't want to jinx it by cheating on her with Misses May through August.

I turned out the light.

• • •

BY SATURDAY I was praying that she would come to her senses and back out. I was nowhere near ready for this. I pictured myself leaning in for a kiss at the end of the night, but instead of kissing back she would shudder in disgust, and I'd break down and bawl like Chet when he's overdue for a nap. Or, if I managed to get a little farther, I imagined staring down at my uncooperative, still-mourning cock while Sabina hurriedly dressed and speeded out the door. Or, I imagined myself getting farther still, yet the instant after I came, sobbing uncontrollably while Sabina looked on in horror, clutching the sheets to her breasts.

I needed to calm down.

I showered and dug up some old cologne, Acqua di Parma, a birthday gift from Carmen from several years back. Cary Grant had used the same brand, so she'd picked it out for me because she said I reminded her of him. I hadn't bought a new article of clothing in two years, so I cobbled together what I thought the young single folks might be wearing these days.

I was too nervous to bathe the kids, so that night Linda did it for me. Later, she was down in the kitchen making herself dinner when I tripped down the stairs dressed for my big night.

Hubba hubba!

I didn't say anything back. I was just trying to get out of there with a minimum of embarrassment. She was making a salad.

I guess I won't wait up!

We're just having drinks, I mumbled.

If you want, I'll tell her yours is bigger.

She was holding a cucumber.

One of the many blessings of being black is that it is very hard to see you blush. I muttered something incomprehensible as I stumbled out the door.

Sabina lived in Hollywood, so I had a long drive from the beach. Unless it's raining, I drive with the top down and ostentatiously loud and fast. She had chosen our rendezvous, this cavernous Irish bar in the middle of the Sunset Strip. Fighting my way inside, I was greeted by eighties-era Hall and Oates trumpeting from omnipresent, yet hidden, speakers. The place appeared to be a cross between a drunken frat party and a drunken frat party inside Satan's rectum. I didn't see Sabina, so I called her on her phone, but both Hall and Oates were screaming in my ears. I was sure that my long-awaited first new date in over a decade would end in the tragedy of never even meeting her. Then I looked again, and there she was propped on a stool just in front of me, enjoying my distress.

She sparkled like a diamond in a dung heap. I had forgotten the depth of her beauty, the kind of beauty that makes my eyes cross. I had forgotten her endless legs.

My heart leapt like a puppy just released from doggy intensive care who was just about to run right back out on the freeway.

Ellis. I see you found me.

You kind of stick out. Nice and quiet, this place of yours.

I don't trust you enough for someplace quiet.

I'm the least dangerous guy on the planet.

That's what the really dangerous ones always say.

Oh God, I think she's flirting with me. Is this the way women flirt these days? Why? Why the hell isn't she running away?

What are you drinking? I asked her. Bourbon?

I'm Scottish. We drink scotch.

I don't really drink. After a drink and a half, my bones turn to rubber. I don't smoke either, can't stand it, but I have twice accepted cigarettes from girls just because I liked the height of their heels. If Halle Berry ever offered me a speedball, I'd do whatever it is you do with one.

I'll have what she's having.

She was having turpentine.

It's the only single malt they carry that isn't shite, she said.

My lips were stinging, but I forced myself not to cough. Besides, I am a sucker for dialects and always wanted to date someone who could get away with pronouncing *shit* shite.

Somewhere in the middle of my second Scotch, all nervousness drained out of me and I was deeply, hopelessly infatuated. Her obscenely ripe lips, pulsating as she talked, hypnotized me utterly. Had I had just one more sip of scotch, she would have turned into a giant ice cream cone, and I would have tried to lick the mocha right off her face.

Ellis, there's a party down the street from my house.

We drove together, and when we arrived, she took my hand to lead me inside.

I was holding another woman's hand. I hadn't held another woman's hand in twelve years.

It was a small party and apparently we were late. She kissed friends' cheeks and fell onto a couch and waved me off to get us more drinks. Nothing felt familiar. Suddenly everything about my life, not just this strange house, was utterly new. I found the kitchen, but the beer was gone and most of the liquor bottles spent. A very drunk Persian woman grabbed my arm to steady herself then leaned toward my lips. Instinctively, I turned my cheek so that was where her red lips landed, and she grinned at me with only one eye open. I poured what I hoped was vodka into two possibly clean plastic cups and withdrew from the room. But before I rejoined Sabina, I first stopped and breathed.

I am single now. I am free. Why did I waste so much time on tears? There was so much to look forward to. Drunken women might sometimes kiss me. Untold adventures awaited.

We didn't stay much longer. Soon we walked down the silent street to her house. She insisted that I was too drunk to drive home yet. Sabina couldn't get her key to work, so she handed it to me, whispering pointers on her door's eccentricities from so close behind my back that her breath made me wriggle.

Seeing inside her place made me like her even more. It was littered with her paintings—abstract, angry—as well as with dirty clothes and actual litter like old newspapers and polyhedral Styrofoam takeout containers. Even after her beauty stops surprising me, I thought, even after I start taking for granted the plums of her lips, she will still be a very interesting person.

I sat on the couch, and she joined me with mismatched glasses of water.

Ellis.

She studied me from beneath her eyelids, arms folded, seeming to rehearse in her head some sort of critique of my personality. I just had to tell her something first.

Your lips are like plums.

She sucked them into her mouth like a startled mollusk.

Don't do that, I told her.

I kissed her, and the power of that kiss made my inner self, for a moment there, disappear into the infinity of the cosmos. Then I remembered who I was again, and the old chatter started again flooding my brain.

Just keep kissing her, your heart couldn't take much more than that tonight, but what if she wants more? Didn't you read that women today routinely give it up on the first date? Give it up? What are you, some drunken frat boy? She's grown and likes an orgasm as much as you do. Damn, you still have so much to learn about women. But you also read that blowjobs are now seen as just an extension of making out, and you're already making out and . . . ? I'll have to tell her that I can't stay the night. I have to get back before the kids wake up.

She pulled away.

I think you're bloody all right to drive home now.

So that was just your routine, sober-up kiss?

She took my hand, hauled me to my feet, and walked me to her door.

Driving home with the top down, the stores shuttered, and the streets long and quiet, I couldn't stop myself from touching my lips.

The next day I padded our little red wagon with pillows, loaded in Ava and Chet, and pulled them the quarter mile down Main Street to the Santa Monica farmer's market. Of course everyone stopped and cooed as if I were wheeling a litter of puppies. Ava's overly wide eyes told me that the adoring swarm of Venice and Santa Monica white liberals was beginning to freak her out, especially the people that cried, Your hair! Wow! And tried to reach out and touch it before I cut them off with a look.

I see in her so much of me. Shy, smart, complicated universes collide inside her head. Chet, on the other hand, waved and giggled at the fawning onlookers like a grand marshal at a parade.

My kids' local exoticism was so familiar to me. I too grew up a brown spot in a pink sea. Back in Hamden, Connecticut, our dinky little suburb outside of New Haven, I was once called *Oreo* by an older, head-wagging black girl bussed in from New Haven and also *nigger* by some local Italian Stallion wannabe—*on the very same day.* Many years later, when I was writing an adaptation of Anna's novel for Spike Lee and

Showtime, I dramatized that very incident. Anna's novel told the story of a black, upwardly mobile family growing up in Hamden, Connecticut, in the seventies, who then moved to Greenwich when they got rich. She named the character Tommy Two because he's Thomas Jr. I'm called *Trey* because my real name is William Arthur Ellis III. I had started adapting the novel toward the very end of our marriage, but we never once fought about it. She knew it was my story as much as it was hers and, anyway, in her head, I guess she had already moved on.

So while I was pulling a wagon carrying the two best-looking kids in the western hemisphere down Main Street, Danny Glover was up in Toronto (standing in for Hamden) playing my father. Whoopi Goldberg was my mom.

We arrived at the Santa Monica farmer's market, and it was, as always, packed. Fifty kids and their parents lined up along the low brick wall for pony rides. The lawn in front of the long, snaking line of organic, handpicked or prepared, absurdly overpriced strawberry, nut, oyster, tamale, sausage, pesto, and bok choy vendors was a lake of toddlers on blankets. On this day a band of non-Brazilians in almost matching jungle-print shirts played samba.

I checked my watch and wondered when Sabina would be getting up, wondered what the rules were these days about how long one had to wait before calling. I also kept thinking about the six-month rule in our divorce decree and how hard it would be to hide my new girlfriend from my kids for so long. Since Sabina and I had known each other for years, would I get a special dispensation to fold her into my family sooner? I felt her presence so strongly in my heart that several times a minute all day long thoughts of her invaded my brain and overwhelmed me. However, the thought that never once entered my skull during my dizzy reverie was that it just wasn't normal for a grown man to have to bite his lip so he doesn't burst into song after just one date.

Luckily, in bouts between my raging love drunk, I did somehow manage to parent my children. We three shared two huge apple pancakes on the lawn. Ava could feed herself the pieces I cut up, but I still had to feed Chet. He'd bird his mouth open, and I would deliver square after square varnished with syrup.

Pulling them home like pharaohs, I could still feel the dry warmth of Sabina's hand in mine as I imagined us pulling the kids together, a family of brown superheroes parting a sea of adoring white Santa Monicans. I imagined finagling them into simultaneous naps so that Dada and Stepmom could nap too. We would make love in the cool shade of the early afternoon, then drift to sleep ourselves until we were awakened by Ava and Chet giggling into the baby monitor.

The wagon was suddenly rocking my wrist, but I was too busy test-driving new baby names (and positions that would lead to the creation of said baby) in my head to turn around.

Whap!

Ahhhhhhh! Chetty hit me!

He wasn't even one yet, but my Bamm-Bamm could already pack a punch. And he usually landed them on his victim's eye. The kids had their hands on each other's necks and were leaning dangerously out of the wagon like brawling cowboys. Instantly my hands encircled their wrists, and my big head descended on them like an angry T. rex.

Stop it, you two. Right. This. Instant. (If that tone was good enough for my mom, it was good enough for me.)

Silence, as their eyes fattened. Then came the storm of tears, the shrieking, the wailing. If I had boiled them in a french fryer, they wouldn't have made more noise. A Santa Monica mom passed by, eyeing me as if she had social services on speed dial and was just itching to make the call.

Quiet. I didn't mean to yell but . . . *please!*

I pulled faster, but we were still ten blocks from our house, where the walls would muffle their cries. After three more blocks, their shrieks had started to lose their sharpness, settling into an almost musical, albeit still continuous lament. If they had had a larger vocabulary, they might have been wailing:

Oh Daddy, what a terrible life we have just with you. Where is Mommy? She is the one we really love. Why did you drive her away? You have ruined our young lives so we will be condemned to be as miserable and as lonely as you are. Ohhh, if only we hadn't been born to you but to some normal couple who would push us on the swings more often and let us watch TV.

By the time we reached our front gate, they were silent, however tragedy still seemed to envelop us. I felt like a surgeon at a MASH unit coming off of three days of repairing chest wounds. I carried Chet right to his crib, and he was almost already napping before I fitted the blanket around him.

I went downstairs to read Ava *Hop on Pop*. Soon, she was again giggly and light while I still felt spent, rattled. I wonder if I will ever learn to let these storms blow through me as quickly as they exit my kids.

• • •

SABINA CALLED THAT EVENING and asked me if I played pool. Of course I lied and said sure, and we made a date for the next night. The evening of our second date, I took the longest shower of my life, water conservation be damned. I was a wreck.

Actors have stuntmen to step in to perform the acts too dangerous for them. I wish regular people had emotional stuntmen. I would just sit on the sidelines and watch as a guy who looked sort of like me from a distance put his heart through the psychological extreme sport of seeing if a woman would ever like me again. After I was sure it would end well, the director would yell *Cut!* and I would saunter in and hold her hand.

The me in a movie would play pool effortlessly, like Montgomery Clift in *A Place in the Sun*. The real me should have been expelled from the pool hall for nearly ripping the felt.

Ellis, your hands are just gorgeous, you know that. Pity you're so disastrous at billiards. Or are you just pretending to make me put my arms around you to show you how?

Sabina sank shot after shot. Bent over the table, her ass in my mind was a ripe apple dangling from a low branch. Overwhelmed by the image, I closed an eye.

What, Ellis?

Would you like to come over and see the new house?

Sure. I'll follow you.

Never have I driven so slowly. I'd be damned if I'd come this close to taking her home only to lose her in Los Angeles traffic.

I opened my front door with hardly a shake. I was grateful that Linda was already asleep.

Sabina sat herself in the middle of my couch. Whichever side I chose would be next to her.

Scotch?

No, thank you.

I sat next to her and said something about Frank Gehry and the house and God knows what else before I kissed her and kissed her again.

She pulled away and stood. When I opened my eyes, I saw her hand reaching out to me.

Where is your bedroom?

Her body tasted so different from Carmen's. Less fruity, more bourbon. The curves had different amplitudes. Holding her ass, my hands felt electric. Every place I touched her, every place I licked, pulled deep sounds out of her, made her body dance. I had forgotten how much I loved making love, discovering what unlocks a new woman.

She came hard under my tongue, digging her back into my bed. A good sign. That took off some of the pressure from other body parts to perform. If I didn't make her come a second time, at least she wouldn't go home empty-handed. I pulled the condom out of the night table's drawer. I had placed it faceup in there that afternoon. I'd even opened a practice one to remember which way they unrolled. Though I hadn't touched one in twelve years, I still remembered the endless, awkward purgatory of trying to unroll one the wrong way.

I looked into her eyes as I entered her. Now. At that very instant. By any measure. I was officially, irredeemably single.

I could have just stayed inside of her and ruminated on how the chapters of my life had unfolded in the most unexpected ways, but thankfully I soon realized that this was not the time. I started moving, and she locked me with her legs, and the condom actually anesthetized me from overexuberance so I lasted forever, greedily trying out every position Carmen was never a fan of. It was all very sexy and pleasant, but it also forced me to remember how being inside of Carmen I often felt as close to her as if we shared the same nervous system.

Sabina started coming again—very loudly—and I felt like beating my chest until I remembered that I had two sleeping little ones in the house. I came *this* close to hushing Sabina by whispering, *Inside voice! Inside voice!*

Then I remembered that since she didn't have kids, she probably wouldn't have understood.

She slept in my bed as if she'd been born in it.

The next morning, as I was coming back to consciousness, I smelled her next to me, filled myself with her air. Then I opened my eyes, and my heart nearly burst as I watched her tranquil beauty sleeping still. Then I drank in the blue of the morning sky as somewhere far off someone's gardener began blowing leaves.

6:58. In two minutes my perfect young angels were about to be permanently scarred.

I grabbed the used condom from the floor with one hand as I picked up my pajamas with the other, ran to the urinal, threw away the condom, hopped into my pajamas while nearly catapulting myself down the stairs, then dragged on a T-shirt and ran up the stairs to the kids' side of my crazy house.

There they were, happy, smiling, and sleepy.

French toast! Who wants French toast?

I hoisted up Chetty, and Ava hurried down after us. I stuffed both kids with half a loaf's worth of French toast and flooded each piece with syrup, I guess hoping they would sink into some sort of temporary diabetic coma long enough to sneak Sabina out of the house. Alternatively, I was praying that Sabina would take it upon herself to climb out the window and shimmy down the jacaranda tree. Instead, she flounced downstairs and sat next to me at the table.

Wearing my robe.

Well, good morning! I've heard so much about you two wee ones!

Ava looked at me. I have no idea what she was really thinking, but in my mind she was saying, *You just bought yourself thousands of dollars in therapy and my entire adolescence in hell, big boy.*

Ava. Chetty. This is Sabina.

Mmmm. French toast! You made it yourself? What a daddy! chirped Sabina.

It was right then that I remembered that, for the first time in the entirety of either of their short lives, last night I had not checked in on them as they slept.

Ava was monosyllabic to all of Sabina's queries. I was already rinsing the kids' dishes before Sabina had taken her first bite of French toast and was trying to telepathically convince her to hurry back up the stairs to dress and go home. Not waiting six months was one thing but introducing them to a new woman the very next morning? Hadn't I vowed never to be *that* divorced parent? I couldn't blame Sabina. I had meant to tell her that she would have to leave before the kids got up, but last night, before making love, I didn't want her to think I assumed we were going to sleep together, and afterwards I guess it kind of slipped my mind.

I left the kids alone and unsupervised for the first time in their lives while I walked Sabina out to her car. They were both still too short to look out the window so I grabbed Sabina and kissed her hard.

That was the best night of my life, I told her.

Oh, Ellis. I love your drama. It was wonderful for me too. And your kiddies are perfect. I knew they'd be.

That evening, little Ava was acting strange, looking me up and down, studying my eyes. All day she hadn't asked me anything about Sabina, but I was sure that her odd behavior now meant that I'd have some difficult explaining to do.

Ava. Sweetheart. Listen, I—?

Daddy . . . I have to go poop.

She pushed down her skort and waddled to the bathroom. I breathlessly raced after her, and, yes, there she was sitting on her little Elmo potty next to the real toilet. Her eyes didn't leave mine. I held my breath. The sounds I eventually heard were music to my ears.

Ava. Ava! *Ava!* You did it, baby. Wow!

She giggled. I wiped her tiny ass with toilet paper for the first time in her three and a half years.

Now do I get a piece of chocolate raspberry cake, Daddy?

No, baby. You get the whole thing.

4

I fall in love too easily,
I fall in love too fast.
I fall in love too terribly hard,
For love to ever last.

ON JUST OUR FIFTH DATE I took Sabina to a mutual friend's engagement party, so thrilled to be able not only to show her off but also to show us off together. She sprayed on a red dress and never stopped holding my hand. Thanks to her, we made a deliciously enviable couple. As soon as she went to the bathroom, three friends surrounded me. I just smiled graciously and accepted their awe. Most of the people at the party, however, were strangers. I usually hate them, but this time I wished we'd all been forced to wear name tags. Mine, if I could write small enough, would have looked something like this:

HELLO!
My name is

Trey, and you can all stop feeling sorry for me. Being abandoned was the best thing that ever happened to me. Sure, I had a few months of misery, but now here's an exotic model hanging on my bicep, ready, even if I'm not, to have my child. Sure, my emotional rebound was a lot faster than most, and you probably think it's nuts that I'm so into somebody new so fast, but I've always been precocious, what can I say? Maybe I should go on a lecture tour, advising other formerly heart-broken souls how to rebound on the double. Dr. Trey.

After we'd shown ourselves to everyone, we skittered back to my car and sped back to her place with her hand in my pants. We made out at every traffic light. Her lips were plums. Her lips were steaks.

By the next week, if we didn't see each other all day, she'd call at ten, come over, and leave at three. I had by now explained to her Carmen's and my six-month rule regarding the kids, and she said of course she understood. Now when she saw them on the weekends, she was coming over, not downstairs in my robe, and she and I never so much as brushed against each other in front of them. (All right, maybe there was a little brushing and a lot of dreamily inhaling her scent every time she passed.)

I think it was our second Saturday together when Chet crawled past me to Sabina's feet and she expertly hauled him into her lap. Seeing them together sent my heart instantly into an Olympics-worthy gymnastics floor routine, including a double layout salto piked full-in back out. The next time she came over, she brought Ava a rhinestone barrette that she'd swiped from a photo shoot for Calvin Klein.

My internal early-warning device for relationship trouble ahead is famously flawed, but what she said on the phone a few days later set off alarms even in me:

Ellis, you know my brother ended up marrying someone with kids already too.

It was the *too* that got me. Up to this point, our conversations had mainly centered on where and how often we were going to attack each other with our body parts. I'm someone who loves the idea of being married. I'm the marrying kind. Yet, technically, I was *still married* to Carmen. For twelve years, I had been with the same woman. Even I realized the dangers of moving too fast.

Yet what did I do with this new information? Did I call her on it right then, clear the air immediately so there would be absolutely no misunderstanding? No. I dealt with it like a man.

I pretended I didn't hear her.

A few days later there was this e-mail from her:

```
Ellis: You are dreadful at billiards and darts.
Fortunately you are brilliant in bed. I did not
expect this to go so deeply so quickly, but it has.
I can't understand how Anna could leave a man like
you and your two little ones, but I am thrilled
that she has.
```

Part of me realized that we were a volatile combination of mutual romantic delusion. And yet much of me welcomed her overenthusiasm, because for the several years before Carmen had finally left, I had been treated only to the opposite. Was I really so special that I could make this sought-after, exotic model fall for me before she even really got to know me? That sounded more like something that I would do. And I was not well.

For some reason I wanted Linda's opinion on her.

Well, they sure grow 'em long wherever it is she comes from, said Linda.

I know. Isn't she amazing? Did you ever see *Nash Bridges*? She was the assistant coroner.

Wow.

Linda's *Wow* was flat but fat with meaning. I wondered suddenly if she could be jealous. I remember she was watching *The King and I* with the kids the weekend before and I overheard her explaining this to Ava:

See, she's a nanny! Just like me!

Ava looked hypnotized by Yul Brynner and Deborah Kerr's ballroom dancing. Chet was preoccupied with gnawing a curve into the corner of a book about a truck.

Linda held Ava in her lap, and her eyes found mine and she raised an eyebrow and then ignited her dimples. I was petrified she'd hold out her arms for me to dance with her, delighting little Ava immensely. Knowing me, if I hadn't just met Sabina, I almost definitely would have.

Two weeks into our relationship, Sabina and I made plans to go to a college friend's wedding up in Sonoma a month later and had even started talking about visiting my American friends in Capetown at the end of the year. I didn't tell anyone about our plans because I already knew they would berate me. Even I realized that someone had to slow us down. Unfortunately, that someone had to be me.

Two days after having scheduled the next six months together, we were making out on the couch. Linda came in and we suddenly stopped.

Excuse me, guys. Pardon me. Excuse me. Good night.

Your nanny doesn't like me, does she?

She actually likes you very much.

Liar. She is most certainly going to diddle herself thinking about you this very instant.

You think?

Damn you! Look how hard you got!

I was already hard.

You're harder now.

Well you're grabbing me.

If I find out you're shagging that cunt, I'll rip it right off.

I'm not, I swear, but—

But what? she sputtered and she was almost instantly back on her feet, her hands rocks. I laughed at what I thought was her joke—until I saw the burn in her eyes.

Carmen and I almost never really argued. From what I remember of my parents' relationship, they started shouting at each other when I was about twelve and didn't really stop until four years later and my mother was dead. When my dad was out of town, which was more and more often toward the end, she yelled at me as his proxy. To this day a woman's glacial stare jabs at the parts of me most hidden.

Eventually Sabina sat back down next to me, and we even

started making out. When she stood up again this time, her eyes were completely different.

Right. Straight to bed, Ellis.

Perhaps this wasn't the best time to remind her that she couldn't spend the night, but for some reason I did anyway.

Chet's so little, I don't think he would really care, I told her. But it's best for Ava.

Ellis, I've put up with this for three weeks! I feel like a fucking hooker when I have to leave in the middle of the night.

I know. I'm sorry, I told her. That's why your place is better.

She's gonna love me, your little girl. They all do.

I'm sure. It's just . . . I was with the same woman for twelve years. I like you so much, and right now I don't want to see anyone but you, but I think I need to feel, at least for the moment, that I'm, you know, free.

How dare you! Promise me the moon to get into my knickers and then pull this shite. Where's my coat?

I don't think you brought one. It's hot tonight.

Her hand snapped into the air like she was readying to slap me.

Sabina, don't go. Let's talk.

But she did and so we didn't. Ever again.

• • •

AVA AND CHET NEVER again asked about Sabina, but I still felt like an imbecile when I thought about how clumsily I had introduced them to their daddy's first special friend. How could I have actually thought that I was falling in love? How ridiculously juvenile I must have sounded to all of my friends. I'd had a great love, an epic love, a once-in-a-lifetime love. Shouldn't I have been satisfied? A rational adult male might have been, but even hurtling toward forty, I still thought of myself as some sort of writerly cross between James Bond and a Jedi. I'm sure one reason I learned to speak first Italian and French and then some Spanish and Portuguese was because it seemed like something a 007 should be able to do. My BlackBerry's ring is the James Bond theme. One of my all-time favorite films ever is *On Her Majesty's Secret Service*. In it, Bond, played this time by George Lazenby, isn't yet a callous ladies' man. In fact he is hopelessly in love with Diana Rigg. (She, most famous as Emma Peel on *The Avengers*, and Cher were probably the first women to elicit from me an erection. FYI. TMI?) I'm not one hundred percent sure that this is how the scene really plays out in the film, but this is always how it unspools in the multiplex in my brain.

```
EXT. ENGLISH COUNTRYSIDE—DAY
The wedding is formal and lovely. Lazenby and Rigg
gaze lovingly into each other's eyes. The vicar
stands behind them grinning while a few dozen family
members lovingly look on. Lazenby and Rigg kiss.

                                      JUMP CUT TO:



LAZENBY AND RIGG


Ducking under a rain of rice as they slide into the
backseat of a decorated Rolls.


INT. ROLLS ROYCE—DRIVING
```

Lazenby and Rigg are kissing passionately, contentedly sighing in each other's arms, when . . . RAT-A-
TAT-TAT, machine gunfire slams into the back of the
car, shattering the rear windshield.

BLOFELD

Alive, miraculously, is racing right behind them and
FIRING.

THE ROLLS

Veers and swerves to try to escape, then flies off
the road and stops in a cloud of dust.

LAZENBY
Darling?! My darling?! Are you all right?

Diana Rigg can't answer. She's dead. Lazenby rocks
her lifeless body in his arms as a police car races
up to the tragic scene.

POLICEMAN
Everything aw-right, sir?

LAZENBY
She's just . . . sleeping.

See, that's why James Bond went on to have an unbreak-
able heart and was later interested only in sport sex with

evocatively named international beauties. When it had been so wonderful with Anna, I had always thought that would be me too. Back when we were good, I even told her that after such a powerful, storied love affair, I wouldn't even dare to look for love again. Instead, I would have to content myself with serial affairs with supermodels, round-card girls, and yoga instructors. When Sabina showed up, I temporarily forgot my plan.

The biggest problem with a grown man still clutching to the fevered fantasy of a fourteen-year-old? Fourteen-year-olds don't have kids. Commander Bond is the ur-bachelor. Obi-Wan Kenobi never had to debate with his daughter the merits of taking Señor Charlie Ham, her kindergarten class hamster, home for Easter break.

Since becoming single, I was developing a different fantasy for my tiny family. I imagined my kids and me as a family of hawks perched on a desolate, angular cliff in the midst of a slanting ice storm. My little ones would nestle under each of my brown wings, warm and dry against my heart, while I would squint stoically into the cold needles of icy rain. In this fantasy, I luxuriate in paternal martyrdom, but it is only now that I'm writing this that I realize that not only am I keeping my little ones dry under my wings, their lovely little bodies are keeping me warm too.

5

I HAVE TO ADMIT THAT SO FAR I'M pretty pleased with the image that I've given you of me. I've told the truth, but the truth is supple, and so far I've shaped it to create, I hope, a sympathetic hero. A nerdy, brainy, bighearted dad laid waste and abandoned by his SoCal, New Age, name-changing wife, left pretty much alone to raise their two preternaturally adorable kids and in the process begin to again peek out of his emotional mouse hole to start to look, however tentatively, for adult love. If I were to stop here, maybe I could actually snag that Father of the Year trophy; maybe even a couple of the sexy divorcée mommies at Ava and Chet's new elementary school would scratch each other's eyes out for a playdate.

If only reality were so simple.

Eventually, however, I know that someone would come forward with the whole story. I guess it might as well be me.

Still, it's difficult for me to write about my wilding phase.

You never saw Bill Bixby in *The Courtship of Eddie's Father* naked with two women on a round, red bed in front of a mirrored wall in a high-class Brazilian valet-parking-equipped brothel. He didn't have sex with his kids' former nanny while the little ones were asleep in the other room. Or maybe he did. Perhaps they will one day broadcast on cable *The Courtship of Eddie's Father: The Lost Episodes*. Maybe then I won't feel so guilty.

See, I went a little crazy during those first two years alone. In between mashing up bananas and changing two sets of diapers, I confess I acted out, and I'm still not at all sure how much of that I want to let you in on.

And yet, when I just wrote that I felt guilty, that was not exactly a lie, but it was certainly an incomplete truth. To be more honest, I would say that in reflecting on my wilding days, I am unproud and unashamed in equal measure. Some of the things I did made me feel sexy and dangerous, which, for a recovering nerd, is no small feat. In some ways, I'm as proud of this period in my life as the fact that I have jumped out of an airplane, whitewater kayaked, rock climbed, iceboated, surfed, kite surfed, snowboarded, hang glided, and bungee jumped, twice, once out of a hot-air balloon over the California desert and once off of a construction crane high above the gulf of Saint-Tropez.

In the first months after Anna left, I of course was too emotionally gutted and too preoccupied with getting Ava to preschool and bribing her to poop in a potty, changing Chet, bathing both of them in the evenings, and singing them to sleep at night to think about dating. The Playboy Channel was the closest thing I had to a lover. Satellite TV with benefits. I was fishing for sympathy about my plight with a wild friend when he suggested CyberSkin.

I thought he was talking about Internet porn, of which I was already familiar, until he explained that it was a space-age substance that was actually quite spongy and lifelike.

I told him that it sounded like something they should pass out in prisons.

It will change your life, my friend, and save your wrist.

Though there was a sex shop just minutes away, for weeks I could not bring myself to enter it. Finally, however, I did, and I bought the floppy rubber thing from a woman behind the counter who weighed more than I do. I can't tell you what she looked like, because I pretended to be hypnotized by the dirty floor at my feet. I even feebly tried to disguise my voice when I said thank you and hurriedly scooped up my change. Anything to make it harder for her to recognize me in a lineup if the cops were ever looking to round up the neighborhood perverts, losers, and freaks.

As soon as I got home, I buried the thing at the back of my dresser drawer. Now that it was safely secreted inside my house, I was actually very excited about our date this evening, after putting the kids to bed.

Then I rushed off to yoga. Two hours later I was driving home singing to myself. A few of the yoginis in class had been especially flirty; maybe soon I wouldn't even need the thing that waited for me at home. And the class itself was an ass-kicker. Every part of me sweated. My eyeballs sweated. For the first time in weeks, my brain was pleasantly stewing in endorphins. I was persevering through what was so far the hardest test in a fairly hard life. I was proud of myself. Each day, I could almost feel the wound inside me closing just a little bit more.

I opened the door to my house and heard Ava and her playdate screaming happily as Chet lizarded after them. When I came in, they all gathered around my knees like sheep. Carmen was in the kitchen, my kitchen, chopping a hill of kale. Her newest obsession was raw vegan cooking, so she was using my kitchen to prepare food (I guess you can't call it cooking) for rich raw foodies too lazy to chop up their own.

As had happened every time I saw her again ever since the night she left, as soon as our eyes met, my stomach lava lamped and I had to look away or fall over. It was all so fucking hard. How could I pretend she was dead when here she was in my fucking kitchen five afternoons a week?

I hurried past to take a shower.

Um, Trey, she began, speaking so quietly that at first I did not hear her. The girls were playing in your room and they found your thing. I took it from them but—

On the counter by the sink, far away from the chopped-up kale and my soon-to-be ex-wife, lay my new, spongy, pink plastic pussy.

If it were only sharp and pointy instead of springy and soft, I could have plunged it into my chest and instantly ended my humiliation.

The girls were fighting with it, Carmen added helpfully.

A coherent verbal response eluded me. I marched the forty-bucks worth of silicon (or whatever the hell it's made of) out the back door to the trash, then took the back stairs up to my room. To begin our new lives apart, she had Doug, her white Rasta guru boy. I had been willing to settle for a lousy rubbery cutlet. And even that was denied me. I'm a Zen Buddhist, not a Tibetan one; we're not supposed to believe in karma, but goddamn, if karma is real then in my past life I was Vlad the Impaler, I was Mister in *The Color Purple*, I was Ike Turner times ten.

The next day I accepted my friend Paul's invitation to Vegas. I figured at this point my choices were either to replace my heart with one made of CyberSkin or get myself near a real woman. I had never been the kind of guy who liked strip clubs. For years I just couldn't understand the logic of paying someone to frustrate you with their lame sexual pantomime. Then, several years earlier, a studio commissioned me to write a script based on the true story of a coed who descended into dancing nude and eventually pulled herself out. Being a trained professional, I researched the subculture thoroughly and finally came away with an understanding of the appeal.

The real world is complicated and relationships are sticky and ever-changing. Inside a strip club, however, everyone knows their part. Inside a strip club would seem like one of the least romantic places on earth, but so much of romance is fantasy already; it's what we have seen in film, what we have heard celebrated in song. Romance is rarely about the hard work of loving someone else.

The dim, colored lights, the music, the gowns, the heels, and the booze all conspire to make the inside of a strip club one of the most romantic places on earth. For at least the duration of the small talk leading up to, along with the length of the song itself, you can kind of squint and kind of convince yourself that the junior college dropout mooning into your eyes has never ever loved anyone as much as she is loving you right now.

Also, for me, strip clubs have the highest concentration of high-heeled mules, and those shoes are a shortcut to the very epicenter of my libido. I don't know why. Perhaps since they're shaped like miniature ski jumps they catapult my psyche into orgiastic abandon. Anthropologist Helen Fisher, PhD, insists that they tilt the woman's buttock into a copulatory pose. Actually, my best guess is that on one of those scraps of magazine pornography turned brittle from the rain and the sun that my friends and I inevitably discovered when cutting through the water company's woods on the way to the mall when we were twelve, I must have seen an image of a woman—this was back in 1974—wearing those shoes, and I was forever imprinted with that as my gold standard of erotic imagery.

Whatever the reason, I needed to be surrounded by women who pretended to be desperately attracted to me.

The only thing that stood between me, dim lights, a cacophony of cheap perfumes, and five-dollar sodas were two little kids that depended on me for every aspect of their survival. I was just going away for two nights; however, that would be the longest I had been away from them since their mom moved out. Between Carmen, Lucia, and Linda, I figured they could keep my kids alive until I returned, but our schedules were already so complicated, so subdivided down to the half hour that my sudden absence would be complicated.

So when Carmen came to the house with the kids, I asked her if they could sleep over at her apartment this coming Saturday night and she'd watch them Sunday until I flew back that morning. Sundays were usually her day to be completely off, so I promised to be home by noon.

Trey, Sundays are very sacred to me, she said. That is when I go out into nature.

I understand that, I told her, and offered to trade her that one Sunday for two Saturdays.

I don't think so, she said. My place is very small.

I took her at her word on that. I had never seen her place.

The kids had never before spent the night there; they'd only stopped by sometimes after Ava's school before coming home. After some clever questioning, Ava had once revealed that her mother lived in a tiny studio and that Doug, her white Rasta, was almost always there.

I guess I didn't want them sleeping over at her house anyway.

What was going to become of me? Would I never be able to get away again? I felt the claustrophobia of single parenting. My last hope was Lucia.

I called and meekly asked her if she would mind spending half her weekend with the kids. She said yes before I'd even finished my sentence. They are about the same light brown color as she is, and when she is out with them and strangers ask if they are hers, she always always says that yes they are. She'd recently asked me to change my will so that if I ever got pureed by a cement truck she'd get custody of them. I had to break it to her that their mother would get them.

Lucia just sucked her teeth.

I loved Anna so much, she said. But this Carmen? Aye! I don't know her.

• • •

PAUL WAS COMPED a couple of suites at the Excalibur, one of the cheapest hotels on the Strip. The entire place looks like an enormous plastic castle. Burger King is more authentically regal. I would be sleeping on the couch in his outer room unless the stripper who would be hypnotized by my animal magnetism later that night insisted that I spend the night with her and her roommates, where I would both alternately and simultaneously pleasure the four of them until sometime before the next afternoon's all-you-can-eat keno buffet brunch.

But before the games began, I needed to hear my little ones' voices. On every single night of both of their lives, I'd either put them to bed and checked on them after they'd gone to sleep or, if I was away, I at least called them before they went to sleep.

Linda answered.

Hello, sir, she sang. Get into any trouble yet?

The night is still young.

Well, don't do anything I wouldn't do. Or if you do, do it longer and louder.

Once again, I didn't respond. I mean, I responded, but I didn't speak.

Can I speak with the kiddies?

Ava-lita! Chetty the bear. It's Daddy!

I could hear Ava galloping to the phone. Chet was still not quite walking, so I pictured him throwing his weight across the floor, racing after his scampering sister, then grabbing her foot and hoisting himself up her leg. He was still more than a year away from speaking but already intuited that if his big sister wanted it, he wanted it more.

Chetty! Get off me!

Hello, baby girl.

Hello, Daddy.

I miss you.

I miss you.

I love you.

I love you.

Silence on her end. Then the hurried, wet breathing of a large reptile.

Chetty?

More sloppy grunts and, in the background, Ava singing to him, It's Da-ddy.

Hello, little baby. I love you.

Linda came back on.

You should have seen the drool that came out when he heard your voice.

Five hours later, I was cradled in an upholstered chair on wheels inside a place called the Olympic Gardens when Debbie floated by and asked if I would like a dance.

I told her that I would, and for those famous three and a half minutes, I felt like the king of desire.

What's that bracelet for?

I'm only eighteen. I can't drink yet.

But you can dance?

I know. It's nuts.

I bet that gets you even more business.

So far, most guys don't bother even to ask. This is my first week.

My friends enjoyed the parade of women, catching them like butterflies and releasing them after a single dance. Me, I'm serially monogamous, even with a stripper.

You're terrific, you know that? I gushed. You're so sweet and open.

Wow. I didn't think I'd meet a guy like you in a place like this.

Aren't I the one who's supposed to say that to you? But what do you mean?

You're so nice and cool, she said. But if you want to go dance with some other girls . . . ?

No. I'm fine right here. What are you wearing?

CK1.

Wow. I love it.

This is probably a good time to mention to you, dear reader, that I was as high as a kite.

All through the night, she nestled on my lap and told me about the old factory town in Maine that she'd just escaped from and that Debbie was her real name because she felt too stupid making up a fake one. She only squatted and wiped her hips over me when one of the floor managers patrolled by with his clipboard. Otherwise, she just lounged on my lap, running her fingers through my scalp and sipping Sprite as we chatted.

A friend of Paul's had heard about an after-hours club, and when I mentioned it to Debbie, she almost jumped off me in her excitement. She had already been in Vegas three months and had yet to check it out. I asked her what time she got off work, and she said five in the morning.

That's perfect, I told her. The club doesn't open till five.

She threw her head left and right to make sure the floor managers were elsewhere then whispered in my ear that she couldn't be seen leaving with me, she'd get in trouble, but she could meet me there.

This was not the first time that I had ever been hypnotized by a stripper and not the first time since being single again that I had asked one out. This was, however, the first time that my advance was received with anything approaching enthusiasm.

The next thing I knew it was 5:30 in the morning, and I was outside some after-hours club somebody knew about, far off the Strip, at the edge of the desert, waiting for Debbie to arrive in the cab that I gave her money for. None of the guys thought she'd show, so they had gone home straight from the club. The desert seemed angrily, menacingly cold, but the arriving dawn backlit the mountains in reds and oranges while higher in the sky lorded the richest of blues. The bouncer, bigger and blacker than me by several orders of magnitude, kept me company. I took a deep breath and explained to him that my friend who was meeting me had lost her ID, and, as I palmed him a twenty, I asked him if he could look the other way just this once. Me. The Boy Scout Tenderfoot. The ill-adapted nerd. Here I was slipping a bouncer a tip to sneak an underage stripper into God-knows-where as suavely as Ray Liotta in *Goodfellas*.

As often happens when you wait a long time for something that you intensely desire, just when I gave up on Debbie ever showing up, she did.

My new bouncer friend just nodded us inside without a wink or even a barely perceptible up-jerked chin of *attaway, boy*. Now what? This was already so much beyond what I had imagined that I was at a loss for what to do next. For the first time ever, I had convinced an exotic dancer to come out with me for free. In and of itself that felt like enough of a victory of seduction, while the idea of actually having sex with her suddenly seemed a helluva lot less glamorous. While I had been waiting for her, I had started contemplating the reality of fucking some way-too-young recent high school grad from Maine who had fled to the safety of Las Vegas after her big sister OD'd yet again on northern New England smack. Was that really a memory that I wanted to carry around with me for the rest of my life?

Luckily for both of us, moments into the club, her girlfriend/

mentor called and was berating her so loudly about meeting a guy away from the club that I could hear the shrill yips from Debbie's cell phone even through the horrible, tinny techno of this horrible little club.

The magic and the marijuana had both worn off, and suddenly it seemed as if the only major decision left to make that evening was whether to shoot myself now or after I bought her a Long Island iced tea.

This could not possibly be my life. I was a romantic and, when my adult acne wasn't acting up, not the worst-looking of men. When had I become De Niro in *Taxi Driver*?

Neither Debbie nor I wanted to dance, and she was under orders from her pregnant friend to escape immediately. Still chivalrous, however, I felt it was my responsibility to escort her home. We left the club, and I mistook a club rat outside for a limo driver, but for some reason he ended up driving first Debbie then me home for free. She lived with her friend in this endless subdivision that had been spat out on the desert far out of town. By the time I got back to the Excalibur, it was 7:30. I passed great herds of seniors heading to their breakfast buffets as the aggressive sun needled my eyes.

That evening, when the cab dropped me off and I entered my house, I realized that this was the first time that I had left and returned to our new home. I smelled the mildew I used to smell in the hippie houses of my friends in the seventies. The smell instantly made me feel poor.

It was then that I noticed the two ponds on the concrete floor, one down the hall, while the other I happened to be stepping in.

Who's that?

Lucia said this to the kids as if they were puppies, which immediately set them off, so I heard Ava running to me, her little feet tambourining the floor. I didn't have time to warn her before she hit the water, slid, fell, crashed, and cried.

Instantly, I had her in my arms and rocked her and kissed her.

Chet was cruising in fast, on two feet, but palming the wall like a miniature blind man. He'd be walking, unaided, within days. Lucia plucked him up before he hit the water.

Trey, you didn't tell me the bathtub upstairs still leaked. I was just going to clean up the water when you came in.

Ava was fine now but hiccupping from the residual sobs. I was less fine. My magical daughter had almost suffered permanent brain damage just because I'd felt the need to convince some barely legal semi-runaway that I might be someone she should consider having sex with.

I vowed to do better. I vowed not to be that guy.

We all know that guy. The one who keeps saying that age is just a number and insists that since he feels inside like he's still in his twenties, it is only natural that that's the age of the women he's continually attracted to. The one that dyes his hair at forty and by fifty has had a little work done around his eyes. You know that guy . . . the oldest guy in the club.

I vowed there and then to seek out women that were not paid to flirt with me and whose age was greater than or equal to twenty-seven.

Unfortunately for my new plan, I was invited by the Sundance Institute to fly down to Rio to teach screenwriting for a week. That city lives in my heart. Years before, I had taught myself Portuguese with Berlitz tapes then had found a Brazilian student and had paid her $10 an hour to talk with me once a week. My reward for my resolve was flying down to Rio and Salvador da Bahia for two weeks with Anna. She liked it well enough, but I was smitten. The entire nation is always outside and social, eating and laughing and dancing. If it were not for the machine gun–toting police and the endless *favelas*[1] carpeting every hill surrounding Rio, I would have emigrated years ago.

This time, going alone, I did a little—all right, a lot, you might even say exhaustive—research into how best a divorcé drowning in months of loneliness might get himself laid. At that point in my life I would have paid anything to lighten its heavy fingers on me for an hour. In fact, because President Bush blundered and spoke about Brazil's "collapsed economy" when he really meant to say Argentina's, the Brazilian cruzero cratered, and suddenly for an American buying anything, including an hour with a naked woman, would cost thirty percent less.

If I did end up paying for sex in Rio, it would not be my first time. When I was nineteen and about to begin my junior year at Stanford, I drove cross-country with a friend and stopped off at the Mustang Ranch to drop off my virginity. There at the end of my teens, I imagined myself an American Sartre or Truffaut, being delivered from my intellectual timidity, loneliness, and despair into the vivid world of adulthood by a cynical yet secretly loving, unfiltered-cigarette-smoking, and well-read *fille de joie*. Instead, my virginity was released in a trailer in the Nevada desert under a mural of a deserted beach, airbrushed in neon colors very, very badly.

---

[1]Slums

I describe the event precisely as it really happened in my second novel.[2]

I prayed Rio would be better. From what I could tell before arriving, unlike Nevada, there was a spectrum of choices, from a large café on Ipanema beach where every single woman was a hooker, to a vast nightclub where every woman inside was a hooker, to *termas,* bath houses that were much more expensive, clean, and supposedly stocked with women whose beauty would elevate your soul.

This time I would be away seven days but had a month to plan, so I organized Nora, Lucia, and Carmen into an elaborate grid of their child-minding duties, distributed hard copies to each of them, and posted another on the bulletin board in the kitchen.

I arrived in Rio a day early and was greeted by Alice, a long beauty with hair that dangled halfway down her back in extravagant curls. She spoke English magnificently. *That was easy,* I remember thinking. *I land in Rio and Sundance sends me someone to love.* It took a moment to divine that she wasn't Brazilian but British-born and half-Turkish, recently graduated from the London School of Economics. We fell into each other immediately, and by the time night fell, we had shared three meals together and had never once been silent.

When I finally asked how old she was, I crossed my fingers and prayed.

Twenty-five.

While studying her eyes, my heart suddenly several sizes too big for my chest in that familiarly addictive way, I decided

---

[2]Trey Ellis, *Home Repairs* (New York: Pocket Books, Simon & Schuster, 1993), page 111. Rereading the section right now, the sentence that most sums up that experience is "I came, I guess."

that ages, like shoe sizes, didn't exactly translate across conti-
nents. I wear a size 13 shoe in America, a 46 in Italy, a 12½ in
England. In that same way, I decreed that a twenty-five-year-old
woman in the UK is the equivalent of a twenty-seven-year-old
woman in the States.

By the time Alice and I met the rest of the local Sundance
staff at an outdoor bar in the garden district, we were so comfortable with each other that our eyes would find each other
across the long table of laughing Brazilians and we would smile
so sweetly at each other.

Of course someone knew of a party somewhere afterwards, and we all divided into several tiny cars and drove dark
roads to the house. I breathe better when I travel, my heart is
bigger when I travel, and down those dark roads with this lovely
new woman on my lap because there was no other room in this
absurdly small car, I felt an exhilaration I hadn't felt since studying in Florence. I felt as young and as free as the rest of them.
There was no hyperactive room parent hounding me with weekly
e-mails to help paint a banner for the upcoming jog-a-thon at
Ava's school. There was no ex-wife loading my refrigerator with
bowls and bowls of sprouting beans.

This night there was just me and the possibility of her.

The young guy driving, a lanky Brazilian hipster in
skinny glasses, introduced us all to the guy giving the party. The
house seemed to have endless rooms. Everyone was young and
drinking and talking close.

Alice and I separated, and I found myself meeting one
new extraordinary person after the next. They always gushed
over my Portuguese and I always shrugged, falsely bashful. I
hadn't seen Alice in almost an hour so I started hunting the

rooms for her. I finally found the Brazilian hipster making out with a girl in the middle of a doorway. Just as I was wondering if I should ask him if he'd seen Alice when he came up for air, I realized that it was with Alice that he was snogging.

I backed away, a sudden ringing in my ears.

Did I really need to fly twelve hours to be rejected by yet another woman? I made myself smile when I saw her again. I made myself kiss both her cheeks in our hotel elevator when I got off at my floor, but she and her hipster continued upward.

I taught for a week in Petropolis, a mountain resort above Rio, with the other mentors, including John Cameron Mitchell, the writer/director/star of *Hedwig and the Angry Inch* and Bráulio Montovani, the Brazilian writer of *Cidade de Deus* (*City of God*). Three days into the session, the Brazilian hipster disappeared, and I spent the rest of my free time cornered by a crying Alice in the dining room trying to answer hours of questions about why some men can be so viciously unfeeling.

We returned to Rio and everyone scattered on various planes. My flight wasn't until the next morning, so this last night I planned on visiting Centaurus, the most luxurious *terma* in town.

I showered again and dressed and triple-checked my map of the city before setting out on foot. Each step closer sent my heart beating faster. Of course I soon got lost, but how could I ask anyone for directions? Although it is legal and a time-honored part of Brazilian culture, I could not shake a persistent sense of shame. It reminded me so much of my first time in Amsterdam. I entered the "coffee house" and started to whisper for some pot when the tattooed woman behind the bar just handed me a long menu of international choices of varying potencies.

The valet parking finally gave the place away. I circled

the block, still unsure if I had the courage to enter, and then did. A smiling older woman took my $200 and gave me a locker key on a wrist band. I stepped into the men's locker room, which was luminously white and smelled of steam and lavender. Another smiling old woman, this one heavy and round, handed me a towel and some terry-cloth slippers. I found my locker and discovered a short white robe inside. There was just one other man in the locker room, but it was getting naked in front of the round old woman that embarrassed me. I had read that the spa was lovely, and the blog I'd found encouraged one to enjoy it before meeting the women. I took a wet sauna and then plunged into a small indoor pool that must have been twenty feet deep. I dried off, put on my tiny robe, studied my eyes in the mirror, and then stepped out into a dim corridor.

I heard American house music coming from the smoked glass door in front of me. I held the handle before I opened it. Inside the club at first I could not see, only hear. As my eyes adjusted, I realized that I was the only man in a room full of dozens and dozens of women in tight gowns and sharp heels whose skin tones spanned the entire range of human possibility.

It was how I imagined the adult world to be when I was fourteen years old.

It was the Make-A-Wish Foundation for desperate, international divorcés.

I was a space explorer still trying to comprehend this wondrous new planet when the prettiest woman in the place walked up to me and said *boa tarde*, good afternoon. She introduced herself as Biya, and because she was so much prettier than all the rest, I assumed that she was the nonsexual hostess there to shepherd me to the right choice.

Then she backed me up to the bar, reached into my robe, and grabbed my cock.

I let out air, noisily, as if from a balloon.

She held my hand and led me out of the disco, down the quiet hall, and into a room with a round bed and a mirrored ceiling. She stepped out of her heels and unsnapped her halter, and her dress collapsed to the floor. I asked her to put her shoes back on, and she wagged her finger at me.

I dove into this hour of condom-wearing sport sex with the gusto of an amateur adult film performer/director. There were no feelings to be hurt, no expectations of a future, no love to watch fade. There was just playful biology, geometry, and of course physical education.

Afterward, she snuggled into my side and we breathed together.

On the plane ride home, I would close my eyes and try to remember her smell.

• • •

OF COURSE THE RELEASE gave relief only for a short while, and loneliness soon welled again within me, to the level of about my throat. The wives of friends continually threatened to fix me up with someone, but the dates and dinner parties rarely came.

Then, after six months of emptiness, Angela, our Uruguayan former nanny, called. You might remember that she was the one that I had kicked out because I had been advised not to shit where I ate.

How are the kids? How is little Chetty?

She was always closer to Chet than to Ava. That bugged me.

They're fantastic, I told her. They're doing just fine.

I miss the kids.

You should come over. With your sister. Any weekend.

Aye, Trey, you know you missed my birthday. I sent you an invitation.

I swear I didn't get it. I'm sorry. Maybe. Maybe we should, um, go out for dinner. Celebrate.

Okay, she said, so softly.

No, it is certainly not okay. You just turned twenty-one. I'm about to turn forty. It's creepy. It's wrong. It's sick. It's sick and also pathetic and the worst sort of cliché and completely beneath me and irredeemable, absolutely, the actions of an antihero instead of the superhero that I have been striving to grow into, and stupid too, impossible to ever live down.

And just about the only thing that my brain would ruminate on between the time of its utterance and our dinner date three days later.

I convinced myself that dinner with Angela was just dinner as I drove to pick her up. Sure, I bought condoms and changed the sheets, but that was just theater. We would go to dinner, flirt, and then awkwardly kiss on the cheeks good night.

At her door, my kids' former nanny greeted me in jeans, a blouse, and high-heeled Lucite mules. I took her to a hulking Asian fusion restaurant on the Promenade in Santa Monica, and at the bar I ordered a martini. The bartender turned to her and asked for ID.

She fingered through her tiny little purse then gasped. She'd left it at home.

To tell you the truth, not all of me was disappointed. When you might or might not be having sex with your until recently not-underage former nanny, alcohol should be nowhere within reach.

Still, my drink had already been ordered.

When our table was ready, I balanced my martini up the stairs and, only moments after sitting down in a dark corner booth, our waiter beamed at her.

Ma'am, you don't have a drink! What can I get you from the bar?

Apple martini, please.

We waited until he was several yards away before laughing. The booth was so deep that I felt as if I was watching her from across the room. Nevertheless, I felt myself dissolving into the cushions. She didn't work for me anymore. In fact, Linda, her replacement, was so inappropriately flirty that perhaps I actually needed this ex-nanny with benefits. The guy who fucks his kids' ex-babysitter has gotta be at least a rung higher on the ladder out of the pit of midlife, puerile irredeemability than the one who fucks his current one.

We talked about her school, Santa Monica College, and how hard it was. We talked about Chetty and how many hearts he was destined to break. We talked about her sister and her new boyfriend and how it finally seemed like she'd found a boy who would respect her. The remains of the kung pao chicken were still on the table when I confessed:

You know. When you were living with us. Especially at the end. If I ever made you uncomfortable, I didn't mean to.

What do you mean? she said, her eyes immense.

I mean I was a little flirty.

I was flirty too.

Yeah, but that time I talked about Tantric sex outside your room.

I thought you were going to come in.

Did you want me to?

Of course.

If my life were a musical, I would have burst into song.

We both giggled, and I asked if I could sit next to her. I did, and suddenly we were making out like wolves. Then we'd take a breath, laugh, and dive back into each other's mouths. I thought I felt someone tapping me on the shoulder but ignored it. Who on earth would interrupt somebody at a time like this?

Yo, man. Some customers are complaining, said the manager, a fellow black guy that I sort of knew.

I looked around our floor of the restaurant for the *playa-hata,* but it seemed empty. Who would complain about young romance? Or at least one of us was young. Wait. Do you think that's why somebody complained? How can they tell? I thought *black don't crack.* I don't have any gray hairs. How could they discern from fifty yards away that I could have had a child her age if I had had a child when I was nineteen?

Then there was the fact that I'm black and the Uruguayan Angela looked white. Could some otherwise enlightened Santa Monican housewife have mistaken me for her pimp?

We left, making out more in the street and in the car at every stoplight. As we drove into my carport, I saw that Linda's light was on. My plan was to spirit Angela inside without an inquisition from her successor.

Ah yes, hello, Linda. This is Angela. She used to have

your job. Kindly lock yourself inside your room because we plan
on making love on every available surface in this house.

Fortunately, Linda didn't come out. I held Angela's hand
and led her up on the roof. You can't see the beach from up
there, but when the tide is high and the swell is strong, you can
hear the thunder of the waves. I had put a condom in my wallet
before going out, and we made love on the roof. Her beauty, the
night, our history, those shoes, everything should have conspired
to make it the most charged coupling since Richard Burton and
Elizabeth Taylor (this was three years before Brad and Angelina). Instead, a sudden guilt softened me somewhat. Though
she had lived with us, I barely knew her. Suddenly, powerfully, I
just felt the overwhelming hunger to be loved.

We went inside to my bedroom and, as she lay naked on
my big, king-size expanse of NASA-certified memory foam, I
felt that I had rarely seen anyone as beautiful. I stowed my neu-
roses, postponed my search for love for the night, and jumped
on the bed. I set the alarm for six o'clock so I'd have time to
sneak her out of the house and return to dress the kids and get
them off to school. However, we didn't need an alarm. We alternated making love and napping in each other's arms until the
sun started warming the fronds of the shabby palm outside my
window.

6

Gosto muito de te ver, leãozinho,
Caminhando sob o sol.
Gosto muito de você, o leãozinho
Para desentristecer, leãozinho,
O meu coração tão só
Basta eu encontrar você no caminho.

THANKS TO ANGELA, the fever in my brain broke, and I could concentrate once more on my only important job. I was just beginning to recognize this pattern within myself of loneliness for an adult connection welling up within me until a sort of temporary madness set in. Then, after even the most fleeting contact with a female, I was prepared again to try to be the father that I had dedicated myself to becoming. The other side of desire is such a peaceful place. Too bad it never lasts as long as I'd like.

So before my resolve again faded, I rededicated myself to

spoiling my kids. My fantasy is that, when they are much older, they will tell me that they had an absolutely magical childhood and had no idea that our situation (and my mental state) was so tenuous.

The con I hope that I will have successfully pulled on them has been made enormously simpler by their magnificence. If they were half as whiny as I was as a child, I would have shipped them off to one of those British boarding kindergartens when I had the chance.

In general, they almost magically seem to intuit that I could easily be overwhelmed by the task at hand, so they usually cut me some slack and get along. I had heard that having a girl first makes everything easier, and that has certainly been true in my case. From the day Chet was born, Ava has been the poor kid's bossy mini-mom. Anna and I had read all the books on sibling rivalry and followed everyone's advice simultaneously. As Anna's belly swelled like a sail, we read *I'm a Big Sister Now* to Ava and somewhere picked up the trick of heading off her jealousy by conning her into believing that Chet had brought a little present from wherever babies come just for her. She was barely three when he was born, and it wasn't until a year later that she cornered me and said, Chet didn't get me that jean jacket from the Gap, did he, Daddy?

• • •

MY MOM WAS A FEMINIST SQUARED, so growing up in the seventies, I didn't have a choice but to believe that a woman's place was in the House and in the Senate and, in my mom's case, Yale Law School. She graduated magna cum laude from Howard, was done with all but her dissertation for her PhD in psychology from the University of Michigan, where she also taught, and when I was a teenager and Mom was thirty-three years old, she enrolled in the best and hardest law school in the country.

So I was singularly unprepared to find myself raising a four-year-old girl who was passionate about cooking, baking, her nails, edible makeup, and anything having to do with princesses.

I am terrified that she is going to grow up and become a Republican.

But she loves me like teenaged girls loved the Beatles in '64, at least at this point in our story, when she is four and three quarters, during our first summer with just the three of us. She's eight as I write these words, and I have to say that, thankfully, she still loves me without condition. Chris Rock, also a parent of a little girl, says our job as dads is to *keep them off the pole*; that is, raise them so that they don't grow up to become strippers. The film *American Beauty* crystallized this dilemma for me. Near the very end of the film, moments before his death, Kevin Spacey stares at a picture of his once happy family. It had been taken only a few years before, but the smiling little girl in the picture clutching her father's neck bears almost no resemblance to the Goth teen dad-hater we see in the film. Even Anna's experience with her own father is one of devolution—from adoration to disappointment to hostility to indifference. My job is to strive to disappoint little Ava as little as possible.

In fact, almost every woman whom I have ever dated has had a troubled, contentious, aggressive relationship with her father. Perhaps for me it's a prerequisite. At my lowest points, when everything around me seems to be disintegrating, I terrify myself with the thought that my own little girl will one day stop loving me. After all, there was a time when her mother looked at me the way Ava looks at me now.

On my deathbed, whenever that will be, the degree to which my kids still love me will be the only criterion by which I will judge the worth of my journey.

• • •

LITTLE AVA'S QUIET reminds me so much of me. I mumble, a big black man talking quietly, low and quickly from just the front half of my mouth, tall and awkward and often desperate to disappear (except when I'm disguised as a movie star in my loud, vintage convertible or wearing my Gucci sneakers or I whip off my shirt in yoga).

Ava, when she's near strangers, is even quieter than I am, moving her lips with no sound coming out at all. She is already so beautiful that that is always the first thing anyone ever says about her. Like her mother's, her beauty is rare and loud. It often scares her when adults gush over her looks. I'm so used to how this makes her withdraw that I automatically reach down and help her hide into my side. Then of course as soon as we get home, she's like the talking dog in that old joke (*DiMaggio!*), jumping on the couch, dancing, and singing a medley of the best of Hilary Duff.

Chet is our opposite in almost all things. He's a chubby love ball quick-crawling to every single friend or stranger in his path. His charm is so genuine and infectious. I may be a little biased, but to me he's a genetically engineered hybrid of Bobby Kennedy, Muhammad Ali, and Elvis.

The Caetano song I quote at the beginning of the chapter is the perfect portrait of my son. I memorized it when I was teaching in Brazil, so far from him and his sister. After the fourth day away, I was beginning to remember, albeit dimly, the timbre of my life before marriage, kids, and divorce. I'd heard the song for years and knew that it was one of Caetano's most popular, but it was only on this trip, after I had taught myself Portuguese, that I understood what he was saying:

> *I love watching you little lion,*
> *Walking under the sun.*
> *I like you so much little lion.*
> *You take the sadness out of my heart, little lion,*
> *Just by meeting you on the path.*

A lion cub is not only cute—any baby animal is cute—but a lion cub is also goofy and yet at the same time full of the promise of magnificence. That's all that I see in my son.

I forced the unfortunate Brazilians at the screenwriting workshop with me to patiently teach me all the words, and that very first night back home it was my new lullaby for the kids. Ava, as usual, laid motionless in her toddler sleigh bed until I finished the song and leaned over her. That's when her arms rose and captured my neck. I kissed her twice, and she turned into her pillow with a smile.

Chet, on the other hand, had kicked off the blanket I had just tucked around him in his crib and was sitting up and smiling at me.

Go to bed, now.

I wrestled him into my arms and held him against his squirming as I sang him the song again. By the time I delivered him back to his crib, he'd been tranquilized, and nuzzled his tiny nose against my bicep. Not this night, but often, he would mistake it for a breast and tickle me by trying to take a sip.

7

I HAVE ALWAYS LIVED for the summers. Perhaps it comes from having grown up in Michigan, where the winter days are about four hours long but the summer light oceanic. Growing up, the only thing my family ever spent a dime on was vacations. Whether we could afford it or not, my family spent every August on Martha's Vineyard as well as a week in the winter in the Caribbean. Another friend who also grew up as a faculty brat explained it this way. When you are raised in academia, you acquire upper-class taste although in fact you earn less than a spot welder. My dad was a psychiatrist for the neurotic spoiled brats at Yale, and after my mother died, he moved us to Manhattan, where he ran Columbia University's Harlem Center for Child Studies, a mental health facility for at-risk little kids. Though he was never paid well for what he did, he lived very well indeed, thanks to ingenuity and creative credit contortions.

I inherited directly from him my compulsion to jet-set on

a budget. I know he'd be so proud of me. Yes, he took us to the tony Vineyard for the month of August, but we couldn't afford to stay in Oak Bluffs with the rest of the bourgie black folks, you know, the ones with actual money. Instead, every year we rented one of a series of sorbet-colored prefabricated tract ranch homes in the woods behind the town of Vineyard Haven. The rooms had walls but no ceilings, like office cubicles or a movie set, so at night no one could make a sound. If there was any place on Martha's Vineyard that you could call the ghetto, we lived in it. Of course, we would drive over to visit friends in Oak Bluffs and pretend we belonged.

My dad was always figuring out ways to scam free flights: a symposium in Rio, consulting on Saint Thomas. When frequent flyer programs began, he lost his mind and became obsessed with hoarding miles from any available source. Now I do it too.

People who don't know me well assume that I am exceedingly rich. I like their misconception. It makes me feel like a spy. Those who know me well enough to know something about my erratic finances can never seem to grasp how it is that I manage with no visible means of support. Traveling is simply what I live for, so I dedicate myself to finding a way. For our honeymoon, I arranged to exchange our Santa Monica house for one outside of Saint-Tropez. In other years I rent out our house for the month that we're gone and combine miles and special offers dug out from the deepest crevices of the Internet.

This summer, however, the first summer after she left, I was too broke and our new house was too broken down to subsidize globe-trotting with the kids. In some ways I measured the success of each year by the quality of our summer vacation. The concept that this summer was going to be vacationless, my first ever (I think), took all but the minimum possible volume of air from my lungs.

One morning Caroline, Chet's godmother, called. She is one of the most vibrant people I have ever known, a sexy French version of Fellini's tiny muse and wife, Giulietta Masina. She told me that she had been invited to teach acting for a week to aspiring French filmmakers in France in a chateau in Brittany.

I told her I was very happy for her.

You don't understand, sweetheart, she continued. The Writers Guild envoy who was to teach screenwriting to the filmmakers dropped out at the last minute. Do you want to go?

I opened my mouth to breathlessly shout *yes* when it occurred to me that, in this first year of our experiment, I had already left the kids for a week to visit Cuba and for another week to go to Brazil.

Damn it, Caroline. I can't leave the kids.

Darling, they'll fly you business class!

I smiled. Not because I was looking forward to abandoning my kids while I reclined in a fat leather seat and feasted on hot nuts and warm chocolate chip cookies at cruising altitude. I smiled because I knew and Caroline knew that a business-class ticket is about four times the price of coach. Thanks to one lucky phone call, I could fly myself, my kids, and Lucia from LA to Paris for free.

Whenever fantastic good luck comes my way, I immediately think of Captain Grimes in Evelyn Waugh's first masterpiece, *Decline and Fall*. Grimes is a pederast, a bigamist, and a drunken schoolmaster at a private school in Wales. At the end of the novel, he's finally been tossed out of the school and finds himself—where else—downing pints of beer at a pub. The man next to him, impressed by his bottomless thirst, introduces himself as a representative from Guinness and on the spot offers Grimes a job driving around the countryside in a company car, sampling Guinness across the land to make sure it isn't watered down. After all he's been through, Grimes can no longer even conceive of fortune again smiling upon him. Convinced the Guinness man is a fake, he boxes the man's ear and kicks him in the ass and out of the pub.

After first reading that passage back in college, I vowed never to let an opportunity pass me by just because I couldn't believe that it could happen to me.

My luck continued. Lucia's classes at Santa Monica College were just ending, so she could actually drop everything and come with us. It had not occurred to me that she might not have been able to until just before I asked her. Though she had been helping raise our kids since Ava was six months old, it was not until this year that I really began to get to know her. Over the years she and Anna had become best friends. They could talk for hours about rebirthing and the higher beings from Pleiades and their plans for the enlightened Indigo Children, a club of which, evidently, Ava and Chet were members.

It was not until after Anna moved out and moved into the shell of someone named Carmen that Lucia pulled away from her and closer to me.

Plus, she would always greet me with some variation on the words handsome, gorgeous, *guapo,* and *guapissimo.* It never failed to make me smile even though my friend Tommy, her previous employer, got the very same greeting during her tenure with them.

She made soup for Chet a few times a week and started

surprising me by bringing a bowl up to my office. The first time, I almost wept. I so want to be taken care of, at least every once in a while.

She often threatened to set me up with her gorgeous friends from school, but months would pass and finally when she did introduce me to someone, we were always drastically incompatible. One was a Yemeni virgin saving herself for a good Muslim boy. Another drank so much at Lucia's birthday party that I let her hold at my house that the girl threw up in and around my downstairs toilet.

Carmen was the first one to ask why I didn't marry Lucia. Every friend who saw how she was with Ava and Chet eventually asked the same question themselves. During this first year, when all was so new, we grew more intimate than lovers. It was as if we'd slept together once years ago and it just hadn't worked out but we'd remained friends. Some of her friends delighted in referring to me as her ex-husband.

I cobbled together a two-week vacation out of one free plane ticket. After the first week in Normandy, we would fly down to Ramatuelle and stay with our friends Kasi and Vondie for a week. Caroline and Howard lived only minutes away in the village.

Ava was a champion traveler, having already flown silently to France twice and several times to Atlanta to visit her grandmother. More than once, after we had landed, we were congratulated by the passengers seated near us who had almost held their breath, waiting for Ava's shrieks, during the length of the flight.

However, this would be Chet's very first long flight, a vast twelve hours from LAX to Charles de Gaulle. In general he's the world's jolliest baby—except when he's not and he sirens endlessly. The little round guy is so powerful that, if he so chose, somewhere over Greenland he could force the 777 to turn around and head back to Kennedy.

Thanks in large part to Lucia's feathery chest, Chet slept through the entire flight. Ava took turns either sleeping with her head in my lap or watching *Babar* dubbed into English on the little brick of a screen on the seat back.

We arrived in Paris in the evening. We were booked to spend the night there before training to Brittany in the morning. Because the French government was sponsoring the program, they booked us that night in a five-star hotel, the Raphael, on Avenue Kléber, just behind l'Arc de Triomphe. I'd never before stayed anywhere so posh. Every centimeter of the place was covered in an ornate rug or a baroque chandelier or a lush romantic painting framed by a dense, gilded bramble. Though my room had a sleek glass booth of a shower, the kids' and Lucia's room had a marble bathtub perched on the golden paws of a lion. Each fifteen-foot-high Burgundy velvet curtain weighed more than I did.

I like hotels, Daddy, said Ava.

I bet you do, baby. But don't get used to it.

I had read Ava *Eloise* just a few weeks earlier, and New York's Plaza Hotel, Eloise's home, was a Comfort Inn compared to this place.

Lucia, Ava, and Chet were depleted from the flight, so they went right to bed. One of my favorite things in life is to dive into a great city after having just thrown down my bags. The Champs-Elysées unrolled at my feet like the yellow brick road. It was early June, after nine at night, yet the sun seemed like it would cling to this grand day forever. I couldn't stop laughing and am not ashamed to admit that a particular Joni Mitchell song swelled inside of me. I was the freest man in Paris.

The next day, our life of luxury continued. They'd booked us in first class on the TGV, my first time ever in first class and the kids' first time ever on a train. White linen napkins shrouded every headrest.

I like trains, Daddy. Princess Ava felt very much at home.

I'm glad. But they're not all like this, baby.

The other teachers were with us in first class, all of them French filmmakers except the Directors Guild delegate, Randal Kleiser, the director of *Grease, The Blue Lagoon,* and *Summer Lovers.* On the train, I told Randal that I had brought my then-girlfriend, now-ex-wife to spend six weeks on the Greek island of Santorini because I had become obsessed with the place after having seen *Summer Lovers.* In the film, Peter Gallagher and Daryl Hannah are newlyweds on the most beautiful island on the planet. Gallagher starts having an affair with a French archaeologist. Daryl Hannah catches them, and everyone's quite logical reaction is to have a threesome. I was twenty when it came out, and had just returned from what was easily the most amazing experience of my life, my sophomore year abroad at Stanford's manicured fifteenth-century villa overlooking Florence. When the school year was over, all the other kids backpacked around Europe for the rest of the summer. I, on the other hand, thanks to family friends, had scored an internship at *Newsweek*'s Atlanta bureau, so I had to fly back to a rented bedroom in the basement of a friend of a friend of my grandmother's in suburban Atlanta.

Too cheap and too broke to get a car, I took two buses to work and walked two miles to the movies on the weekends. It was on one of those hot, thick weekends, when my sweat would freeze to the sides of my face as soon as I sat down in the movie theater's exaggerated air-conditioning, that I saw *Summer Lovers* and convinced myself that all those cool, affluent back-packing Stanford brats were rutting like weasels *à la ménage à trois* on a caldera overlooking the Aegean while I was marooned in Dixie, just trying to breathe in enough courage to one day ask for the phone number of the hostess at the local PoFolks. Like Saint-Tropez courtesy of *Going in Style,* Santorini became the second iconic home of all my romantic and sexual desires.

Now here in France, flown in to teach screenwriting, the Domaine des Ormes had the potential to become a third. It was also, however, a study in contrasts. Although it was an elegant sixteenth-century chateau, it was surrounded by kitsch camp-sites, miniature golf courses, a waterslide, and brigades of soft, pale, middle-class English vacationers. Lucia, the kids, and I were assigned one of six Disneyesque Swiss chalets on the property, each the size of a camper. Still, I was the happiest I had been since becoming forcibly bachelored. I felt downright Bondian, critiquing scripts in French all day, and when I saw the kids at lunchtime, they were always giddy and out of breath. Ava would ride the ponies. Chet was the only baby in our group of sixty, and pretty much every woman there cradled him at least once.

Of course, whenever a sizable group of strangers is thrown together away from home, a constant, furious, yet sub-terranean game of musical-chair mating informs every interac-tion. And when they are almost all French and a third of them are actors . . . the French have a word for it: *Oh-la-la.*

I have never been good at it. The fictional version of me would be an excellent *draguer,* picking up women with a few well-placed, provocative witticisms. The real me is forty-something going on fourteen.

So for the first two days, I just watched and suffered as these free, childless young French people paired and re-paired.

Blame it on *The Addams Family*. I must have seen too many episodes because, just as Gomez the dad would go crazy and kiss and lick up and down his wife Morticia's arm whenever she spoke French, whenever I hear a woman speak the language, my brain stops driving and my heart takes the wheel.

So just being in that country, I was already lost even before I met Laurianne. She arrived two days into the session, after most of the others had already mated.

Every day, the French screenwriters and I would go over scripts for the short films the filmmakers had written while Randal and the other directors would supervise them in videotaping directing exercises with a rotating band of actors. Laurianne was a last-minute replacement for an actress who had just booked a better-paying job. As soon as I saw her, that switch went off in my head. That switch has gotten me into trouble repeatedly, but it is also the only force strong enough to overcome my fear of maybe being laughed at, spat at, and chased away for approaching a woman. In *Cat on a Hot Tin Roof,* the alcoholic Brick explains to his wife, Maggie, why he has to drink so damn much. He tells her that he has to drink until he feels *that click*, that click that tells him he's finally at the place he's supposed to be. My desire for a woman is something like that. A love junkie, I never feel quite right until the switch is flipped.

Every night there was *un apéro,* wine and cheeses and breads, always in some new manicured corner of the grounds of the chateau. Her first evening, she found me and introduced herself as not just an actress but a filmmaker who was just finishing her first feature-length script.

She'd just come from the shower, and the clean smell of her torrent of black hair, flowing easily to the middle of her back, made it hard for me not to nuzzle into her neck to better breathe. She was tall, so unlike all the other women there, she could almost look me in the eye and her eyes were vast and dark.

Laurianne was so flirty back to me—when she wasn't flirty with this impossibly handsome and irresistibly charming young Argentine. Nevertheless, I was convinced that I was making great progress. When I introduced her to Lucia, Lucia turned to me in front of Laurianne and asked:

¿Quieres foyarla?

I tried my best not to choke. Lucia was way, way off. I didn't just want to fuck her, I wanted to kidnap her back to the States and eventually retire with her to the Caribbean, where our grandchildren would often visit. However, if Laurianne had spoken even a little Spanish, or if that Argentine had been around to translate, I would have been within my rights to drown bigmouthed Lucia in the water park.

It turned out that it didn't matter anyway. After beating out the Argentine for the privilege of sitting next to Laurianne on the bus ride into Saint-Malo, she admitted that she had a boyfriend. A sixty-year-old semi-known French stage actor. A sixty-year-old semi-known French stage actor who also happened to be married. She was miserable with him but fatally in love. Have I mentioned that she was twenty-six?

Instantly, the vibrant colors of our magical (free) vacation drained into the earth, and, though it was early summer, my world turned gray and chilly. It reminded me of the night that I was sure I was going to win an Emmy. I had written an HBO film, *The Tuskegee Airmen,* that had been excellently received. Everyone said we were the odds-on favorite, and despite myself I tried not to believe them. Finally, however, I did clear out room in my office's mini-fridge. I kept only some water and the manuscript to my last novel inside (it's fireproof, after all), so I was pretty sure that my heavy new statuette would fit. When friends would come by to visit, I'd ask them if they wanted something to drink and then casually fling open the refrigerator door.

Oh, that thing? I was just happy to be nominated.

When it came time to announce the winner for the Best Writing for a Miniseries or Movie, I was wheezing, the tux I'd gotten married in was now crushing me, my spastic heart was rocking me in my chair, and a cameraman was kneeling at my feet, shooting right up my nose.

And the winner is . . . *Gulliver's Travels!*

I and the rest of the losers in my category instantly excused ourselves to go to the lobby bar to join the night's earlier losers.

In this most recent case of crushing disappointment, I just knew that Laurianne and I belonged together. If her old guy were only twenty or thirty years older than he already was, then I could have just waited until nature took its course and she was free of him.

Mercifully, the workshop ended the next day, and Lucia, the kids, and I flew down to Ramatuelle for a week as guests of Kasi and Vondie, the best friends with whom we usually shared this magical beach house back when we were two fabulous couples. Ava's fourth birthday was just three days away, and I dedicated myself to making it so unforgettable that she would forget that which was better left forgotten.

• • •

I REMEMBER my own birthdays when I was little and how they anchored the entire year. I will never forget my seventh birthday, a first for me in our new, cheap condo in Ypsilanti, Michigan, just as Ava's would be her first without her mommy.

We were one of the first five families and the only black one to move into the hundreds of proposed units in various stages of construction in what used to be southern Michigan farmland. There was only one other boy my age, Scott Jackson, recently arrived from Alabama. A year older and twice as big, he used to howl that he was Robert E. Lee and chase me around the still-unfinished lanes of our subdivision. I did not have a deep bench of friends to draw upon. For that first birthday in that new town, it was just the two of us down in my basement, eating premade ice cream sundaes out of little paper cups and taking turns firing off pretend rounds with my one gift, a black plastic, damn-near-life-size M-16 Marauder machine gun. This was in 1969, Vietnam was at its bloodiest, and my dad was a child psychiatrist and my mom was getting her PhD in child psychology. What the hell were they thinking? Were they experimenting to see if they could induce a desire to serially kill? I would never give one to Chetty or Ava. (Though it was maybe the best gift I've ever gotten in my entire life. For Christmas this year I got Chet a lightsaber, with sound effects and weightier than the one I had as a teenager. The day after Christmas I realized that I should have bought us two so we could fight each other with them instead of over who got to play with it.)

Although I loved the gun, two kids is not a party. That night my crying into my pillow was loud enough to bring my mom into the room. The next year, more kids had moved in, and my mom and dad had even invited our old friends from Detroit. My folks gave me a white cowboy outfit—pants, vest, jacket, hat—and a six-shooter and sat me at the head of a long table festooned with multiple paper accordion centerpieces that opened into footballs, pumpkins, and turkeys (my birthday is in the fall). That second year I was treated like a reincarnated lama.

• • •

I WAS DETERMINED to do at least as well by my little girl.

I drove into Saint-Tropez, to the patisserie that actually invented the *tarte tropezienne,* and ordered one as large as a hassock. Though it's not my favorite dessert, Ava loves them. A spongy cake sliced in half and crammed full of cream, it was invented in 1955 by the baker who catered the film that invented Saint-Tropez as a concept, *Et Dieu . . . créa la femme (And God Created Woman).* Legend has it that Brigitte Bardot herself gave the mountain of fat and fluff its name.

The French present their desserts as if Marie Antoinette herself were about to be served. A simple ice cream sundae (*la glace royale*) comes with sparklers. When I asked for a birthday candle, the lady behind the counter gave me one as thick as a cigar.

Back at the house, I gathered Chet's godparents, Howard and Caroline; Kasi, Vondie, and their son; Ava's play cousin Hunter; and Lucia held Chet in her arms. We all gathered around Ava, who was scrubbed and in a flowery dress with flowers in her hair, and I pulled out the cake, so fat it hung over the edge of the platter, and I lit the candle.

I now know that they use *Roman* candles for birthdays in France. A thick and fast spray of sparks blasted from the cake, ricocheting off the iron chandelier and the ancient wooden beams of the ceiling. Everyone stepped back except Ava, whose big cheeks were lit by the white sparks, although it was her eyes that I most noticed. Even brighter than the fireworks they sparkled. I took picture after picture, but what I really wanted to do was cry. When you're raising your kids without the other parent, your still-married friends often spread praise upon you and your kids as thick as peanut butter. *I don't know how you do it. You all are so brave. The kids are doing so wonderfully.* Their words are all very nice, but you know they're just being kind. Not too many friends are going to pull you aside and say, *You know, I think you're doing a really crappy job so I've called social services.* So you really have no idea how you're doing. The kids aren't taking a crap on the dining-room table or lighting squirrels on fire, but beyond that, how can you give yourself a grade?

Yet when I looked in her sparkly eyes, I knew that at least on this day, on the day of her fourth birthday, I got an A.

· · ·

SOON AFTER RETURNING to the States, little Chet decided to join us bipeds. I can't tell you exactly when it happened. Every moment of the firstborn's life is fretted over and stage-managed. The second one is parented by pure chance. With Ava I remember precisely where I was. It was a shiny morning in June, and the two of us were lying on the sisal carpet in our showy old house. Her mom was upstairs sleeping in. Mornings were always just the two of us. When she was as small as a gym bag, she would crawl over my legs like a marine through an obstacle course, arrive at my face, and try to pry open my mouth. Sometimes I would pull out the video camera, put on Joni Mitchell's "The Circle Game," and shoot an impromptu music video. My heart was as heavy with love as the ripest fruit deeply bowing a branch. If I can remember where the tape is by the time she's ready to get married, I will howl and sob at the rehearsal dinner.

That shiny morning, I wasn't taping. I was working up the enthusiasm to convince a major studio to pay me $150,000 to rewrite a comedy about an African American dentist who becomes an Alaskan dogsledder. I tried not to believe in karma. As I mentioned earlier, I'm a Zen Buddhist, not a Tibetan one, and we're not supposed to fall for that crap. Still, it was tempting to think that in a previous life I had slain a whole village and barbecued their entrails. How else to explain the current state of my career?

Ava had been cruising for weeks, holding on to the sides of anything—the walls, a coffee table, the kitchen's island—and navigating their circumferences the exact same way she would three years later, during her first few times on ice skates.

Yet that morning I looked up and saw her standing in the middle of the room. Swaying, smiling, and free.

My breath stopped. I tried not to make any sudden moves. She lifted her right foot and brought it back down like a cute little Frankenstein. My eyes didn't leave her, but my hands felt back behind me for the video like a cameraman just spotting Bigfoot.

Another step. It was official now. I breathed. Anything more was just gravy. She did it. She stepped again and then wobbled, wobbled a lot, and my torso wobbled with her, until she plopped back on her diaper. It seemed all in a day's play to her. There was no gleam of accomplishment in her big round eyes. She just crawled up my legs and tried to pry open my mouth.

Chet seemed to have skipped all the interim steps. One day

he was prone, the next he was upright, and the next he was sort of running, more like perpetually falling, falling forward until he clutched a wall or my leg or bowled over his big sister. His constant baby aerobics turned out to be the most rapid form of weight loss ever. Not only was he no longer hugely fat, hugely fat like some very old lady's overpampered old cat, he was actually turning downright wiry. The change was almost freakishly fast. If he weren't so smiley and charming, I would have been reminded of Damien in *The Omen* and started to worry. I was afraid that I'd come home from the gym and he would not only suddenly speak, *Hello, Father,* but he would be casually smoking a pipe.

It was a year for milestones. I was about to turn halfway to eighty. A few years before, when I was so sick that I was vomiting more often than I was going to the movies, I was not at all sure that I was going to make it. My mom died when she was thirty-seven, so half of my genes were already in overtime. Back when Chet started walking and still today, only rarely do I throw up. Most of the time I feel as fine as I ever have. The heaps of pills I palm into my mouth three times a day, the weekly injections, watching my salt intake, watching the potassium, watching the protein are now just the price of doing the business of living. My goal is to live at least until Chet turns twenty-four, the year I was when I was suddenly all alone. By then I will be sixty, ten years older than my dad's last birthday.

Though that is my goal, my dream, however, is to make it a century. Since I was a teenager, my fantasy was having my hundredth birthday in my simple cottage in the Caribbean. I would be one of those sticklike old black men and my wife of fifty years would help me out of the chair on the porch to welcome the kids, grandkids, and great-grandkids fanned out on the lawn before me.

When I'm not obsessing on being very old, I'm clinging to the idea of remaining relatively young. Forty is disconcerting for anyone, but it was especially troubling for somebody who secretly thought that since he was born in October that that was almost as prodigious as having skipped a grade. I have always craved the idea of being a wunderkind. When my first novel, *Platitudes*, came out when I was twenty-six, I was so sure that I was the youngest new novelist in America that I would flip to the bio on the back flap of any book whose author appeared even approximately youthful. If anyone threatened to challenge my reign, I would remind myself that I had begun the book as a senior at Stanford in the writing workshop of the recently late and eternally great Gilbert Sorrentino and had actually sold it to Vintage Contemporaries when I was twenty-four. I remember quite clearly attending the birthday party of my oldest friend at the time, Jack Barth. He was turning thirty, and I remember congratulating myself on being so open-minded and mature enough to allow a friendship with somebody who, I thought, would soon be crapping into a colostomy bag.

Now forty was rushing upon me like a wave of dirty water.

The only thing I could possibly look forward to would be a vigorous midlife crisis, but unfortunately I had already gone through one when I turned thirty-five. The fact that it hit me early was further proof of my prodigy.

Back when I was thirty-five, Anna was pregnant with Ava. I owned a house. My childhood had definitively disappeared. I bought the '73 Mustang convertible with the lie to myself and to Anna that I would trade it in for a wagon or another SUV as soon as the baby actually arrived. Then one day

Anna came home with some temporary tattoos. I picked one of a Georgia O'Keeffe deer skull, and she laid it on my right deltoid and soaked the paper with a sponge. I had forgotten about it until 4:15 that afternoon, when my ass was skyward in downward dog. Seane, the yoga teacher I've had a crush on for years, squatted down next to me and purred.

When'd you get that tattoo? Wow.

For the rest of the day it was like that. No one, but especially the women around me, could believe that someone as nerdy as me would subject himself to permanent body art. Always, when they asked if it was real, I told them of course it was. Instantly, I saw the change in everyone's eyes. It was as if I'd just killed a man. (Of course, this was in 1998, before the Great Yuppie Tattoo Rush of 2001.) Eventually, however, the Boy Scout in me would confess, and they would all say, Aha! I knew you wouldn't get a real one.

It upset me that everyone assumed that they knew me so well, so for my birthday I made it permanent. I'd be damned if at just thirty-five the book of me would have already been written. I went to this place on the Venice boardwalk alone, and after the guy, a Brit named Swag, had finished with the deer skull and a red poppy, he asked me if I wanted anything else. I told him to write *Anna* in the leaves of the flower. When I came home, I showed it to her. At first she couldn't make out her name through the slab of petroleum jelly protecting my healing skin from infection, but I assured her that it was in there. Ten days later, after the last of the scabs had flaked into the ether, she read it and held me so tightly that my chest could take measure of the health of her heart.

This time, as my fortieth birthday approached, death and disease seemed to hound me. The poet in my brain kept reciting Andrew Marvell's "To His Coy Mistress":

But at my back I always hear
Time's winged chariot hurrying near;
And yonder all before us lie
Deserts of vast eternity.
Thy beauty shall no more be found,
Nor, in thy marble vault, shall sound
My echoing song; then worms shall try
That long preserv'd virginity,
And your quaint honour turn to dust,
And into ashes all my lust.
The grave's a fine and private place,
But none I think do there embrace.

I was taught the poem in boarding school by the brilliant and randy novelist Alexander Theroux, and right after college had used it to so successfully seduce Sally, the Yale comp-lit PhD candidate/runway model that she immediately used the poem and our experience with it as an example of successful hortatory discourse. (Then, after just a month, she pillaged my heart, leaving the husk to be picked over by hungry crows. I mention her in the first paragraph of chapter one. My heart crashed into Anna as I rebounded off Sally.)

However, on this morning a few days before my fortieth birthday, I told the kids I'd be right back and excused myself from the breakfast table because one of those relatively rare yet sudden urges to vomit was upon me. This time I was hearing the Marvell poem in my head not as a ploy to score but because my own death seemed to be coming sooner than I would have liked.

I threw up as quietly as I could so Ava wouldn't ask questions. She's worse than Columbo. *Where are you going? Didn't you go there last night? Who are you going with? What are you reading?*

I palmed water into my mouth and spat a few times before brushing my teeth and then jogged back into the room smile first.

C'mon, Ava, finish your cereal. As soon as Lucia arrives, we have to head off to school.

Daddy? she said.

Yes, baby.

Happy birthday.

Thank you, darling, but it's not my birthday yet.

Not Mommy's either.

No, not hers either, I told her. Remember, Carmend and I have the same day.

I just love listening to my daughter talk. It's like having a songbird free of its cage. When she was just two, she would bump into you, stretch her arms skyward, and chirp *Hold you. Hold you.* That never failed to melt her mother and me, and we'd immediately lift her into our arms. Neither of us ever corrected her, and the day, a few months later, when she self-corrected to *Hold me,* I obeyed but with the sadness of loss.

Earlier that spring some not very attractive great-tailed grackles had camped noisily under the eaves outside our old house. I kept updating Ava on the progress of the life cycle of these ugly little birds.

The mommy is sitting on the eggs and soon the babies will hatch, I informed her.

See! That very little one is just learning to fly.

Then one day as I was hurrying her to preschool, I suddenly hopped so as not to step on a dead baby grackle, matted little wings, broken old lady neck.

What's that, Daddy?

Nothing, baby. Go back inside.

Instead she pried open my legs and squatted down to get a better look.

What happened to the birdie?

It fell and it died, I told her.

When I fall I don't die.

No. You're a tough little girl.

I loved how death neither frightened nor repelled her. We went together to fetch the dustpan and the broom, scooped up the almost weightless former being, and laid the little body on top of the yard trimmings in the green trash bin.

My friends all know how attached I am to the concept of youth, especially my own, so they kept pestering me for my exact plans for the catastrophe of my fortieth. All I knew was that my birthday celebration would have to involve travel. Besides falling in love, travel is the only other activity that so elevates me. I travel when I am flush. And I travel just before it looks like looming bankruptcy will prevent me from ever traveling again. A friend in college theorized that people love to travel because, when they are traveling, they don't have to be doing anything else.

What are you doing with your life?

You mean right now? I'm traveling.

It's only when you stop that the problems have a chance to catch up with you.

I traveled from my old high school in New Haven to finish up high school at Phillips Academy, Andover, and then I traveled as far away to college as my dad would allow. I took my junior year abroad as a sophomore and returned to Florence soon after graduating. My dad accused me of confusing myself for one of the spoiled preps I met in boarding school who bum around Europe before the trust fund activates, but he was not-so-secretly proud of my restlessness. He was restless too and visited me when I was in Italy. He never offered and I never asked him to subsidize my adventures. James Bond didn't ask Daddy for handouts, so neither could I. Instead, in Florence I worked three jobs under the table while writing *Platitudes*. I had walked into a ski shop on Viale dei Mille to buy some gloves. The owner had said he'd just seen a documentary about a black skier, and he had never before heard of such a thing. I told him I too skied, and he clapped his hands to his cheeks and immediately offered me a job as a ski salesman. Suddenly I realized that my race in this place could bring me some good. So I ran across the street to this gym that I had wanted to join though I was so poor I could barely afford pasta and butter. I told them that I was a very famous American football player, and they immediately offered to let me use their facility for free. A few weeks later, they offered me a job as a trainer. Eight months later, to celebrate having finished a first draft of *Platitudes* (by hand in seven notebooks), I hitchhiked for four months through Kenya, Uganda, Zaire (now the Democratic Republic of the Congo), Central African Republic, Cameroon, Nigeria, Togo, Burkina Faso, Niger, Algeria, and Tunisia and then ferried to Sicily and took a train back to Florence, where I slept on the floor of the station, Santa Maria Novella, until the sun rose and I could wake up my Italian friends to let me use their shower.

This time, nearing forty, I was poor again but had 90,000 frequent flyer miles. With them, almost anywhere in the world was within my reach. But where? Then one of my best friends called to say he was getting married in London and he asked me to be his best man. The fact that that friend was the same Jack

Barth whose thirtieth birthday fifteen years before had so horrified me seemed an obvious omen of either future good luck or impending disaster.

I drew up a chart for the five days I would be away and plugged in the names of the team members I would need to pull it off.

WEEKDAY SCHEDULE

0700h Linda takes over my shift, wakes with the kids and feeds them breakfast.

0800h Lucia arrives. Takes both kids to Ava's preschool. Returns with Chet.

1200h Chet naps. Lucia stays and takes over my shift till Carmen returns with Ava at **1415h** Carmen stays with kids, as usual. Until:

1730h Tuesday

1900h Wednesday

1730h Thursday

1900h Friday

Tuesday Linda takes over for me. Watches kids from **1730h** to overnight.

Wednesday Lucia takes over for me. Watches kids from **1900h** to **2200h,** when Linda returns from her night class.

Thursday Linda takes over for me. Watches kids from **1730h** to overnight.

Friday Linda does her regular Friday night babysitting from **1900h** to overnight.

WEEKEND SCHEDULE

SATURDAY

0700h to **1200h** Linda does her regular schedule.

1200h to **1900h** Carmen does her regular afternoon with the kids.

1900h to **2300h** Natalia, Brazilian pinch-hitting sitter stays with kids.

2300h to overnight Linda.

SUNDAY

0700h to **1200h** Linda does her regular schedule.

1200h to **1900h** Lucia takes over my shift.

1900h to **2100h** Linda watches kids until I return from airport.

USEFUL NUMBERS:

Trey: (310) ████████ (My cell will work. Remember, England is 8 hours ahead.)

Lucia: (818) ████████

Carmen: (310) ████████

Linda: (310) ████████

Natalia: (310) ████████

Tenth Street Pediatric: (310) ████████

I printed a half dozen copies, e-mailed the itinerary to everyone who had e-mail, and pinned another to the bulletin board in the kitchen. I folded one into my jeans pocket and another in the secret lining of my carry-on, where it joined a waning photocopy of my passport.

Before I left, I thought I'd call my film agent to remind him that since we had last spoken, a month and a half ago, I had been neither abducted nor incapacitated. He is an older, balding man with narrow eyes and an impressive scold. Except for that giddy afternoon two years earlier, when he first signed me, he seemed perpetually irritated by my presence. I guess you could call him paternal, yet nothing like my own father. My dad was always easy to talk to. Talking with this guy was like talking with your best friend's mean mom, the one who wouldn't think twice about berating you for some apparent shortcoming while your friend was upstairs finishing his homework before she would allow him to come out and play.

I called his office right before lunch to get my name down on his phone log kept by his assistant so a return call before nightfall would not be beyond the realm of the possible. I was already starting to hang up when his assistant put him right on.

Hi! Um . . . I'm heading to England for a wedding and for my birthday, on miles, and I was just wondering if . . . um . . . there were any projects out there that looked interesting?

I send your stuff out there. There was this project, sort of a *Booty Call* meets *Mannix*. But they passed.

My office is on the second floor of my new house, and I wanted to dive over the balcony headfirst. I wanted my agent to worry when I didn't answer him and to send the paramedics. I wanted him to go to his grave knowing that he had killed a father of two.

I . . . um . . . I have cash reserves for maybe another four months. So if . . .

Look. If you need money, wait tables.

I stared at the phone long after I had hung it up.

The tears surprised me, but it was the bellowing moan that scared me into stopping soon after I started, even though the big house was empty.

I added my agent to the list of people who didn't believe in my capacity for significant advancement. A list that included my best-friend-while-growing-up's mom, my boarding school precalculus teacher, and my ex-wife. They would all receive anonymous invitations to the ceremony celebrating my MacArthur fellowship.

My flight wasn't until the evening so I had the afternoon to play with the kids. We feasted on organic macaroni, cheese, and broccoli, and I gave them an extra-long bath and an extra-long story before laying Chet in his crib and Ava in her tiny little platform sleigh bed.

In London, Jack housed me in his members-only club in swanky Soho, the Groucho Club, where bitter, extremely funny London writers, filmmakers, and television personalities get hammered several times a week. Because I was his best man, the day before the wedding, Jack and I got fitted with spats, gray waistcoats, gloves, and top hats. Had we not been in England, I would have felt as ridiculous as the banker in Monopoly.

Like at all good weddings, the singles in the crowd played that musical chairs game I hate to see who would hook up with whom. Penny and I seemed instantly linked by our mutual and unlikely childhood devotion to Simon and Garfunkel. Her father is Trinidadian, her mother Welsh, and she's a celebrity chef who cooked Italian on the Sky Channel.

After the ceremony, many of us returned to the Groucho Club to continue drinking. In the middle of our large crowd, Penny kept giving me the type of smile that could feed a healthy ego for weeks. However, it was past one in the morning, and the rest of the dissipated crowd showed no signs of dissipating.

Damn it. I forgot to call my kids.

I said this to the crowd in general, but the following I addressed only to Penny:

The phone is on the second floor. There is also a snooker table.

A Yank that plays snooker, she said. Fancy that.

Now as an internationalist, jet-setting man of mystery, yes, I should know the rules to snooker, cricket, and rugby. Just as I should have a pressed tuxedo always at the ready, and I should know how to silently sever a man's spine with a bent cocktail straw. However, since that image of myself exists uniquely in my imagination, I know none of the above.

Now was not the time to tell her that.

We left the party to head upstairs. Penny set up the snooker table while I called. Ava still wasn't very good on the phone, and Chet was hopeless. Pretty much she would just repeat what I said.

I love you, I began.

I love you, she replied.

I miss you, baby.

I miss you, Daddy.

I got you a present.

She giggled.

A baby doll, I told her. From Hamley's. People say it's the best toy store in the world.

When I asked to try to speak to Chet, I heard her shout, Chetty! No! And then, Come here. It's Daddy.

I think I heard panting on the phone. I'd like to think that at least a little bit of the sweet things I was putting into my end of the line were actually making it into his little ears. I told him about the toy London taxi I bought him and about the replica red 1973 Mach I that Sean Connery drove in *Diamonds Are Forever* that I bought for myself. All I heard on my end was more dragon breath.

When I returned to the snooker room, Penny handed me my gin, now thankfully watery.

How are the little ones? she asked me.

Excellent.

D'you really know how to play snooker?

I can't even play American pool. But I have some absinthe in my room.

I guess one sort of balances out the other. Just a drink and then I'm off. I've got an early taping tomorrow.

She entered my small, velvety room and everything seemed possible. I had bought the bottle of absinthe around the corner and was weighing different possibilities for smuggling it into the States. I chose this bottle, *La Fée,* from among the half dozen others for the unblinking green eye on the label and the slotted spoon that came with it. I poured just a finger of the green monster into two tall glasses, placed the slotted spoon over the first glass, put a sugar cube that I had swiped from the restaurant for just such an occasion on the spoon, and drizzled water over the sugar into the glass. Like a cool ninth-grade chemistry experiment, the thick green instantly turned milky upon contact with the water. I tried to look as cool as the reincarnation of Balzac as I mixed, and not like a guy who had only learned the proper absinthe ceremony by Googling it the day before my flight.

You get off on these types of things, don't you? she snapped. They're such crap.

We toasted. It tasted like poison, like what I imagine the kids' ipecac syrup must taste like, and it could easily have had the same emetic effect on me. It also made me almost instantly very drunk.

She sat on my bed and I moved to join her.

You sit in that chair, she ordered with a point of her finger.

I obeyed and she ridiculed my shoes (So posh. What a waste.), one of my professions (Hollywood is crap.), my nation (You Americans won't be satisfied until the rest of us are all either your slaves or dead.). I, however, was undeterred.

May I sit next to you now? I asked.

Why?

Because it's time for us to kiss.

She actually bit her lip, and her sourness was suddenly devoured by a cute little girl.

We kissed like teenagers, working our tongues like we were stirring fudge.

And that Spielberg fellow, she continued. I honestly can't see why—

I swallowed her words by kissing her some more. Later, when she broke us apart a second time, she laid her hand on my chest.

I really must be on my way.

I pulled off my sweater so I was just wearing a T-shirt. Her eye instantly caught something.

Is that . . . a tattoo?

She pushed up my sleeve and inspected it.

It's a deer skull, I told her. By Georgia O'Keeffe.

She glanced at me sideways.

Right, then. We're shagging.

8

BACK IN LOS ANGELES, I e-mailed Penny several times a week. I informed her about the latest repairs to my leaky house. She complained about her new segment producer. We vowed to meet in the middle, in New York, maybe at Christmastime, when the kids would be in Social Circle with their grandma and Carmen and I would be off duty for about a week.

By mid-November, however, she said she couldn't wait and that the flights from London to New York cost about the same as from London to LA. Would I mind if she flew in?

Mind? I told her I'd love her to come. I'd figure out a way to get a weekend off from the kids so we could go to Palm Springs.

As her arrival neared, my heart began to fill like a hot-air balloon until it was tethered to the ground by the thinnest of ropes, straining to pull the stake out of the ground and take flight with the next significant breeze. Could I have a girlfriend who

lived in London? Could she come here often enough? Could the
kids and I go there? What if she got picked up by the Food Channel in the States and taped in LA during the school year and we
all returned to England for the summer? Did she like kids? Would
she like to have some of her own? Would I like to have more? We
had only talked about politics and Hollywood and snooker the
night that I pulled her. Where would she stay? I knew Carmen
and I had the six-months rule, but hotels are so expensive. Neither
of us could afford it. There had to be a loophole for out-of-town-
ers. I'd have to inform Carmen before Penny arrived, of course.
But damn! What if it worked and I had found my new love at a
friend's wedding in London and now I was done? That actually
hadn't been so bad at all, that whole being single thing. Still, I was
glad that those days would soon be again behind me.

Then she stepped off the plane at LAX and my heart
knew instantly.

I didn't feel that click.

But she was staying a whole week.

She was chatty, I was silent, during the endless twenty-
minute drive back from the airport. What the hell had I been
thinking? When we entered the house from the garage, Ava ran
to me and, as usual, tried to disappear behind my legs. Chet
waddled up to Penny and cackled as he wrestled her calf. Carmen was on duty and she hung back in the kitchen until my
words freed her.

Uh, that's Carmen, their mom.

Hi! If you're exhausted I have this homeopathic oint-
ment—

I'm actually quite fine, snapped Penny. Thank you.

As if on cue, Linda the live-in wrestled herself through

the backdoor with a bag of groceries that was pinning her miniature T-shirt even higher up on her flat brown belly.

Hello, world! Linda shouted to all of us.

That's Linda. She lives behind the kitchen.

That sounds 'orrible! said Penny.

Yeah, Trey, said Linda. Like I'm some cousin of Shrek.

This has probably occurred to you already, but it only hit me at that very instant: My existence was encircled by women. If Lucia, Marta the once-a-week housekeeper, and my mother's ghost had all showed up just then, my Amazon would have been complete. When I lost a wife, I gained a sorority.

After fleeing to my bedroom with Penny, she spoke as soon as my door clicked shut:

Quite beautiful, your ex. Stunning, actually. The chippie *au pair* as well.

That's true.

Bastard.

I made myself grab Penny and kiss her.

That night, I didn't know what to do. When she wasn't insulting my bourgeois taste in decorating she was purring under my arm. I couldn't send her home early. I'd never had a woman fly so far to be with me. Or was it better to be honest up front before she dug herself in even deeper? Who knew? My brain was a warring parliament of incompatible ideation.

And the sex was spectacular.

Immediately after she'd turned me inside out with an orgasm, a voice inside me started chattering: *Give it another chance, Trey. You are so adept at self-sabotage. What did that therapist say soon after Anna turned into Carmen and fled? You write a script in your head about how you'd like a relation-*

ship to progress and when it doesn't adhere to the words on
your page, you act surprised. Guess what? Magical thinking is
supposed to disappear in early childhood.

As I stepped down the stairs and into the kitchen in my
robe to get Penny and me some cranberry juice, I decided that if
I could feel that close with this woman while we were making
love, I should be able to find some of that same intimacy with
our clothes on.

I had my head in the refrigerator when I heard:

British chick. Classy.

I had no idea how long Linda had been in her doorway,
but automatically I found myself tightening my robe.

She's great, I told her.

You really think so? I mean, I thought she was really
cool, but you don't seem too into her. But hey, what do I know.
I'm just the thing that lives behind the refrigerator.

As I studied the juices, milk, and the chopped almonds
Carmen was soaking until they made some sort of raw vegan
nut cheese, Linda limboed under my arm to extract a Diet Coke.
Her hair smelled like fruit.

Sweet dreams, Linda.

Sweet dreams, tiger.

The next morning Penny was sniping at me again, as
insistent and annoying as the bird that inspired the verb. In fact,
every day of the entire week followed the exact same recipe:

1. Bicker, snipe, and nag.
2. Three, maybe four orgasms between the two of us.
3. Cuddle.
4. Repeat.

I resolved not to tell her while she was here that we were doomed, and certainly not before putting her on her flight. I could never send somebody sobbing across the continent, let alone across the expanse of the inky Atlantic as well.

As I drove home alone from the airport, depression curled up on top of my brain like an old fat cat. I went straight to my computer and signed up with Nerve.com. Sure, Internet dating is about as humiliating as public masturbation, but what choice did I have? If my heart didn't make a new friend soon, it would raisin and then petrify. In six minutes, I had thrown down a clatter of words describing myself and then hit send. If the universe wouldn't send me someone to love, cyberspace seemed my last resort.

Meanwhile, Penny called as soon as she landed at Heathrow. Of course I couldn't break up with her right then, as she'd be addled by jet lag and parched by the stingy airline air. The next day I called, but only her cell's voice mail responded. As tempting as that opportunity was, I left no message. On the third day, still without nibbles from Nerve.com, I was still determined to free Penny. I had just put Chet down for his nap when I decided to call her again.

Hi.

Hi.

Where are you? What's that noise? I asked.

I'm back at the Groucho. I sort of despised it for the longest, however, now I am rather fond of it again.

I listened to hear if she was already drunk, but had yet to decide how that might affect my resolve.

Sweetie, I was thinking we could meet in New York at Christmastide. You mentioned Ava and Chet would be with their mum and grandmum in Atlanta.

I . . . I'm not yet sure . . .

Or, if you're really good, I might come to California. How strong is the sun in January?

But the distance— We had talked about the difficulty of the distance, and I was planning on leveraging that into my escape.

I reckon the more you do it, she said, the shorter it becomes.

The distance doesn't really work for me, I told her.

I heard women laughing in the background, but for a moment I did not hear her at all.

Just good for a shag? That it?

No! Of course not! I just . . . This is just all so new to me. I'm . . . confused.

You sleazy bastard. I spent a small fortune flying to see you while all the bloody while you—

Not all the while.

All the while you just wanted your bloody knob gobbled. Piss off, you fucking cunt.

I stared at the phone for a beat after she had clicked off, as if the camera filming my life was still running.

Well, that went about as well as could have been expected.

I said this aloud. To the audience of me.

On the monitor I heard Chet complaining in his sleep, so I tiptoed my way into his room. He'd stopped moaning, but had started rhythmically pile-driving his little forehead against his mattress. The doctor said it was normal, that some babies and toddlers like the rhythm of the banging to help them get back to sleep. I didn't give a damn what the pediatrician said. It freaked me out, so I hurried to comfort him. Besides, I'll take any excuse to hold his hot heaviness in my arms.

How can a woman compete for the oceanic love I feel for my two soft miniatures? No two other beings on the planet can pull my cheeks into a smile just at the thought of seeing them again. Why waste my time on romance when I could be learning to be a better parent? I don't play enough ball with my son. I don't tell my daughter enough stories. With their mother exploring her solitary consciousness, I don't have the luxury of settling for mediocre parenting on my end. A B– is not a passing grade. Women are a luxury that I cannot yet afford.

Chet was now motionless and napping between my elbows. I maneuvered him back into his bed and drew their door closed as silently as a spy.

My office is just outside their new room and the washer and dryer my roommates. I was in the late-middle of writing my very exciting spec script, a thinking man's international espionage adventure called *August Welch*. Nothing in my life would change until I finished this script, so I worked on it every moment that I wasn't watching the kids. With Chet napping, I had maybe another twenty-six minutes of productivity.

I sat down at my desk prepared to take control of my future. I reawakened my PC and on my computer a small window appeared asking me if I would like to accept an instant message from someone named FelaLover325. I had received an instant message a few months before from someone named *hARDcore VerGINs!!!* offering to enlarge my penis, so my first reaction was to decline the invitation lest some worm, Trojan horse, or virus eager to exploit the depths of my reckless loneliness steal in and paralyze the only machine in my house that had the potential to someday make me some money again.

But I love Fela Anikulapo Kuti myself. When he was alive, I never missed a chance to hear the Nigerian James Brown live. It was not until I had crossed my fingers and clicked *accept* that it occurred to me that Fela was probably short for fellatio and FelaLover was undoubtedly either spyware or a combed-over, middle-aged Midwestern trigonometry teacher named Chuck. Just as I tried to exit and get back to work, my computer chimed:

FelaLover325: Saw your profile on Nerve. I love Fela too. Hence the name.

TreyTreyTrey: Um. Hello. And you are?

FelaLover325: Cynthia Montoya. Here is my link.

Immediately I clicked, and she looked good. Very good. Thirty-four. Long brown hair and tricky, active eyes. A bit of a double chin, but I can have one too at certain bad angles. She was tall, five-eleven, and solid, 165 pounds. But I had to get to work, didn't I? The damn Internet makes writing on your computer like writing on top of a TV screen. It takes a tremendous force of will not to peel back what you're working on and take a peek. My plan was to just flirt for a couple of minutes and then, I swear, get back to writing.

TreyTreyTrey: I saw Fela in concert every time he visited the States.

FelaLover325: I missed a couple of shows. I just love his middle name.

TreyTreyTrey: *Anikulapo.* He who keeps the devil in his pocket.

FelaLover325: Wow! I never knew anybody else who knew that!

TreyTreyTrey: So. I've never instant-messaged before.

FelaLover325: So you're a virgin☺.

TreyTreyTrey: Please be gentle.

Wow. And I had thought that instant-messaging was only for Finnish teens. This was going to be fun.

FelaLover325: I'll be right back. My daughter's school is calling . . .

Daughter? Fela? Beautiful face? What if this becomes something real. Something pretty cool. Something great? What a terrific story that would make. *So, how the heck did you two kids meet anyhoo?*

FelaLover325: I'm back. She's fine. She just cut her lip at recess.

TreyTreyTrey: How old is she? I have a four-year-old and a sixteen-month-old.

FelaLover325: Lucinda is nine. So. U married?

TreyTreyTrey: I wouldn't be here if I was.

FelaLover325: You are new to IMing, aren't you?

We went on like this—lovely like this—till I heard Chet moan awake like a small dinosaur. I excused myself and was changing his diaper on top of the dryer when Carmen arrived to pick him up and then go pick up Ava at school. I let her finish pulling his pants back up so I could quickly minimize the IM screen. The instant she took Chet downstairs I maximized it again and with it my hope.

TreyTreyTrey: She takes them every afternoon.

FelaLover325: My ex comes by about every leap year.

TreyTreyTrey: You sound lovely and amazing. Sexy and beautiful. He's an idiot.

FelaLover325: He is. You too. Not the idiot part. The sexy part.

TreyTreyTrey: Should we talk on the phone?

FelaLover325: That's not how this works. Patience.

TreyTreyTrey: You're the expert. I'm in your hands.

FelaLover325: Maybe one day.

An erection is a dangerous thing. The enemy of logic and reason. It was kicking at the barn door, threatening to escape and dragging my heart and then my head along with it into the dangers of the night.

And did I mention that I very much had to get back to writing?

TreyTreyTrey: Where do you most like to make love?

FelaLover325: Well that very much depends on how comfortable I am with my lover. How open our communication, etc. But if we both seem to understand and respect one another, then . . . anywhere it fits.

That ejected me from my chair, set me pacing the floor, palming my forehead. The conversation continued, careering from parenting to pornography, from G to X and back, till it devoured not only the entire afternoon, but much of the evening. For three days, more on than off, our computers mated. I would have gotten so much more work done had we just met for coffee. However, she was fascinating, so smart, like me had traveled in Africa, like me worshipped her daughter's every twitch. We agreed to dinner on Friday and every other IM was one of us saying how much it felt like Christmas was coming.

She lived in the Valley, and the Wednesday before our Friday I was in the Valley visiting friends when my cell phone rang. My phone said number unknown, but I had dared her to call me earlier in the day. I pleaded with her that I needed to hear if her voice was as sexy and as inviting as her words. She had just laughed and typed that interesting things come to those who wait.

Do you know who this is? asked the voice on the phone.

I can guess. How are you?

I'm fine, she cooed. How are you?

Nervous. Excited.

Me too.

You know I'm in the Valley tonight, I told her. How'd you like to meet for a drink? If we wait till Friday I'll pop.

We don't want you to pop. But I don't have a sitter tonight.

Shoot.

Would you like to come over here for a drink?

It was already ten o'clock in the middle of the week.

Sure!

She gave me meticulous directions, which I double-checked with her as I wrote them down. The couple I was visiting, Brett and Kendahl, quizzed me the moment I hung up. Married friends are fascinated by the torture of adult dating.

Dude, said Brett. After ten? Midweek? That's a booty call.

You think?

Kendahl just threw up her hands and said, Men are such idiots.

She shoved me a bottle of wine so I wouldn't show up with just my idiotic grin.

It was all I could do not to run every single stoplight between Burbank and Pacoima. I had my excuse all ready for the cops when they finally pulled me over:

Officer, I can explain. She said anywhere it fits and my penis's driving skills are limited and . . .

I stopped right in front of her sweet little cottage and tried to steady my breath. What a wonderful life I lead. What adventures. Even if we just date for a month or so, I thought, I will have discovered a rich new vein of promising potential mates. We're all so single and alone, speeding past maybe a dozen people who could be significant lovers in our lives every time we drive down the 405. Every trip to the mall brings us within the orbit of at least a few people whom, were we to get to know them, it would be a pleasure to kiss and whose hands it would be a warming pleasure to hold.

The night was very dark, but the cottage glowed bright from its windows. As I raised my hand to knock, I remembered the old commercials for a girls' board game, *Mystery Date*. Cute white teens rolled the dice to see if they'd open the door to a dream! (*Ooooh!*) Or a dud. (*Ewwww!*)

My mystery door opened to Cynthia Montoya's very

pretty face on top of a body that health-care professionals could only classify as morbidly obese.

I forced the shell of my face to keep smiling, but my eyes and everything inside me started to cry. She was wearing a beige negligee large enough to bivouac a company of marines. Behind her, a skyline of wine, hard liquor, and glasses shot up from the coffee table. The fireplace was bright and noisy and of course Fela frenzied the speakers. Her daughter, Cynthia informed me, was a heavy sleeper.

Before we even sat on the couch she was talking, talking, talking, but my head was too distracted by my own thoughts to hear her.

She invited you into her home. Her face is pretty. You pride yourself on your eccentricities, well what about your embarrassingly pedestrian taste in women? Do they always have to have had their picture taken professionally for you to be interested in them? Do they have to fit society's fucked-up, puerile, Barbie and Baywatch notions of what is and what is not stimulating? Her face is very pretty. There must be lots of men, those that are into three-hundred-pound women, for whom Cynthia would be a dream date. And weren't you the one who always said carpe diem? Who always said if you have a choice between the known and the unknown, go for the unknown? Well have you ever had sex with a woman the size of a Sub-Zero? Couldn't you be a gentlemen, conjure Halle Berry and Angelina Jolie making out backstage at the Oscars, and do it for England? Isn't it a better story, aren't you a better human being if you just lean over and start kissing her? C'mon! Chicken! Bok-bok-bok!

I took several deep breaths, preparing myself. I've jumped

out of airplanes, bungee jumped out of a hot-air balloon. Surely I can make out with a fat chick. Daredevil that I think I am, each time, just before almost kissing her, I collapsed.

My eyes found a clock in the room and I resolved to stay forty minutes. Forty minutes seemed polite and uncowardly enough for me to claim a cold and a school night, kiss her cheek at the door, and escape.

Maybe her life was not as sad as I imagined. If one had a fetish for the superfat, she would have been quite the catch. Botero, for example, would have sculpted her for decades. However, the cavernous loneliness that I perceived in her and that echoed within me as I sailed home down fat, dark, and empty highways, the 101 to the 405 to the 10, made me think hard about my mother.

9

PRETTY MUCH ABSOLUTELY EVERYTHING
I REMEMBER ABOUT MY MOTHER

By Trey Ellis

I'm looking at a picture of the two of us. Washington, DC, 1962. I couldn't be more than three months old and am as cute as a puppy, enveloped in a white blanket and in her arms. She's so full of love for me, drunk with it and twenty-two years old. I'm staring at the camera, she stares at me. I look happy too, but coy; a quarter of my face is buried behind her flexed shoulder.

Her smile in this photo showcases the gap between her white teeth. I got my gap from her. For years I restrained my smile, drew the upper lip over the emptiness or used my tongue (in vain) to try to suck my two big front teeth together. The gap closed thanks to the pulling of tiny, translucent rubber bands during my dark, braces-wearing adolescence, only to open again post-retainer. Now I usually like it and habitually probe my tongue inside the intimate in-between.

From DC we moved to Dayton, then to Detroit, then to Ypsilanti, Michigan, when I was five. There I remember Mom driving me home from kindergarten and me leaving my groovy leather satchel on the roof of our Ford Country Squire and it falling off and Mom stopping traffic with both palms to run and get it.

Mom and Dad got along well enough when we were all younger. The viciousness, me frozen outside the side door, waiting for them to finish making noise, burning at the thought of the neighbors—watching commercials, washing vegetables—suddenly stopping to eye each other and tilt their ears, didn't erupt and swallow my life until junior high and we had moved to Connecticut.

Ypsilanti (still one of my absolute favorite words) is a suburb of Ann Arbor. Mom was getting her PhD in child psychology at the University of Michigan because Dad was beginning his psychiatric residency there. Mom and her colleagues often experimented on me. I made a pretty good living for a seven-year-old, playing with blocks and dolls and plastic guns in front of prehistoric video cameras and two-way mirrors.

One day my dad discovered the university had mistakenly been underpaying him since he arrived. With the windfall, the three of us summered in Europe. I was tenish and had bad diarrhea in Florence, and I remember my mother, sure she could communicate with the Italians with her advanced college Latin, asking for and finding a place where she could rinse out my underwear. I remember her, this young black woman, flanked by old and heavy Italian women, all wringing out wet clothes in a medieval public trough. Later, in the Rome train station, while my dad went to find us a cab, some Italian men mistook her for a prostitute. Ten years later I would study in Florence, then, after graduating, return there to live and to write my first novel.

When we moved to Yale, as I mentioned earlier, the terrible fights began: Mom smacking Dad in the stomach with a plate, dumping an entire liter of Pepsi (which he adored with an addiction I have inherited) into the sink in galloping, noisy gurgles. I never once remember them kissing or holding hands.

As a child psychologist, my mother, soon after my thirteenth birthday, explained to me what nocturnal emissions are, how they are a natural part of puberty, and how I would have to wash the befouled sheets myself. I nodded seriously, as I imagined adults did during business conversations, then marched to my room and collapsed with shame.

She taught psychology at Quinnipiac College for a few years while she was also supposed to be finishing her dissertation. Then she wrote a play about her father, who died when she was sixteen, and sent it everywhere to try to get it produced. She had graduated magna cum laude from Howard University and was several orders of magnitude smarter than my dad, who was sweet and silly. She would have graduated summa cum laude, except she blew up the chemistry lab. My uncle Fletcher says she used to sleep through class till the teacher called on her. She would slowly raise her head from her desk, give the correct answer, and then go back to sleep. It's probably not true, or could not possibly have happened more than once, but I insist on perpetuating the legend. I like to think how pleased she would be if she knew that I grew up to write novels, movies, articles, and essays and to teach.

Her final career change was entering Yale Law School when she was thirty-six. She already knew she was sick, already knew that her marriage was fatally corroded by my dad's secret, and yet she dove in, the older mom among the aggressive young jurists.

As a teenager I fought with her pretty much constantly. My dad was more often away on business or in Manhattan visiting friends than sharing the house with her, and somehow I seemed to have volunteered to battle her as his proxy. In truth, I was under the roof only a little more often than he was and it was my absences that were the subject of most of our rows. Most every weekend night I invited myself to sleep over at either Ben's house or Danny's.

I didn't want my friends coming around the house much during the week, either. As she was getting more and more tired and sleeping on the couch all afternoon under a Day-Glo-orange afghan that her mother had crocheted, I just saw her as lazy. I didn't care that she'd been studying constitutional law till four in the morning and I didn't know what was happening inside of her body, so when my friends came over after school, I was just petrified that they'd peer inside from the driveway basketball half-court where we were playing H-O-R-S-E and tease me about her. When I would finally enter my own house, she would still be sleeping, her mouth open like a cave. More than once her robe was open too and I could see her underwear and more, and my lungs stopped as if somebody had thrown a switch.

Once, she was cooking something (probably her signature wintertime dish, hamburger with two undiluted cans of Campbell's soup, one Cheddar cheese, the other golden mushroom. Her summertime dish was Crab Louie, crabmeat from a can mixed with Thousand Island dressing on iceberg lettuce. Both were excellent.), and she asked me to move our biggest iron skillet to another burner. Maybe I refused, or just further slowed my shuffling feet, I don't remember, but I remember her trying to do it herself, the skillet dropping, banging loud against the vinyl floor and scattering ground-beef BBs, and the two condensed soups still holding most of the shape of their cans on the floor. She was so mad at herself. I thought she was just weak, and weak willed. I didn't know till later that multiple sclerosis had invaded every one of her synapses.

They told me they were separating after her first year of law school, and I was looking forward to being able to breathe. The plan was for her to move to Washington, DC, after law school. I had just applied to Andover and if I was accepted, during most school breaks I would live with my dad. Mom said she was going to buy me, a fourteen-year-old, the hang glider I'd been whining about with her forthcoming lawyerly riches and I believed her—believed she meant it when she said she'd purchase the means by which I could quite possibly kill myself. Actually, I'd always believed she was that cool until just now, as I was writing this down. I like it now, knowing that I fell for her ruse. I feel warmed by this, a new memory about her twenty-eight years after her death.

I wonder how much she forgave how badly I treated her. It must have been heartbreaking for her, feeling that her only son would scowl and roll his eyes every time her lips began to part. Promise him a hang glider, a luge, bomb-making materials, anything, she must have thought, just so he will smile at me again, like he couldn't stop doing when he was a baby in my arms and my marriage was promising and my body obeyed my commands.

The year before she died, I remember going with her to Philadelphia to visit her mom, my grandma. Mom took me to a fancy hotel restaurant on a high floor, almost like on a date. She said she was sorry we fought so much, said we were both going through a phase. At first I mumbled and cleared my throat instead of actually communicating, but eventually she coaxed whole sentences out of me. I liked her more by the time the fat slice of German sweet chocolate cake was in front of me and she was smiling as she watched me dismantle and disappear it. This dinner, with the grown-upness of my only sport jacket and the panoramic view, is often the first thing I think of when I think about her.

When she didn't come home from the law library one night sometime before Easter (I can't tell you the exact day), my dad and I were absolutely convinced that something was permanently wrong. He let me stay home from school and the television babbled from seven in the morning until after dark, when I heard my dad's little Fiat enter the driveway and his footsteps approach the side door, then saw him enter. Crying. There were five low steps from the side door to the kitchen and he made it up them to where I was waiting and then collapsed on top of me as he said through his sobs that my mother was dead. At the time, he had four inches and fifty pounds on me, but somehow I kept him up.

When I was a kid I used to pray every night. First it was the Lord's Prayer, but from about thirteen to sixteen, words of my own invention. I knew all the lines to every song in *Godspell* and *Jesus Christ Superstar*. I loved this idea of Jesus: a gentle, beleaguered hippie/martyr who was quietly cool and preternaturally unflappable. That night, in my bunk bed, I saw how little the rest of the world cared about my mother's death; how *What's Happening!!* and *Barney Miller* on my tiny black-and-white Sony had not altered their story lines; how the sheets were just as freezing till I bicycled my legs between them. I haven't prayed since.

They found her Audi in the parking lot at Yale's Paine Whitney gym and in the car they found a note for me saying she loved me and was sorry we fought so much and I don't remember what else. I put it in a locking steel box years ago, but in the move to California it seems to have disappeared. The combination to the box was 1-2-4.

The day before the funeral, I taught myself to juggle. I had a lot of free time and the house was too crowded with people toting casseroles, so I spent the day around the side of the house with three tennis balls. When the balls dropped, they would often find the rubber toe cap of my Jack Purcells and fire off in wild directions. By the end of the day I could sort of do it, and can still do it today, sort of.

Battell Chapel is Yale's biggest and the place was packed. My dad and I were in the front row, but I felt suf-

focated by the hundreds of other mourners, the entire law
school, every single person who had ever known either
of us, all behind us filling every single unforgiving pew.
My dad's crying was sometimes shrill and sometimes
profoundly guttural. My embarrassment silenced me.
Although it was her body on view in the open casket, I felt
as if our whole family was onstage. It would not be until I
gave a reading at Lincoln Center with Amos Oz after the
publication of *Platitudes* that I would find myself before
another audience so large. I wonder if that is why I have
such an ambivalent relationship with fame.

Seeing her body in the casket must have been horrible,
but I don't remember much about the feeling other than
the vibration of its oddness. I do remember that you
couldn't tell where the bullet entered. The police cleaned
the blood out of our Audi and delivered it back to us a
week or so later. I didn't know what had happened to the
gun till years later, when my cousin told me that my dad
had gone back to the gun store where my mom had bought
it, handed the manager the weapon, and told him that his
wife had used it to shoot herself in the heart. I don't know
why I never knew. Years later I totaled the Audi on the
Long Island Expressway coming home from my first and
last hang-gliding lesson.

10

I DEACTIVATED MY PROFILE on Nerve.com. I couldn't be bothered right now. Christmas loomed like an iceberg and I had to commit myself now to some fancy emotional navigation. Christmas was when I had proposed and nine years later Christmas was when she told me we were terminal. Ava knew that she, her brother, and her mother were flying back to her grandmother's in Social Circle, Georgia, for the holidays.

Are you coming too, Daddy? she asked.

Of course I'm coming, baby. I've told you before. I'm just flying out later.

And you're staying the whole time?

I'm staying for Christmas and then I'm going to New York to see some friends.

I wish you were staying the whole time.

I know you do, sweetheart. But if I don't see these friends they will be sad.

That seemed to hold her reservations for the moment. She nodded.

I flew in on the 24th and Carmen and I slipped out to the Mall of Georgia on Christmas Eve to shop for the kids. The drive and the shopping were the longest we'd been alone together since she moved out. I felt as if I was acting in some poignant, indie relationship movie of the 1970s—a black remake of *Chilly Scenes of Winter*. How odd it is to be so pleasantly formal with the person who used to share your soul. Together we fought the crowds through Barnes & Noble and Toys "R" Us and Old Navy, me paying for everything though we'd agreed to write "From Mommy and Daddy" on most all of the presents and "From Santa" on the rest.

Since Carmen is a raw vegan, eating out in the South is complicated. We settled on what looked the most upscale, a simulated Yukon fur-trapper's lodge with a moose over the bar who got animated and lip-synched to classic Motown on the half hour. I ordered the Eskimo wings, and she, two house salads.

I'd been coming to her mother's house for twelve years. I call her Mom. She makes extra chocolate chip cookies just for me. It's as close to an ancestral home as I've got. Christmas Eve, before going to bed, Ava dictated to me a note for Santa Claus and she laid it on a Styrofoam plate by the fireplace with three cookies and a glass of milk. Carmen and I kissed the kids to bed and then wrapped all the presents in front of the television. She hadn't had a TV since she'd moved out so she was wide-eyed at the new reality shows. Finally, we were done.

Good night, Carmen.

Good night, Trey.

And she disappeared up the stairs to her room. I ate most

of Santa's cookies, carefully sprinkling the remaining crumbs around the plate. I drank almost all of the milk. I moved the fireplace screen over to the side, as if Santa had forgotten to replace it. I wanted to leave sooty boot prints, but Carmen's stepfather had just cleaned out the fireplace.

Up the stairs to my room, I had to pass Carmen's. When we were just dating, her mother had made us sleep in separate rooms, but she would sneak to mine nightly. This Christmas Eve her light was out, and as I passed her doorway, something made me bow just my head into her room, but that was enough. She was asleep and so beautiful that my chest hurt. On her dresser she had arranged a half dozen photographs of half-naked swamis. All of the men in the photos were skinny, old, and Indian except Doug, her boyfriend, with his mop of blond dreads, lotusing under a pine.

After finding my way down the hall in the dark, I turned on the light in the spare room to make sure that another drowsy mud dauber wasp wasn't dying on my mattress. For twelve years I've shared this room with them at Christmas, and thanks to my hypervigilance, they've only stung me once.

For my New Year's resolution, I (yet again) swore off women. I needed to dedicate the coming year to raising my kids and course-correcting my career. Which, by the way, was starting to show signs of life again thanks to, of all people, Carmen. The script that I had adapted from her novel for Spike Lee turned out pretty well. He told my agent that it was the best thing he'd read that year. Whoopi Goldberg and Danny Glover had signed on to star, and it had been selected to premiere at the Sundance Film Festival. My surly agent, never an optimist, was beginning to hint that at least one interesting and moderately lucrative future assignment might be born of its heat.

Also, to celebrate the New Year, Chet would be graduating from the crib to Ava's toddler sleigh bed, so she would graduate into a real bed. Though he was only seventeen months old, he had already staged several almost-successful escape attempts from the crib. He was already so strong that when he and Ava would wrestle, she was the one who usually ended up crying. He would keep cackling as he reached out to knead her face. Ava, on the other hand, had luxuriated in this same crib until she was well past two, content to wait on her back, play with her hands in the air, until her staff (me, her mom, Lucia) arrived to attend to her.

The kids and I shopped for her new bed together. Luckily, Chet did not yet understand that most every major purchase in their room goes to Ava first. Ava and I settled on a high storage bed because she sleeps like a stone wherever I lay her down. I wasn't too concerned about her tumbling the three feet past her built-in drawers to the carpet.

That first night I put them to bed with the usual improvised story and related improvised song, but tonight's theme was that a pair of magical beds cruised their passengers over clouds, past mountains and farmlands, until they reached their grandmother's house, where she stuffed them with cookies. I closed the door, still singing, stuffed a load into the washer, and then sat down to write. The noise of the washer has never really bothered me. It was the dryer and the rhythmic clack of zippers on the metal drum that would steal so much of my concentration that I wouldn't turn it on until I went to bed.

Before going to bed, I habitually checked on them, readjusted blankets whether they really needed it or not—any excuse to smuggle some of their peace before I slept. This first night out of the crib, this first of the thousands of steps little Chet will take between infancy and manhood, I found more than half of his body hanging out of Ava's old, low toddler bed. The next night he was not only out of the bed completely, he was face-down, several feet away from his bed, on the carpet. I worked my fingers under him as carefully as if he were a landmine, but once I got a good hold on him, I encased him in my arms and kissed him till his unconscious complaints threatened to wake him. I delivered him back to his little doll bed and flanked it with pillows and a sheepskin.

Now that Chet was freed from his cage, our morning ritual changed as well. Ava used to play in their room, maybe pull a red plastic Ikea chair up to his crib and dangle her fingers for her little brother to play with until I arrived. Now that Chet was mobile, however, they both started coming into my room.

I usually heard them before I saw them: Ava's fast trampling, racing Chet up the stairs, as he pulled himself up the treads like a Slinky in reverse. Just as my eyes were opening, Ava would dive onto my legs. My platform king was too high for Chet to knee himself up onto the mattress, so he growled. I raced to drag him up with us by his armpits before he started to cry in earnest. I tried to get them to snuggle under my arms the way my cat Pearl used to when I was a kid, but after only a few moments they both would start to squirm and crawl under the sheets.

One day a memory triggered a smile that grew so big it might have floated me away by my cheeks. I remembered play-ing under my parents' sheets. I remembered the magic of the light.

Now with my kids happily wrestling under my sheets,

squealing and giggling, there was only one thing left to do to pay them back for waking me up and its initials were S.B.D.[1]

Eeeeew! Daaaaady!

Ava threw the sheets off of her, operatically pinching her nose with the fingers of both hands, and ended up tangling Chet in the mess of Egyptian cotton. I freed him and, laughing not so much because he understood but because laughter is his default position, he made something of an *eeeew* sound himself.

So much promise of the new came with this new year. Chet was about to start going to preschool with Ava Mondays and Wednesdays, and in the fall Ava would graduate into kindergarten.

Kindergarten. There is nothing more huge.

Where she would end up next year had already busied the majority of my mental faculties for months. See, our old house was just a long throw away from Canyon Charter, the best public elementary school in the city. Our new house in Venice was exactly right behind one of the worst. Families rent studio apartments in the Canyon school catchment just so their kids can qualify for admission. The annual lottery for the few open spaces has parents bringing lawn chairs and fat books to wait in line all day. My parents, educators themselves, were fanatical about education. Before Ava was even born we had found out about RIE, a sometimes cultish but nonetheless beautiful and commonsensical philosophy of child rearing. Unfortunately RIE is an acronym for Resources for Infant Educarers, but behind that mumbo jumbo is a commitment to treating infants like human beings, not like a warm accessory for that cool new Bugaboo

---

[1] S(ilent). B(ut). D(eadly).

stroller. Carmen and I talked to Ava constantly, told her what we were going to do before we did it. We didn't urge her to roll over, crawl, or walk until her body told her she was ready to. The preschool we chose was an extension of that ethos, founded by a heretic Waldorf teacher. No TV, wooden toys, healthy snacks. Yeah, we were that kind of parents. I wanted to continue with progressive education at least through elementary school, hoping to cultivate in my kids a love for learning before the real hard homework kicked in in high school. Canyon Charter was great, but the fancy, hippie private elementary schools seemed like a better fit. The tremendously bad news was that private kindergarten in LA at that time ran around $18,000 (it's now around $25,000). Of course I did not have the money yet but, if you haven't already gleaned this about my personality, when it comes to my own personal prowess, I am hopelessly, relentlessly optimistic. I will always bet it all on myself. So although for a few months I convinced the bachelor that I'd sold my old house to to allow me to keep paying his gas bill so I could pretend that I still lived near Canyon, I eventually gave up the con. Ava was doing magnificently as one of the only black kids in her pre-school and now the only one with divorced parents. I couldn't bring myself to load her with even more emotional baggage by having to lie about where she lived. I vowed to pull in a fantastically lucrative new writing assignment after Sundance and god-damn it my Ava was going to be sharing circle time with Spielberg's kids. Had my seriously boojy parents been alive, they would have insisted.

The day of our visit to the Wildwood School, Chet stayed home with Lucia. Carmen came over so we didn't have to take two cars. Ava was so excited to have the two of us back together and all to herself for an entire morning that her energy, had it been harnessable, could have powered our car.

While the kids were read a story by the director of admissions, we parents giddily milled in the courtyard, as tentative as that day our children were born, drunk on the enormity of this new passage. The intimate little campus seemed magical and nurturing and personal, everything that a public school has a very hard time achieving. Everyone seemed to smile and to know everyone else's name. I was smitten. If she got in, even if I had to knock over liquor stores or sell my body to aging heiresses to pay the bill, I pledged to myself that she would go to that school.

The Sundance Film Festival was not only my ticket to the A list, it was, more importantly, Ava's ticket to an unforgettable education.

I had not been back to Sundance in over a decade, not since I had been invited to the institute as a student after they read my very first paid assignment, a musical called *Staggerlee*. I was tutored by some of the most brilliant screenwriters ever, Tom Rickman, who wrote *Coal Miner's Daughter*, Terry Southern, Oliver Stone. They were teaching us for free, just for the love of the art of screenwriting. The Sundance Film Festival was new and alternative then, and as it grew in importance, I had several friends who would fly up every year to try to massage the noun *network* into a verb.

Me, I try to keep my nouns and my verbs separate. In fact, my first experience there was so transformative that I pledged only to return when I was invited, either as a creative advisor at the institute or with one of my films.

They've never asked me back to the mountain as a creative advisor.

Of course by now I had heard that the film festival had turned into Hollywood's version of spring break, a wintry bacchanal of drunken mating. I don't really drink, don't really talk to strange women in bars, but friends assured me that even with my limited skill set I could get laid in those mountains in Utah.

Besides condoms, I was also bringing my snowboard. The hotel room that Showtime had booked for me was steps from a ski lift in the center of Park City. I figured Carmen could spend a few nights on my couch and watch the kids so I could wallow in the freedom that she enjoyed every other night of the year.

Just as I was drawing up the babysitting schedule for my absence, she surprised me by saying she wanted to go too.

What do you mean you want to go? I asked her.

I mean I wrote the book, so if you get to go, I should get to go.

Maybe she had a point. But I had plans.

It's probably too late, I assured her. The hotel rooms and flights book up a year in advance.

She immediately picked up the phone and soon found herself a room and a flight and Showtime agreed to pay for them.

I scrambled into action, enlisting Lucia to pull triple shifts, but in the gaps Linda would have to pretty please step in. She had been spending a lot of time at her boyfriend's house on the nights when she wasn't babysitting for me. This night, however, she was in her room behind the kitchen. I was about to knock when she opened the door herself in her robe, holding a tube of cream. (It might seem as if she was always in her robe, either going to or coming from taking a shower, but I think that's just the way I like to remember her.)

Oh, hi, handsome.

H-hi, I stammered.

I've got to go put on the cream.

Oh.

Yeah, I had this, like, boil thing on my coochie lip. I made the Fossil pop it. After all, he's the one who probably gave it to me.

I think I then made some sort of sound that I hoped would give her whatever type of answer she was hoping to elicit.

I decided to wait to ask her.

• • •

SUNDANCE WAS ODD. I'd first started adapting Carmen's book when we were married, and when Spike Lee agreed to produce it, we joked that our dream of being the black reincarnation of Dashiell Hammett and Lillian Hellman was finally coming true. Two years later the Ellises were walking down the red carpet together, smiling for photographs and later waving to the sold-out audience during the film's standing ovation. During the Q and A afterward, in the middle of answering a question about the progress of race relations in America, microphone in hand, it occurred to me that sharing the stage with Carmen meant that almost certainly I wasn't going to get laid by any misguided groupie in the audience. Here I was, dressed up, famous for an evening, and cock-blocked by my ex. It wouldn't have gone over too well had I announced to the crowd, Ladies, don't be fooled by our shared last name. I am *definitely* available.

I know I should have seen other people's movies, but the slopes beckoned. The year before, I hadn't snowboarded once.

The year before that, just one day. So during the daytime on the mountain I instead tore down the slopes, deliciously sore in the evenings as my friends and I careered from party to party like sailors on leave. I only ran into Carmen twice on the streets of Park City, and thankfully never while I was in the middle of trying to divine which combination of words might convince some starlet or drunk development exec to sleep with me.

My biggest disappointment was Rosario Dawson. I had somehow managed to talk her up at some Hollywood party months earlier—she had even accepted my phone number—and had heard that she was loose on the mountain. My fevered plan was for her to have seen or at least to have heard about my film, to vaguely recognize me at some after party, and then for us to fall in love, marry, and make more tremendously beautiful and gifted babies. Of course I didn't see her until the last night when, as luck would have it, another moderately well-known black actress was burning me with her eyes, laughing louder than anyone else in the loud room at all of my jokes, and several times steadying herself against my forearm. Each time this actress touched me, she seared me with her heat. That was exactly when Rosario walked past and, I think, maybe, I hope, checked me out.

My first reaction was to sprint after her, but I didn't want to be rude, and this person in front of me was quite lovely in her own right and actually demonstrating an interest in me. I took a deep breath and refocused my attention on the actress at hand.

I'm telling you, this actress gushed at me. You did just a genius job. I mean it. The camera angles in that party scene. You cracked me up.

Um, thanks, I told her. But of course the director was more responsible for that part.

The actress's forehead contracted like a mollusk.

What? she asked.

I wrote it. I didn't direct it.

Yeah! Yeah. I mean. Of course.

Never again did she steady herself on my arm. Soon we excused ourselves and I ransacked the party for Rosario, who had of course disappeared like a thought.

Once again I heard the sitcom sound effect on the soundtrack of my life: *Waaa-WAAAA*. Charlie Brown was Warren Beatty compared to me. Once again the song had stopped, the game of sexual musical chairs was over, and I slogged through the slush to my condo alone.

And yet I did return from Sundance with a good line on a new assignment. My producer introduced me to an executive at HBO who said what they always say in Hollywood: I'm a big fan. However this guy seemed to mean it, said that my surly agent had put me up for an assignment with them, and seemed to hint that I was the front-runner. At least that's what I took away from our fifty-second conversation yelled to each other in a Park City bar while Beck moaned onstage. The next morning, after calling the kids, I called my agent and he confirmed that I was up for a job and it looked pretty good.

Are you a big fan of basketball? he asked.

Of course, I lied.

Back home I was still in the doorway when I had to crouch to catch my running children. After I presented them with their presents, two small stuffed moose, and before I had unpacked, I was already studying the packet that HBO had had messengered to my house. It was a biopic of a high school phenom who had gotten ensnared in drug dealing and ended up in prison instead of the NBA. He was just getting out and trying to make it into the league now, both a felon and no longer young.

Basketball. Prison. Of course I was an obvious choice to write the script. I did two years at Phillips Academy, Andover. How different could that be from Attica?

Look, of course I'm kidding. Of course I immediately saw the inherent dramatic arc in the story, and the guy came from Dayton, Ohio, my dad's, granddad's, and great-granddad's hometown. I would dedicate myself to creating an unforgettable treatment that would elicit a standing ovation from the suits in the room. Still, just once I'd love to be considered for a story that did not involve basketball, hip-hop, and/or crack. A decade previous, in an essay I wrote for a book entitled *Why We Write: Personal Statements and Photographic Portraits of 25 Top Screenwriters,* I had likened the position of the black screenwriter to that of a lion. Everyone on the planet is an amalgamation of adjectives; however, if you are fortunate enough to claim those two—*black* and *male*— in America, they subsume every one of the others. Although you enter the room ectomorphic, right-handed, moderately witty, polyglottal, clean-shaven, pantsed, nephrotic, paternal, and broke, all the suits seem to see are mane, teeth, and claws.

Of course the preconceived notions do not always work against me. Because of my skin color I'm assumed to be much cooler than I actually am, and who wouldn't want to be stereotyped as being in the possession of a magical penis?

My agent told me that in the meeting with the producers and the HBO exec, I just had to be enthusiastic and give them the broad strokes of an outline and the job would be mine. I was determined to do much more than that. I was constantly on the phone with the junior executive, acting as if I had already gotten the job and was preparing to write the *Chinatown* of uplifting sports movies. Instead of a page or two treatment, I wrote up a thirty-page bible detailing minutely the beats of not just the three acts and their act breaks, but every single scene. I poured myself into it, making sure that it was both emotional and inventive. This was HBO, the Patek Philippe of premium cable; they wouldn't accept a conventional, moderately uplifting biopic; they always wanted something more. I was thrilled to be about to begin working again with one of the only outfits in Hollywood that encouraged both unconventionality and excellence.

When I didn't get the job, my agent told me they just didn't think I was enthusiastic enough in the room. He didn't bother to hide the contempt in his voice, like a father who was not-so-secretly pleased that the outside world had finally confirmed what he had always suspected: that his son was a retard. My own father was absolutely the opposite. Although he begged me to learn some sort of marketable skill besides writing, *just in case*, I always felt that he'd be the least surprised person in the world to discover that I'd simultaneously won a Nobel, Pulitzer, and MacArthur. When I graduated from Andover on the honor roll and was on my way to Stanford, his present to me was a gold Bulova with the words *Soar, Carefully* engraved on the reverse. I had always wished that he left off the second part. It wasn't until I fathered the grandchildren that he would never meet that I understood that you cannot help but add the *Carefully* to even the most extravagant wishes for your kids.

Look, my agent continued, if you write me an urban comedy, *that* I can sell. But if not . . .

I didn't hear whatever else he had to say. I looked out my window over the rooftops of Venice Beach. Wow. What a beautiful sky. I mumbled something so I could hang up and then I collapsed to the carpet and whacked my forehead with my palm. Mom dies. Bad. Dad dies. Terrible. Kidneys start giving out. Not so good. Wife leaves. Vast acres of sadness. Did fate really have to throw in downward mobility? I mean, give me back my mom or my dad if you're going to saddle me with all the rest of this shit. Or if I'm going to need a kidney transplant in the next few years, couldn't fate at least be kind enough to keep me in the fucking upper-middle class?

I've kept a diary since I was sixteen. My second novel, *Home Repairs,* was based on my actual journal entries from ages sixteen to thirty. Since then I have only written in it sporadically, usually just when the reality in front of me threatens to collapse under its own weight. By writing it down, I instantly distance my life into art (if you consider a live-action, African-American, NC-17-rated version of *You're a Good Man, Charlie Brown* art). I appreciate the fact that it is better drama if the schmuck at HBO doesn't give me the job. It is better drama to see how our protagonist handles the news. Does he proceed with his plan to put his daughter in private school even though it costs more than he actually earned that calendar year? Does he allow himself, at forty-one, to be forcibly retired from Hollywood? Does he burn down this new house for the insurance money and then sign up for a degree in network systems administration at DeVry?

I had been threatening to write a memoir ever since my dad died, and it is at this point in our story that I actually began to write the words that open the book you are currently reading. When people ask me what I am, what is it that I do, I tell them that I am a writer. I write novels and screenplays and now I blog and I have just written a play. I'd write a greeting card or a menu, I'd write a prescription if you asked me nicely. I just love to write.

I had wanted to write another novel, but my last novel, my favorite, *Right Here, Right Now,* sank like Salvatore "Big Pussy" Bonpensiero's bound and bullet-riddled corpse off the Jersey shore in *The Sopranos.* Nobody would advance me the money to write another one. I'd have to first earn enough in Hollywood to not only feed the kids, but also bankroll enough reserves that I could write a book for a year on spec with the hope that at the end, somebody might possibly consider buying it. I didn't envision that time coming anytime soon, and the thought of never writing another book petrified me. I hadn't had a regular job, you know, the kind where you have to actually put on clothes and show up someplace five days a week, since I was twenty-two. And even then I hadn't kept regular hours. I worked as a field producer for RAI, Radiotelevisione Italiana, prowling Manhattan film premieres with a cameraman and a sound guy, wrestling our way past the other paparazzi to get a clean shot of Sharon Stone. I loved speaking Italian every day, so I tried to put up with my evil, screaming Turkish boss named Gul. I lasted about six months. I was living at home on the Upper West Side, my dad was threatening to charge me rent, but he was a softie, I knew he wouldn't go through with it. I was working on a second draft of *Platitudes,* my first novel, so I needed more flexible hours than *La Rai* allowed. I had interned for *Newsweek* in college and my editor there had moved on to *Rolling Stone* and I got him to hire me as a freelance proofreader there. That was only three nights a week, so the rest of the week I could transcribe the seven hand-written notebooks of the first draft of my novel using my Smith-Corona electric typewriter.

My dad was getting sicker and sicker while I was sending out *Platitudes* and getting back from publishers only sympathetic rejection letters. I finally sold it four months after he died.

Shortly afterward, my first script was accepted at Sundance, and embarrassingly lucrative writing assignments soon followed.

However it was not the money that had kept me so long in Los Angeles. I arrived a very successful, bratty young novelist who loved great movies as much as I loved good books. My life-long dream had been to publish a novel. I did that at twenty-four. My new dream was to direct a film. That looked like it was about to happen three months before my thirtieth birthday. Then it didn't.

I am convinced that my delusion of seeing the story of my life as just that, a grand story, is the only thing that has staved off even more debilitating mental illnesses. At this point in my life, eleven years after turning thirty, with my film career in ruins, I didn't just visualize packing up and leaving Los Angeles; in my mind I heard a soundtrack, turned way up. In Hollywood this is called a trailer moment—a scene that absolutely, positively has to be in the movie's trailer. And there is only one song in the world that can do this image justice. Ladies and gentlemen, please give a warm *Bedtime Stories* welcome to Gladys Knight and the Pips!

So as the music swelled, I'd buy one adult and two kids' tickets at LA's Union Station for that famous midnight train to Georgia.

11

THE PROBLEM WITH LOS ANGELES IS YOU GO TO
SLEEP BY YOUR POOL ONE DAY AND YOU WAKE UP
AND YOU'RE SEVENTY-FIVE YEARS OLD.

—Buddy Hackett

AND YET I DIDN'T GO ANYWHERE. Where was
I gonna go? I was determined to avoid the Hackett curse, but
every perfectly sunny day, every biblically ostentatious sunset,
every deliciously crystalline iced blended mocha recemented my
attachment to the instantaneously gratifying.

Change, however, was thrust upon me. Lucia started telling me that Linda felt taken for granted, that I worked her
harder than I had advertised. I found that odd in that she stayed
in a large room rent-free in exchange for three nights a week
babysitting and watching the kids until noon on the weekends.
With me, however, Linda was, as always, pure flirt. I tried to get

her to talk to me about anything that was bothering her, but she always just smiled and sang, until one day she said she was leaving. I felt as if she'd broken up with me. I felt as if an impossible situation was just becoming possible, but her sudden leaving threw me back into the chaos of those first months alone. I'd be under house arrest until I found someone new.

Lucia and I were just starting to write out an ad on Craigslist when Ornella, our first live-in back at the old house, called and said she was divorcing her husband. I immediately invited her to come back and live with us.

New to Miss Beth's preschool, Chet, since he still couldn't talk, would just wobble after the bigger kids, who either ran from him screaming or gathered around him as if he were their second pet rabbit. For me, until the end of the year, it was heaven. I finally had both kids going to the same place at the same time. Lucia still arrived every morning to make their lunches, but I drove them both to Miss Beth's. I could have made their lunches myself—at the time they only ingested cream cheese and jelly sandwiches and baby cut carrots—however, I wanted Lucia around. Not only would I need her again in the fall when Ava would be at Wildwood and Chet at Miss Beth's, she was also the closest thing they had ever had to a traditional mommy.

One day in the morning at preschool drop-off, while we were walking back to our cars, another father asked me this:

Hey. Do you know who Amber Valletta is?

Obviously, this guy didn't know me very well. I know the names of supermodels the way other guys know RBIs.

My wife told me her kid might be coming here, he whispered.

Is she single? I asked him.

The other dad just laughed. I did not. How could it be that I did not know a supermodel's marital status? I must have been slipping. If she was single, then it was theoretically possible that she could fall in love with me and possible, theoretically, that we could get married and raise our laughing, love-filled blended family together, dividing our time between Los Angeles, Soho, Saint Barths, Paris, and the South of France. She could support us just until I finished my book, but once the reviews came in and the film rights sold to Will Smith and we were often photographed dining with Seal and Heidi Klum, then I'd start taking care of her so she would only have to work when Tom Ford or Karl Lagerfeld called in a favor.

Who knows how long I stood there watching a future that only I could see. I heard the other dad's car mumble and leave.

I started wearing sleeveless T-shirts to drop the kids off at school. January mornings by the beach in Southern California feel as icy as Michigan, but somehow I reasoned that the sight of my biceps would instantly enchant this supermodel.

The last time I was that stupid was when I was sixteen. Miss Rowen, my boarding-school English teacher from the year before, had invited me to dinner at her house in Boston. What other possible reason could she have had for calling me than to relieve me of my virginity? I breathed maybe twice on the long bus ride from Andover into the city. It was raining, and my simple yet elegant plan was to get soaked so that when she opened the door, she would invite me out of my wet clothes and into her vagina.

The rain stopped somewhere between Medford and Somerville and yet I was undeterred. All the master thieves and con men in every film I'd ever seen always had their meticulously rehearsed plans scuttled at the last minute. It was their bold improvisation, not their organizational skills, that proved their brilliance.

I found a puddle of dirty, oily rainwater outside her townhouse and, after checking to make sure that I was unobserved, I threw myself in it.

When she opened the door, she did indeed suggest that I take off my pants. And my response? I looked at her and the fever broke. I realized that I had been actually insane ever since she had called. Uh, no thanks. I'm okay, I said to the parquet floor.

And yet a quarter of a century later, there I was shivering in the morning dew in a goddamn sleeveless T-shirt. I studied the goose bumps on the tattoo on my bicep and once again the fever broke. As I started to pull on a sweatshirt, I finally noticed it.

My tattoo!

Though over time it had gotten harder and harder to see, *Anna* was still inked into my flesh, each letter camouflaged as part of a leaf on the Georgia O'Keeffe poppy above the deer skull. Had I really been too busy over this year and a half to never find the time to get her removed (or at least inked over)? I'm not superstitious, but how could I ever hope to once again fall giddily in love with that woman still under my skin?

The office of Swag, the tattooist, was perhaps one hundred and fifty yards from our new house. I drove home from Miss Beth's and walked over. Twenty minutes later I was done. The moment felt weightier than the one several weeks earlier, when I had finally received our Dissolution of Marriage certificate from the State of California.

A few days later my agent called and said something that I never thought I'd hear him say:

I've got some good news.

I leaned closer to the phone.

You've been short-listed for a PEN award for best teleplay of the year.

Wow. That's great news, right? I said.

It's very prestigious, yes.

Do you . . . think that might be . . . translatable into work? I asked.

Probably not.

Fuck him. I was done crying. I was too busy writing my hilarious yet moving, tender, horrifying, and sometimes sexy memoir. Cash reserves would hold out until the end of the summer. Saint-Tropez was out, obviously. The tail end of the summer would involve packing up, selling the house, and moving into some sort of condo. Embarrassing, yes, especially in the world of Hollywood, where they exclusively assign work to those who are already so wealthy and so busy that they won't have the time to actually do it. If you even hint that you're actually in need of a job, everyone thrills in assuming it's because you've already flushed away your life savings on some combination of crack, boy whores, and the ponies.

We were going to be fine, Ava, Chet, and me. Even if I sold everything and moved us into a van, they were still young enough to see it as an adventure. Around Venice there were at least three school buses converted into rolling communes. I often fantasized about moving us into one and painting it like the Partridge Family's.

When people hear that I'm principally responsible for raising my two kids, they invariably soften their eyes at me as if I
were a cancer survivor. The truth is, they're not heavy, they're my
kids. There are no two people on the planet whose company I
enjoy more. We have our routines. I often run out of liquid baby
soap, so I squirt my own Old Spice High Endurance body wash
into the running water of their bath. Ava's probably the only five-
year-old girl in the world who sometimes smells like James
Coburn. And, slowly, I'm getting much, much better at her hair.

Chet was just beginning to speak. At first I thought I was
just imagining it, but he really was calling me *Mommy-Daddy*.
He started pooping in the toilet just about as soon as I asked
him to, too.

Throughout that spring I met my friends at the movies
twice a week and got out of the house to go to yoga or the gym. I
wasn't unhappy. I was too busy with the kids to be unhappy. In
June the kids would go back to Georgia to spend a few weeks with
their grandma, and for a very short burst I would get to regress to
my life previous. If we weren't going to France, then I knew I had
to go somewhere. I have an old globe, from the forties, I think. I
saw Moscow in front of me, and since I had never been there, I
knew that's where I wanted to go. I called my friend Jack in London and he immediately said he'd like to come with. We both had
mountains of frequent-flyer miles and, like me, he has a gift for
traveling on the cheap. Within a few days he e-mailed me that he'd
found us a youth hostel in Moscow that ran ten bucks a night and
didn't care that our youth was at least a decade behind us.

My flight from LA stopped in Paris and one stopover's
free, so I added a night in Paris on my way back from Russia.

Throughout the year Laurianne, the actress I had chased after last summer, and I had e-mailed. She had sent me a very funny feature-length script of hers and I was giving her notes. As soon as I booked my stopover, I e-mailed to ask her to make herself free for dinner. I didn't ask if she was still seeing the married sexagenarian. I didn't care. My plan was to be the guy who popped in to see her in Paris on his way from Moscow to Los Angeles. For a woman seemingly petrified of healthy, stable relationships, I wanted my arrival and soon-after departure to be an irresistible opportunity for hours of gymnastic and attachment-free sport sex. I imagined boarding my flight the next morning with a sigh and a smile, emotionally fortified enough to begin selling off the rest of my assets and downsizing (again).

Though she'd studied English for years in school, she was not very accomplished. I could not really tell how much she understood when I wrote, and last summer when we spoke it had been exclusively in French. This summer, e-mailing her was slow, tricky work. I write French at about the level of a French third-grader. Most of the subtleties of seduction were hopelessly beyond my limits.

Comprehension was another problem. They are our planet's most famous romantics, the actual inventors of the concept. They kiss strangers on the cheek and use the same verb, *aimer,* to mean both *to like* and *to love. Baiser* used to mean *to kiss.* Now it means *to fuck*; however, *un bisou* is still just a kiss. *Embrasser* used to mean *to embrace,* but now it means *to kiss.* So when she wrote back *J'attend de te voir avec impatience,* did that mean simply that she was impatient to see me or, as it sounded to me in the world's sexiest language, that she burns to have me holding her in my arms? She signed the letter, *Je t'embrasse*. She probably just meant once or maybe twice on each cheek, but what if she was hinting at something more interesting and in the middle? After consulting my Robert English-French dictionary and making, remaking, and unmaking my mind, I finally decided to test her intentions thusly:

```
Salut Laurianne!

Mon aussi j'attend de te voir avec impatience. Ca
fait plus d'un an deja'!

Kisses everywhere,

Trey
```

For years I have been proud of this ballsy e-mail, but on reviewing it now I see that I wrote *mon aussi,* which means *mine too,* when I wanted to say, of course, *moi aussi,* me too. And I accented *déjà* abysmally.

However I have to say that the *kisses everywhere* part, written in English, was masterful. I wanted her to be as linguistically disadvantaged as I was. I knew that her English was good enough to literally understand the two words, but probably not good enough to realize that we don't usually put them together. I wanted her to wonder if I was just using American slang that she did not know or if I was literally saying that I was looking forward to kissing every centimeter of her sweet flesh.

An Italian friend of mine played this game beautifully back in college. His defense was that he had wanted to say *You look good enough to eat.* I never believed him. His English was superb and yet after a very elegant cocktail party he kissed the lovely young hostess's hand, studied her eyes, and said, in a forced accent that would have embarrassed Marcello Mastroianni, *You look-a so good. I would like to eat-a you out.*

All afternoon, dozens of times an hour, while working on the first part of this very memoir, I checked and rechecked my e-mail's in-box. Finally she wrote back, complimenting me on my Web site, impressed by what I had accomplished, asking about Chet and Ava, and starting to tell me about her career plans until she stopped and said she would save all that for our dinner together. And then she signed off with this:

`Je t'embrasse fort, everywhere too.`

`Laurianne`

OHHHHHH! I shouted.

What, Daddy?

Ava was just coming out of the bathroom.

Nothing, baby. I just got some good news.

Her mom was downstairs julienning kale. Chet was waiting for Ava to come back and chase him. I wasn't on with the kids for fifteen minutes, so I quickly responded, encouraging her writing, praising her acting, in general expressing my amazement at how much she'd already accomplished in just twenty-six years. I then added:

`Tu es la femme la plus belle que j'ai jamais vu.`
`Chez moi en dit, "Wow."`[1]

I went on to tell her a little about my life as a single dad, *un père celibitaire*, and that writing *l'histoire de ma vie* was giv-

---

[1]*You're the most beautiful woman I've ever seen. Over here we say, "Wow."*

ing me a lot of pleasure. From there I lost my mind, told her I was counting the days till I saw her, and then slathered it on as thick as spackle, using English with this Frenchwoman as the language of love.

Je compte les jours a te voir. And I cannot wait to look into your eyes again, deep black lakes where I lose myself and forget to breathe.

Thinking of you . . .

Trey

Of course, though I told myself that I would be satisfied with one night with her in Paris, after her *kisses everywhere too,* my dreams now had the four of us living there together or dividing our time between the City of Lights and the City of Angels.

The preschool year was ending, and little Ava was about to graduate. Though when she had arrived at Miss Beth's three years earlier, she had been mute and withdrawn from the other children for the first four months, now she and her two best friends were the preschool's chatty mother hens. They cuddled and scolded the younger ones, they were the first to help set the tables for snacks or put away their cots after naps. One afternoon when I arrived to pick them up, I found Ava helping a younger friend write her letters.

Daddy!

Hey, baby. Where's your little brother?

She answered with her shoulders. I wandered out back to the play structure that the other fathers and I had built the summer before. Chet was trying to wrestle a kickball out of the arms of a perfect-looking little boy. Just as I started to speak—

Hey! Boys! Share, said a mom.

I turned and found myself looking into Amber Valletta's eyes.

Daddy!

Chet dropped the ball and dove at my legs.

Hi! I guess you're Chet's daddy. We love him.

And I love you.

While we small-talked and my heart returned to my control, I eventually managed to focus attention on her ring finger. Which was occupied. That complicated my plan greatly. Now I would have to save up to put a hit on her husband, then console her in her grief.

A few days after Ava's preschool graduation—I haven't seen so many cameras and video cameras since the Emmys—the kids and their mom flew down to Georgia. I was without commitment of any kind for three weeks and did not leave for Russia for a few days. The first few days of my freedom were overwhelming. I felt like Tom Cruise in *Risky Business,* skating around the house in my socks. I stayed up late just because I finally wasn't going to be awakened at seven by kiddie breath. By day three, however, I realized that I was permanently addicted to the demands of my children. Even today, three years later, when they are with me, which is almost always, I sometimes feel like RoboDaddy, parroting almost hourly instructions to pick up, brush, wash, or put something away. Around May I start counting the days until my short few weeks of summer daddy break. Yet only a few days after they've gone, I leave Chet's

Heelys or Ava's Hilary Duff Barbie in the center of the living room floor. When I come home to the odd stillness of my empty house after treating myself to a late show, seeing a symbol of them makes me smile.

I finished my last online Russian lesson the day before I flew. I didn't learn much, but I figured if I made the effort to say *dobry utro* (good morning), *spaseeba* and *pazhalsta* (thank you and you're welcome), maybe throw in a *kak vas zavut?* (What is your name?), they would treat us a little less gruffly. Jack and I also learned Cyrillic online. We were both determined to navigate the ornate, palatial subways, and the station stops, it seemed, were not translated into Roman letters for tourists.

Jack flew in from London, meeting me in Paris at Charles de Gaulle airport for our flight together to Moscow. During the layover I tried calling Laurianne, but had to just leave a stammering message. I instantly imagined that she was in the arms of her old guy and that he, sensing her excitement about our rendezvous, had spirited her off for a romantic weekend far from the city. I would join the *Guinness Book of World Records* as the man who had flown the farthest for a date only to be stood up.

With the time difference it was tricky, but I managed to call the kids back in Georgia every day.

I should have enjoyed Russia more, the Arbat, Lenin's decaying remains, the overnight train to Saint Petersburg and its endless summer nights. I saw it all but I did not feel it. My heart missed the connecting flight and never left Charles de Gaulle airport. Clichés be damned. Paris does peculiar things to my heart.

PARIS DOES PECULIAR THINGS TO MY HEART

By Trey Ellis

For the person who falls in love too easily, who falls in love too fast, Paris is the world's most dangerous city. Even before I'd ever been there I wanted to be the sort of American who often lived there. I caught the fever on a Greyhound bus in 1979, when I was seventeen years old and in the middle of my first grand adventure. For two weeks, alone I rode a bus from the Port Authority Bus Terminal in Manhattan (where my dad and I had moved a year after my mom died) to Los Angeles, then up to San Francisco and then back to New York. My best friend Ben was supposed to come with me, the adventure's cover was the necessity of our seeing Stanford before we applied. When at the last minute he canceled (as usual) I pleaded with my father to trust me enough to travel alone.

I made several, forever altering decisions on that trip. When I saw Palos Verde high school dominating a cliff above perfect, noisy waves and the long row of surfboards leaning against the school, saluting the sky like a squadron of P-51 Mustangs at the ready, I knew that I would come to California and I would learn to surf, no matter what university accepted me.

On my way back from Stanford I soon came to two more resolutions. I would one day become a professional writer and I would one day live in Paris. This because I met an elderly black male writer with his hands in his pants.

I was boarding the bus in San Francisco around eleven at night. One of the few empty seats was next to a black man with an irregular gray beard. As I started to sit I noticed that one of his hands had disappeared inside his pants and was working. Quickly I sought a different seat.

Around four the next morning we pulled into a truck stop in Elko, Nevada, and at the Burger King there he and his Croissan'wich fell into the hard plastic seat across from me as he introduced himself as Ted Joans, V.I.P. V(ery). I(mpecunious). P(oet). He was just in San Francisco, see, seeing his old friend Lawrence Ferlinghetti and he asked me if I was hip to him?

No.

Oh! That's bad man. That is really, really awful. He's the poet laureate, man. The poet laureate of San Francisco. Of course you've heard of Jack Kerouac?

Of course.

A friend from Andover, just two months earlier, had rolled his eyes when I told him I had never heard of Kerouac.

You're gonna love him, man. Trust me.

As you can imagine, *On the Road,* for me, especially at sixteen, was heroin. I instantly added Sal Paradise and Dean Moriarty to the bouillabaisse of manhood that I fed on. The other ingredients were Sean Connery, Cary Grant, Luke Skywalker, Hemingway, the Panthers, my grandpa, and my dad.

Here. Read this.

Ted shoved an open book of poetry over my own Croissan'wich. I quickly read a Ferlinghetti poem that described a police car *sireening*.

Whoa. I'd never before seen a noun verbed like that.

On the spot I committed myself to lifelong literary experimentation.

Ted explained that he lived between Paris and Timbuktu and was on his way to speak at Yale. I was just starting to become less afraid of him.

Did you notice my hand in my pants when you came on?

He was curved over and cackling childishly.

You gotta do that, man, on these buses if you wanna sleep. You need the two seats to yourself so you can *lean*.

I don't know if I can stick my hands down my pants in public, I told him.

Then pick your nose, howl like a hyena! Don't sleep straight up, whatever you do, it'll paralyze you!

For three days and nights, as our Americruiser II feasted on Interstate 80, changing drivers in Cheyenne, Wyoming, and Youngstown, Ohio, Ted told of his adventures with Kerouac and Ginsberg, Burroughs and Baraka (back when he was LeRoi Jones), Bird and Rauschenberg, Giacometti and André Breton.

I thought of Ted six years later, when I was hitchhiking through Africa, although I never made it as far as Timbuktu, Mali. I was next door, however, in Burkina Faso and in Niger. In northern Niger I found a truck to take me across the Sahara into Tamarasset, in southern Algeria, then after a week of waiting and threatened imprisonment the Algerians let me fly up to Algiers. I hitchhiked along the coast into Tunisia and caught a ferry back to Italy, where I was living at the time.

My father was living in Paris for a month, angling to get hired as a State Department psychiatrist, so Stefan, a German friend going to med school in Florence, and I drove up to Paris to visit him.

My dad was so proud of how much I traveled. When I had first mentioned my dream of a big Africa trip, he sent me the pair of calf-high Timberlands that I wore every day of those four months. When he came to visit me back when I was an undergrad studying in Florence, he stepped off of the train in a bright red Stanford hoodie and shouted, *My baby!*

I was proud of him too. I thought it was so cool that he would make such a big career change as a forty-nine-year-old man. I hoped that I would be that flexible when I grew ancient.

He had found a sublet off of Place d'Italie on Boulevard de Port-Royal. Before the door had fully opened I already knew that something terrifying was about to be revealed to me. It wasn't just that he looked older than I had remembered him. Middle-aged dads always do. It was something missing from the green of his eyes. He offered us Cokes, we chatted vacantly for only a few minutes, and then he asked if Stefan would leave us for a little while.

Stefan left, confused. I stayed, confused, my mind indexing through every possible catastrophic possibility in its haste to anticipate this latest, fast-coming tragedy.

Trey, I'm not here to work for the State Department. I wanted to but then I got sick.

Okay. He's sick. He'll get better. I'll help him get better.

Have you heard of ARC, AIDS-related complex?

Did he just say he's got AIDS?

It's not AIDS. They just don't want it to ever turn into AIDS so I came here to try this new drug called AZT.

Rock Hudson came here, right? He took the same stuff and he died.

Not everyone dies, he told me.

He told me that he had been with some men but that he thought he had always been careful.

I told him I had to go for a walk.

I opened the door and Stefan was sitting on the stairs. I walked right past him and into the street.

This is impossible. My mom killed herself when I was still a teenager. That's more than enough tragedy for anybody's first twenty-one years. After she died I loved my dad so hard because I was sure that I'd have him for decades. Lightning never strikes twice. It's against the rules of the universe. But remember, it's not AIDS, just some sort of pre-AIDS. The best scientists in the world are working on only this problem. They'll find some pill. I'll help them find some pill. We'll get through this and say, Phew! That was a close one. And yeah, he's slept with men. Who cares? You've let yourself know only what you wanted to know. How many years ago was it that you were playing spy, ransacking his room, when you discov-

ered under his mattress that International Male *catalog? Duh!*

When I returned I was almost smiling. My almost statistically impossible bad luck would be cosmically counterbalanced by the almost miraculous good luck of having a father who would be the very first person in the world to recover from AIDS.

He stayed in Paris for another week, then had to get back to work in the States. I remained behind to close up the apartment. I often found myself wandering the Seine, usually in the Fifth Arrondissement by Shakespeare & Co., one of the most famous bookstores in the world. Sylvia Beach, the store's original owner, was the first to publish Joyce's *Ulysses* and she was a vigorous supporter of Hemingway, Fitzgerald, Henry Miller, and Gertrude Stein. Later, in the fifties, the new owner, George Whitman, took in the Beats, allowing them to stay upstairs until they settled someplace else more permanently, usually in a disintegrating, starless hotel nearby on a spit of street called Git-le-Coeur.

One day very early I was walking the riverbank thinking about how to line up more doctors that could tell me how to help my dad, when I noticed Ted Joans in front of Shakespeare & Co. He was struggling with a large kiosk carousel that held vintage paperbacks. I hurried to help him and reintroduced myself. I told him that since we had last spoken, six years earlier when I was sixteen, I had decided to become a novelist and had indeed just finished a very rough first draft. He literally tipped his hat and then, Tom Sawyer–like, convinced me to do all the work of opening up the legendary bookstore. For almost an hour I rolled out the other kiosks and laid out all the outside books and swept.

Now you can tell everyone that you too worked at the famous Shakespeare & Co.! he shouted. He was always shouting. Are you hungry?

He pointed at the sky and indeed from Shakespeare & Co.'s second floor George Whitman himself was carefully lowering on a long clothesline a speckled iron coffeepot and a pile of croissants on a tray. I had to breathe deeply so I wouldn't cry.

When my life isn't awful, it's actually pretty wonderful.

Paris was also where I was most drippingly in love with Sally, my very brief but intensely felt girlfriend before Anna. Unfortunately, at the time that I was loving her so deeply in Paris, Sally was back in Manhattan re-fucking her old boyfriend. Sally, you may recall, was the brunette model/PhD candidate whom I seduced by reciting Andrew Marvell. We had spent a few transformative nights together, but then I was scheduled to leave for Paris and Florence. I remember staring at the palm of my hand outside of the Louvre and feeling it vibrate exactly as if Sally were still holding it. I ripped a piece of paper from my notebook and wrote her a love letter, right there, standing up, my chest as full as a sail.

Before the kids came Anna and I had lived in Paris for months at a time, twice. The first time we were breathlessly inseparable. The second time was more complicated, however our love still felt vast and historic.

So in Paris my dad broke my heart and in Paris I had already been very much in love.

And now back to Bedtime Stories, *already in progress . . .*

12

CHET'S GODPARENTS, HOWARD AND CAROLINE, have an apartment in Montparnasse that they generously lend out to friends. After I landed from Saint Petersburg and taxied to Montparnasse, I punched their door code, stuffed my bag into the phone booth of an elevator, and walked up to the sixth floor myself. I called the kids and caught them just before they left for school. I showered and scrubbed and cursed my stingy selection of sartorial choices for tonight's date with Laurianne.

The restaurant I had chosen had moved down the street since I'd last been there, so for an interminable moment I was convinced that we would never find each other. Yet I arrived and she was already seated and I was relieved when I first saw her. She wasn't overpoweringly beautiful. She wasn't exactly the dreamy, young, long-curly-black-haired French actress I had obsessed over in my dreams. Phew. For once my heart was acting sensibly.

Then she tilted her head, or I tilted my head, or she said
something, or it was the night wind wheeling in from the opened
door, but somehow everything suddenly changed, my body cav-
ity suddenly became all heart, and I had to open my mouth to
breathe.

Never, it seemed, had I been so near so much beauty. It is
what I call straight-pin beauty. Anna had it too. It's a woman
who strikes you as so beautiful that you are powerless to deny
her anything. You're James Bond and you know that she has
been sent by Blofeld. You know that while you are making love
she is going to pull out a straight pin and sever your spinal cord,
pithing you like a frog, leaving you a vacant, smiling, yet still
erect corpse.

And still it would have been worth it.

The red wine let me speak French beautifully but also
boldly. Umberto Eco has said that he likes to write his semiotic
texts in English because he doesn't know how to lie as well in
English as in his native Italian. I understand him thoroughly. In
English my cowardice often camouflages my emotions. In other
languages I can only say what I really feel. So only halfway through
my first glass of Bordeaux, where she was from, I asked her if I had
a chance with her, even with the old, married guy around. And she
said yes. We both laughed and my eyes dropped and that's when I
first noticed her breasts. I had been so hypnotized by the beauty of
her face back in that film school in Brittany that I had never once
noticed the rest of her. And yet in front of me now her blouse was
more undone than done. How could I never have noticed them?

I held myself to my seat so that I would not fall over.

When she complained that her lips were dry, I pulled out
my ChapStick and reached across the table to apply it for her,

then changed my mind, pulled back, and applied it to my own lips. For a moment she was confused until I told her I'd rather apply it this way. She just laughed, plucked the stick from me, and rolled it slowly over her top and bottom lips. Then she leaned across the table and kissed me.

We talked and kissed, didn't really eat. As soon as we were out of the restaurant I pinned her against the wall and kissed her some more. I invited her over to see the view from my terrace and every half block or so we stopped and kissed and kissed (FYI, in France, French kissing is not called, as you might expect, *embrasser á la Francaise* but *rouler une pel*). We kissed in the elevator and kissed as we entered the apartment. Once inside she said I was beautiful and offered to give me a massage. She was stealing my lines. She was ruining my meticulously fantasized plans. But I did as I was told, took off all my clothes except my underwear, and laid on my belly. Just as I was preparing myself to be teased and disappointed, or at least to have to cajole for hours before satisfaction, I felt her fingers invading my Calvin Kleins. Soon I was in her mouth and in a dream. I saved myself, barely, because I needed to make love with her. Her *no* surprised me. Over dinner she had told me that she was coming to the States, to Los Angeles, for the first time in her life, in just three weeks. She was visiting with a girlfriend. She explained that she hated condoms but if we both got ourselves tested we could make love in Los Angeles. Then she placed me again in her mouth until I came with an embarrassingly vocal supplication to an Almighty that I no longer believe in. I insisted on reciprocating, but she wouldn't let me because she said she was unwashed. I set the alarm for seven for my ten-thirty flight, but we both woke up at five-thirty and

started making out again. Then she saddled me without a condom and almost instantly came. I had to summon every one of
my Tantric superpowers not to come with her. Sure we'd make
beautiful babies, but this would be a little fast, even for me.

She drove me to the airport, both of us still swimming.
At Charles de Gaulle we were that couple you see hanging on
each other dramatically, unmindful that they occupy a public
space. Until I passed US Customs, I didn't even have any kids. I
was free and young and just a breeze away from falling in love.

Back home her kisses kept me high as I opened the old
mail and made a list of all the calls to return. I did not let myself
dwell on the precarious state of my future, the dilapidation of
my finances. I forced myself to think just about her coming to
visit in a few weeks and not the impossibility of continuing the
relationship, especially if the kids and I were living out of a
homeless shelter or a nonoperational school bus.

One of the calls, however, surprised me. It was from my
friend Danny Halsted, a producer.

Call me. I may have some work for you, was all he said.

I had been hunting for excuses not to call the realtor, so
I immediately dialed Danny instead. By the time I got off the
phone I had an offer for a job. An independent financier was
looking for a screenwriter to adapt a story about a hard-driving
yuppie who becomes paraplegic, goes through rehab, and in an
odd way becomes the man he had never been. I thought about
my kidneys and how I could pour that journey into this script. I
thought about how I would do such a brilliant job that I would
be the only obvious choice to direct.

I hung up and stared at the phone. That call gave me six
to eight more months of career and would keep my health

insurance going for another year. That call was the air bubble DiCaprio finds at the corner of the ceiling in a rapidly flooding stateroom in *Titanic*.

First a new girlfriend and now this. Was I actually experiencing some good luck? Would this be the uplifting, heartwarming ending to my book?

I signed up for an international calling plan and Lauri and I spoke three times a week. She had been planning on staying with her friend and her friend's American boyfriend, but we both decided that it would be unbearable to be so close and yet apart. I know Carmen and I had both promised to wait six months before introducing the kids to our lovers, but hadn't I received a pass when Penny flew in from London? Shouldn't that dispensation apply to all women I meet from the EU?

All right, Penny was a mistake. I was too new to dating while parenting to know any better. Laurianne, however, would be someone unforgettable and irreplaceable in my life, someone I was hungry to share with the kids. That, I understood halfway through our dinner. One evening I called Carmen about something else. I was not quite ready to bring up my (again) breaking our six-month rule.

So, when's your girlfriend coming?

Lucia has a big mouth, I replied.

I hear she's beautiful.

She is. And I'd like her to stay here in the house. I can't afford a hotel.

That's not what we agreed.

I know but . . .

If you really think she's special.

I do.

That is so cute! she said. This is our next step!

Look, I didn't want her to be jealous and I certainly did not have any fantasy of ever getting back together with Carmen, but did she have to be so enthusiastic about my sleeping with someone else?

The more difficult conversation would be with the kids. The morning that Laurianne was arriving they, as usual, thundered up the stairs to my room and overran my bed without asking. As always they bickered over who got to snuggle under which armpit. I told them that I so loved having them in my bed every morning, but I had a friend coming and I wanted to give her privacy.

Ava and Chet immediately sat up like prairie dogs.

Noooo! Ava sireened.

Just while she's here, I promised. I explained that the door would be closed and they would just knock and I'd come out and make their breakfast. They still complained but more weakly now, and then I told them that my guest was probably bringing them presents and they went immediately silent, their eyes wide.

At LAX I was the sweating guy you see holding a rose. Everyone smiled as if I were a puppy. Lauri and I fell upon each other at the mouth of the Jetway, tried to pry each other open with our tongues and our fingers.

Carrying her bags inside the house, I felt the grand weight of this beginning. We made love sweetly and showered before I heard Carmen entering the house with the noisy kids.

Est-ce tu es prête à encontrer les gosses? I asked her if she was ready to meet the kids.

Yes!

She liked to say *Yes*, even in the middle of speaking French.

We descended the big stairs as if onstage. Carmen and

the kids followed us with their eyes. Carmen smiled suspiciously widely and held out her hand, but Laurianne moved even closer and kissed Carmen's cheeks.

Ava and Chet were not hiding for once. They both stood like small soldiers beside their mother.

Hello, Ava. Hello, Chet. I am so happy to meet you! I bring you gifts from me and from my little sister, Eglantine, who is the same age as you, Ava.

She pronounced Ava *Ah-va*, and Chet, *Jet*. I had never heard her speak so much English before. The sexiness of it made me so drunk I had to sit on the stairs to steady myself. Carmen backed out of the house waving and giggling, so there we were, just the four of us.

Who would like to show me their room?

The kids raced each other up the stairs, Chet diving to hold his sister by the ankle when she got too far ahead.

Careful! Not on the stairs! I shouted as Laurianne followed them up. I started after them, but she slowed me with her hand and stopped me with a kiss.

So instead I puttered, I straightened up, I wrote in my journal about how fucking insanely happy I was. Then I checked on them.

The three of them were lying on the carpet animating dolls. Only Lauri looked up when I walked in. Ava gave me a black, shirtless Ken doll to puppet. I made him talk in a deep, daddy voice.

Who is hungry? I am as hungry as a wolf!

Downstairs I had defrosted some hamburger. Hamburgers were Ava's favorite and Laurianne, a penniless actress, liked to call herself *La Reine de l'Economie*, the Queen of Cheap. She

told me that she lived on hamburger, *steak haché*. As soon as I
had turned on the flame, she elbowed me away from the stove.

C'est moi la femme. I am the 'ooman. Ava, can you dress
the table?

Dress the table!

She means set the table, sweetie.

Ava bloomed. She ran to the silverware, ran to the
plates, meticulously folded the napkins, and readjusted the
glasses just so.

The inside of my hamburger was as raw and as bloody as
a war wound, but I ate it all, without a bun and with a knife and
fork, like Lauri. The kids put so much ketchup on theirs that they
did not notice or care that their burgers were *très sanglants*.

Can we have dessert, daddy?

You have to take a bath and go to bed, baby.

Bah! interrupted Lauri. There is always dessert! Tomorrow I will make a chocolate cake. What can we have tonight?

Yeah! The kids shouted and threw themselves into an
improvisational dance.

I grumbled, playing the role of the cantankerous dad, but
inside my heart was tumbling through a complicated series of
energetic floor exercises. I spooned out cookie dough ice cream,
and when we were finished, I clapped my hands together twice,
like a pasha.

That's it. Bath time.

The kids sprinted for the stairs and up. I followed and
Lauri followed me, already rolling up her sleeves.

It had not occurred to me that she would like to help.

The kids were naked, splashing, happy. I scrubbed Ava,
Lauri scrubbed Chet. Chet told Lauri that he liked his penis.

Comme tous les hommes,[1] she said.

What she say, Daddy?

Nothing, sweet boy.

Ava taught Lauri the first song that I ever taught her and soon they were duetting in a French accent and in the accent of a little girl:

Fly me to the moon
And let me play among the stars.
Let me see what spring is like
On Jupiter and Mars.
In other words, hold my hand.
In other words, darling kiss me.

I kept the kids in the water way past wrinkling. I never wanted to leave that bathroom. Was this as perfect as the rest of my life was going to be? I was so used to being self-sufficient, an impervious fireman/lifeguard/teacher/paramedic/pediatrician of a single father. I had forgotten how heavy my life had become until I found someone so eager to take half the load.

Then, after story time and after Lauri and I kissed them good night, we sprinted into the bedroom to make love again.

She was here for three weeks and I tried my best to corral my heart. She lived in France. She lived in France. She lived in France. That's an impossible distance. Isn't it? Just live for the moment, be the Buddhist you say you are, and be vitally present for the three weeks that you have together. Don't go too fast and wreck it. You'll scare her off. Be light and fun, for once.

We were invited to a pool party at a friend's. Southern

---

[1] *Like all men.*

California at its finest. Lots of kids, lots of adults, lots of food
and drink. For the past week Chet had been attached to Lauri
like a monkey. I don't think he'd walked more than a few yards.
At the party he was nestled in her arms while she made medieval
figurines fight for him. My friends' wives kept whispering to me
how great she was, how fantastically my kids were evolving. I
was something of a project for them, and I knew they were grad-
ing me on a curve, but still their praise watered me.

I heard Chet giggle so I turned and saw Laurianne bend
her head like a doe drinking from a stream and kiss the summit
of his left cheek and just like that my heart cracked all the way
open like an egg. Her eyes rose to mine and I mouthed, *Je t'aime*.

Oh, God. I didn't want to say it so soon. I had promised
myself that I absolutely, positively would not fuck it up this time.
Then again, much of me had burned to tell somebody *Je t'aime*
ever since I saw Truffaut's *L'Homme qui aimait les femmes*[2] in
middle school.

She blushed and mouthed back, *Je t'aime aussi*.

That was on our first Sunday. By the next Friday we were
making plans. She had to leave in two weeks. I would come visit
for ten days in October and then she would come back with me
and stay at least through the winter.

During the day while the kids were at school, we both wrote.
I had set up a little desk upstairs, across the way from mine. About
once a day, usually in the late afternoon, I would be so consumed
by my writing that her hands would surprise me on my shoulders.
Then she'd spin around my Aeron chair and drop to her knees.

Oh, God, I'd say.

---

[2]*The Man Who Loved Women*

No. C'est moi. She would correct me.

I was thrilled and petrified. Of course this was going psychotically fast. Of course my friends threatened to conduct an intervention. Normal adults on the material plane don't fall helplessly in love at first sight, *coup de foudre*. But I can't remember the last time I was normal. Since all that abnormally awful shit had already befallen me and I had no choice but to accept it all, why not just relax and accept that a young, tall, gorgeous French actress loves me as much as I love her, delights in my children, delights in feeding me, and her hobby happens to be placing me in her mouth?

That night, holding her in our bed after making love, my heart was so full that it hurt. I told her that I had been so in love with Anna that I could not even dream of replacing that feeling in my heart. I was convinced that I would have only shallow, breezy relationships for the rest of my life, but that that would be acceptable because I'd already consumed more than my lifetime allotment of love.

I told her I had been stupid and so wrong. I told her that what was growing between us was already greater, stronger, deeper than anything I'd ever felt before.

She said that she'd been with the married guy since she was twenty, but had been trying to leave him since the beginning. She'd had other flings before, but no one had ever been able to knock him out of her heart. Now, however, she was ready and grateful to me for saving her. She said I was both the sweetest man she'd ever known and that I *baise comme un dieu*.[3] She said that she could not understand how Carmen could have

---

[3](False) modesty will not allow me to translate.

left a man as wonderful as me, but that Carmen's mistake made her the world's luckiest woman. The next day, walking the Venice Beach boardwalk, I showed her the tattoo parlor where Swag had given me my deer skull and poppy. She said she'd always wanted one and started inside to ask for a rose with my name on the leaves. I talked her down. We were about to leave for Sonoma for a week and the tattoo would still be healing, so she wouldn't be able to get it wet in our motel's pool.

All I will say about Sonoma is that it was perfect. The romantic week against which I judge all others.

She cried all the way back to the airport, cried to me on the phone during her layover at JFK. I was not at all sad. I was fired up. I love nothing more than a challenge. I get off on pulling off what others say is impossible. I guess that somehow I think it irrefutably proves my specialness. So the idea of having a girlfriend who was a twelve-hour flight away only made me want to make the relationship work that much more. I was the magician of love and would prove the impossible to the cynical, heart-armored masses.

We talked on the phone at least twice a day and by Webcam at least once a day. With the time difference, the Webcam was tricky. When I was waking up, it was her late afternoon, and when I went to bed, she was just waking up. We needed to see each other naked, however, so in my afternoon, her night, when I was reasonably sure that Ornella the live-in babysitter was out and Carmen wasn't going to be stopping by to leave a basketball-sized bag of sprouts in the refrigerator or wash a trash-bagful of dust-caked hippiewear from her trip to Burning Man, I would draw the shade, drop my pants, and ignite the camera. I kept my jeans around my ankles, however, and my ear attuned for the earliest warnings of any key in any lock.

13

I TOOK A PICTURE OF AVA standing tall in her favorite ladybug dress before driving her to her first day of kindergarten. I was prepared to break down weeping at any moment, to burst into "Sunrise, Sunset" before we'd even arrived at the parking lot, however, I restrained myself and just smiled at everything, hugged her tight, and took one last look through the window as she and the other kids settled in for circle time. Throughout the various orientation picnics and welcoming breakfasts, the mothers would ask, in ways sly and in ways not, where Ava's mother was. Sometimes Carmen arrived separately, but always late, but other events she said she just could not make.

I realized then this truism: There is no one more popular in elementary school than a single dad. The moms are lovely, silly, and girlish around me. If I hadn't told everyone I met about

Laurianne seconds into meeting me, I'm sure they would have plied me with dates with their single friends.

I realized another truism: The more you pay for private primary education, the more work you have to do. Almost immediately Wildwood became another job. I loved the place, loved how they treated my daughter, but I was there painting or marking or cleaning or baking so much they should have given me my own parking spot. The system is built around the schedules of wealthy, educated mothers who crave some sort of work now that they are not full-time child carers. Carmen couldn't be bothered and I knew Ava already felt different enough as one of the only divorced kids in the class. I refused to have her also be the only child whose parent didn't pull his weight.

Progressive schools should come with their own glossaries. Show and tell, for some reason, had been renamed show/share. Four times a week there was D.E.A.R. time— D(rop). E(verything). A(nd). R(ead).—where the parents stayed an extra fifteen minutes after drop-off to read to their kids. Every Friday was All School Meeting, where we all sang this good morning song:

> *Good morning, good morning, good morning to you!*
> *Good morning, good morning, good morning to you!*
> *Our day is beginning, there's so much to do.*
> *Good morning, good morning, good morning to you,*
> *and you, and you . . .*

Whereupon, if the spirit moved us, we pointed and smiled at a few of those around us. And then, to the tune of "Frère Jacques":

Buenos días, Buenos días. ¿Cómo estás? ¿Cómo estás?
Muy bien gracias, muy bien gracias. ¿Y usted? ¿Y usted?

Sure it is a little cultish, but it is a cult of sweetness, so I soon signed up. Ava's teacher taught her concepts and aphorisms that she later brought home and taught me. *If you can't make a mistake, you can't make anything* is one of my favorites. And to stop a kid from carrying on about how much they hated something that somebody else adored: *Don't yuck my yum.*

· · ·

I GREW TO ACTUALLY LOVE the endless school activities. They were a break from writing the script and this memoir and they kept me from just staring at the phone waiting for the right time to call Laurianne again. I even flirted with the idea of becoming the school's first-ever heterosexual male room parent.

Around that same time Chet told his first joke. Like all great comedians, he stole it. For weeks his sister had been performing this chestnut:

Knock knock.
Who's there?
Banana.
Banana who?
(repeat until obnoxious)
Knock, knock.
Who's there?
Orange.

Orange who?
Orange you glad I didn't say banana?

Daddy I have a joke.
Go ahead, Chetty.
Knock, knock. Orange banana!
Nice, Chetty. You're my funny boy.
No. I'm Mommy's. I came out of Mommy, so I'm more hers.

He was grinning, playing, he didn't mean to hurt me.

I made you too, I tried to explain, without getting too technical. I put you in her belly. And when you came out I cut the cord that attached you to Mommy, so that belly button of yours is all my doing.

He jerked up his shirt and thrust out his belly to better study his navel.

• • •

THROUGHOUT SEPTEMBER I rarely left the house. I wrote and talked with Lauri and banked babysitting credit with Ornella. I took two of Carmen's Sundays with the kids so she would watch them on my two Saturdays while I was in France. Lauri had every day of our two weeks together scheduled. For my birthday she was throwing a party in her apartment so all of her Parisian actor friends could meet me and then we would train to the Alsace to meet her mother, her mother's second husband, her brother, and her half brothers and sisters, then back to the outskirts of Paris to meet her father and his third wife and, nearby, her father's second wife and her half brothers and sisters on that side. I was to be the first man she ever introduced to her family in her twenty-six years.

A few days before I was to leave I had finished the first section of this very book and was so proud that I hurriedly e-mailed it to her. When I saw her face on the Webcam, I could make out the tears still shining her cheeks.

I hadn't warned her about the part about me and the hookers in Brazil.

I know it's ugly, I told her quickly and in English. But I want the reader to see how much I have been through so that when I finally find you, and you save me, they will understand what you were saving me from.

She said her man—*mon homme*—would never do something so low.

I tried again and again, kept explaining, kept begging until she snorted a laugh and I knew she was back.

So, were they better than me?

Absolutely not.

Not even two at a time?

Tu rigoles? I told her. *Tu baises comme trois.*[4]

• • •

W H A T   S U R P R I S E D   M E   M O S T about her apartment was its size. My dorm room was bigger. I could stretch out my arms and touch both her bed and her desk. It was getting cold

---

[4]I swear, it doesn't sound so dirty in French.

outside in Paris that fall, but inside her little nest I felt as safe as inside a heart.

I had shown Carmen and Lucia and Ornella how to use the Webcam before I left so the kids could still wake up to my face every morning. No matter where I was in Paris at 3:30, by four (7 a.m. in LA) I was always in front of Lauri's computer.

Laurianne's family was lovely and never once did any of them hint that the difference in our colors was any issue at all. While visiting her mother in the Alsace, Lauri and I hiked in the woods through the gray of the fall and collected chestnuts and mushrooms that her mother cooked for us in various dishes. At the edge of a farm we came across a massive old pear tree, and I pulled from a branch and bit into the pear against which every other pear I eat is still judged.

Back in the outskirts of Paris, however, her father did tease me about my age. I wanted to say that compared to her last boyfriend, both my age and my marital status are huge improvements, but thought it better to keep quiet.

The night before we left together for America, we packed up much of what she owned in life. She was staying for four months and then we'd see how her writing career was going in France and mine in America. We both knew that it was mainly up to me, that for our experiment to work I would have to find enough steady work to support her transplantation.

That last night I felt like the high schooler I never was, coaxing, teasing her to make love on the sofa bed in the middle of her father's living room. Around four in the morning something woke me up and I turned and saw Lauri grabbing her neck and wheezing.

What's wrong!

She waved me away.

Do you want a doctor?

She shook her whole body no.

Do you . . . not want to come?

She struggled to find a pen and ripped through a magazine until she found a clear patch of white.

I am ill, she wrote in English. *But I will come.*

The attack passed and she clung to me and finally she slept. I had changed so much all my life and had had major changes thrust upon me so often that I had forgotten how hard it is for most people to commit to it.

We arrived without further incident, and back on Venice Beach we were again the giddy little family. One day that first week, Lauri and I took the kids to Malibu to explore a breakwater. She brought her camera and took roll after roll of us all. Then she took it upon herself to find a lab and get sepia prints made and bought frames. Chet was still pretty much attached to her neck and I'm convinced that he will always have a soft spot for beautiful French brunettes. She enrolled in English classes and rode my beach cruiser to her school every morning. To help her acclimatize better to her new home, we also instituted a rule that neither of us would speak French until six in the evening.

Language helped us love each other better. In France we had English as our secret language, in LA we had French to talk about how the ticket-taking lady at the movies had a carnivalesque five o'clock shadow, or Lauri wanted to tell me she couldn't wait to make love again once we'd given the kids their bath. The two languages prolonged our stay in a romantic bubble, keeping the monolingual world, the French and the English, at a distance.

I had never fully moved into this new house. Though it was going on two years, all of the artwork from the old house was still in boxes. Lauri scolded me until one night we stayed up unpacking and hanging. I lost count of how many trips I made to Home Depot. She said the place finally felt a little bit hers.

The next day, in our room, right before heading out to the movies, she stopped me.

Trey, she said, I need to teach you how to kiss.

I frowned. I was forty-one years old. Never once had anyone complained. Still, I obeyed.

She looked me in the eye and kissed me, circling my tongue with hers. I mimicked her motions.

No, she said. *Plus doucement.* Softer.

I tried again.

She wiped her chin.

The outside of the mouth needs to remain dry, she added. No one outside should be able to see what our tongues are doing.

I was feeling very inadequate. I took a deep breath and tried several more times, never with the effect I desired. Finally, however, when I broke away, stepped back, and watched her, her eyes were still closed, she was almost imperceptibly swaying.

Très bien.

The marriage talk began jokingly, I think, but by late November we had set a date: July 10, between her sister's exams and her brother's. Her mother's family comes from Bordeaux and we would find a farmhouse there and get married at dusk and have one of those endless French outdoor tables filled with drunken friends, silly children, and an accordionist. For our honeymoon she wanted to go to Vienna. I was thinking farther afield—say, Thailand. She wanted us to start trying for another child by the next winter so Victor or Camille would be about the same distance apart as Ava and Chet. She picked Victor for Victor Hugo. I loved the name Camille, pronounced *CamY* in French.

She had a complicated relationship with her own two stepmothers and her stepfather and she was determined to avoid that with my kids. Ava was thrilled that we were getting married. Lauri would raise her hands over her head like a monster and march at Ava as she growled:

I am going to be your step-*monster*. Wahh!

Ava would cackle so hard that she would fall over. Chet was still too young to really understand.

My friends were not pleased, but I pointed out that we would have known each other for a full year before we legally vowed to stay together a lifetime. Still, they persisted in trying to bring me down. I finally had to shut them up with this:

Don't yuck my yum.

Besides, I didn't trust their reservations. Laurianne filled my every need in ways that Anna/Carmen had only before we had had children. Many nights, Laurianne bathed them both herself so I could skip off to yoga or finish writing. She cooked for us all—pretty badly for a Frenchwoman, but better than the boxed macaroni and cheese and the old baby carrots that I stuffed them with. We made love at least twice a day. Three times on the weekend. In the afternoon we would usually start somewhere other than the bedroom, then run there and lock the door before Carmen came in with the kids.

She had agreed to come to Social Circle for Christmas Day with the kids at Carmen's mother's house. Of course we'd stay in a motel. Then we and the kids would fly to New York to meet what was left of my family: my grandmother and cousins

in Philadelphia, my old friends and my play-uncles, my dad's
Howard classmates, in New York.

I know it seems too good to be true, I told my friends.
But there it is.

Fucking jog-a-thon.

The jog-a-thon was yet another Wildwood fund-raiser.
Tuition was just the beginning. There was the gift-wrapping
drive, the frozen-food drive, the pledge drive. And then there
was the jog-a-thon, where every kid in the school ran laps
around the field and each lap racked up another pledge from the
parents, grandparents, and anybody else you could rope into
subsidizing your child's private-school education.

Ava was thrilled. Her class had made a great banner and
they were to wear headbands and numbers like miniature mara-
thon runners. Carmen said she was too busy. Ava asked if Lauri
was coming and I was so pleased that I immediately asked her to
skip her English class.

Then that morning Carmen called again. Now she
wanted to come to the jog-a-thon. I knew Ava would be thrilled.
Carmen lived four streets away and asked if I could give her a
ride. I said sure. When I informed Lauri, she snapped that she
would go to English class instead and rode off in a huff.

I was a mess at the fund-raiser. I could not enjoy the carnivalesque cuteness, the hot dog stands, the churros, the athletic
director doubling as the DJ blasting raucous pop that the kids
jittered to as if electrified. Ava ran like a champ, her great pouf
of hair following her like flames. I had no idea that she could
run so fast. I kept calling Lauri, kept texting her, but nothing
returned to me except the terror of losing her.

When I returned home I found a note saying that she

did not want a *ménage à trois,* that I abased myself before my ex like a dog. It was late November and she said she would leave before Christmas, not after, to spend the holidays with her parents.

I howled. I raced my Mustang to her school and pleaded with the fat director to pull her out of class so we could talk. The bitch just stood over me as if I were some penitent wife beater as I tried to calm myself enough to write out a note. I told Lauri that I would be waiting in the parking lot.

She never came out.

This was Chetty's day off from preschool and Lucia offered to stay late while I returned to the English school when Lauri's class was supposed to be over. I returned home, again without her, and that's when I finally noticed that while I had been at the jog-a-thon she had brought back her bike. I walked the boardwalk, I walked Main Street, I walked all the places that we used to go hand in hand.

When I got home again, Carmen was there with a load of laundry. I told her that things had to change immediately. No more washing, no more using the kitchen for her raw food catering. I'd already talked to her about taking the kids overnight one weekend a month, but she had said her studio was too small. This time I insisted.

Carmen is not usually a screamer, but today she got very loud, very fast.

You stupid bastard! she began. Don't you see how much I do for these kids! The laundry is the least you could do for me! And just because some French chick comes here doesn't mean that I'm not still their mother!

Chet was on the floor between us, destroying a truck.

I picked him up and carried him into the other room.

Don't you ever talk to me like that in front of our kids, I told her. Not ever.

She left and I carved words onto a piece of paper with my pen telling Lauri that I understood and would fix everything. *Nous nous aimons trop de laisser personne nous separer. Restes avec moi! Je ne peut pas vivre sans toi.*[5]

Night arrived, but Lauri hadn't yet. She'd left her passport, so I knew she hadn't left the country. At seven she walked in the door and we talked for an hour, usually in French, but when I got really upset, I went Ricky Ricardo on her and broke into English. We made love, then she kicked my ass at Gran Turismo 2 on the PlayStation (Carmen's last Christmas present to me). Then sometime in the middle of the night I woke up inside her mouth. The next morning, as I was driving Chet to school, he yelled from the backseat, over the angry engine and the rushing wind.

Daddy, I heard you screaming in your room last night.

What?

My first defense was to pretend I didn't hear him.

We were now at a stoplight. All was quiet.

I heard you screaming in your room last night, Daddy.

It was just a nightmare, sweetheart. I'm fine.

The kids' room is on the far side of the house. If he heard me, then I was heard as far away as Malibu.

---

[5] *We love each other too much to let anyone get between us. Stay with me! I can't live without you.*

• • •

I HAD BEEN DETERMINED to always be with my kids on Christmas morning. Carmen had said that after her parents had divorced, Christmas Day had forever been ruined. I realized, however, how impossible it would be to please everyone. I finally decided to give the kids two Christmases. Lauri, the kids, and I had a lovely celebration at our house on the twenty-second. In all the years living in LA, I had never bought a tree because we were always down in Social Circle. This year Lauri and I picked out a seven-footer and the four of us hung it with lights, balls, and garland. She baked a cake and we opened presents. She got Chet a massive red fire truck full of oversized Legos and Ava, a fluffy, mechanical cat.

Then the kids flew to Social Circle with their mother. I talked to them Christmas Day and they seemed as happy and as excited as birds. Christmas evening in LA, I put on a suit and she wore a long dress and we exchanged presents and in the living room under the tree ate the dinner she had made.

On the twenty-sixth, I flew Lauri and I to New York with a stopover in Atlanta, where Ava and Chet's grandparents met us with the kids. Then my new little family flew on to New York.

In New York Lauri charmed all of my hesitant friends with the way she helped the kids in and out of their coats, tugged on their mittens, and adjusted their scarves. Everyone was rooting for me to have it easier than it had been.

The night before she returned to France for six weeks, we alternated making love and planning our future. She had come to realize that she did not want to raise a child in the States and begged me to move with the kids to France. I told her that that had been my dream even before I met her, but it was complicated. Their mother is here and for now she will not allow it. However, my fantasy, one that I believed had at least a forty percent chance of actualizing, was that Carmen would tell me soon that a guru on an ashram in India was calling her on the astral plane and that she loved the kids but her spirit guides demanded that she move very far away.

Also, I barely had enough work in America. In France I had not yet figured out how to survive. Still, I promised her that if she just gave me a year to scheme, I would come up with something. I always did.

We returned to our long-distance ritual of phone calls and the Webcam. After a few weeks, however, she seemed reluctant to get naked. I knew the distance and our problems would stress our bond, but she was coming back in less than a month and we would repair all.

During her absence I was as celibate as a priest is supposed to be. It was not always easy. Penelope and I had a long history of flirtation. She is a well-known actress and the daughter of Hollywood royalty, not Angelina Jolie, but actually more beautiful and better educated. To tell you the truth, no matter how friendly she had been with me over the years, I had always considered her out of my league. One day, a year before meeting Laurianne, I had run into her at our local ARCO station, finally cowboyed up, and asked her out, and she had said yes. She said she had always liked me. The next day, however, she called and said no. She had actually just met someone and wanted to give it a chance.

This time, while Laurianne was gone, Penelope invited me to a party at her house and it was really the first time that we ever spent a lot of time together. I felt myself falling. I felt that click. I definitely made a note to self: *If Laurianne is ever crushed by a meteor, console yourself with Penelope.* After my second mojito, my penis started trying to convince me that with Penelope it was tonight or never. Lauri would be back in a week and then I'd be married and the store forever closed. I tried not to look in Penelope's direction because I realized that her gravity was becoming inescapable. I thought about where Lauri was at that moment. Staying with Jean-Philippe, a guy friend in Normandy whom I'd never met. She was helping him finish a short film. Just a friend, she'd promised, although they had once slept together years ago and she had said it was awful. The fact that they had once slept together actually consoled me. At least between them there wouldn't be the thrill of the new.

Finally I made myself leave Penelope's party. I knew that in the movie of my life, if I was making love with Penelope, it would be intercut with Lauri bent over the bed by Jean-Philippe. I'm only superstitious when it comes to love.

Four days after that night, three days before she was to come back to me, I began my customary daily rituals. I hurried to the computer to read my good-morning e-mail from her and then see if she was logged on and I would switch on the Webcam for a quick hello before I had to run Ava or Chet to one of their schools. Of course this was between racing downstairs, dumping cereal into Chet's and Ava's bowls, running them upstairs to brush their teeth, and then downstairs again to ask Ava to go back upstairs again to change her dying T-shirt. (It's my favorite, Daddy. Yeah, but it's ripped and has a blue stain on the front the size of a quarter. But *Daddy* . . . ? But *Ava* . . . ? Up the stairs. Right now.)

On this particular morning the computer started up normally. It had been having problems and from time to time would get hung up or crash. I was in the habit of reading Lauri's e-mails last, of purging the spam and reading whatever my New York friends had written me while I was sleeping first, saving her words for dessert.

One friend had forwarded an animated George Bush singing a rap parody about global domination, another a game involving guessing which celebrity belonged to which celebrity breasts.

Finally it was time to open Lauri's and just seeing the subject line, *Mon Trey,* made me smile. The house was already immaculate for her. We'd stay in the States until June, when the kids finished school. They would go to their grandma's while Lauri and I planned the wedding. I'd fly back and bring them. Of course Chet would ring bear and Ava would flower girl.

Her e-mail began normally enough. She was asking me to forgive her for not writing the day before. She was in the middle of shooting her own short film, so was feeling overwhelmed.

Then she told me that she wasn't ever coming back. She'd canceled her ticket. She'd *beaucoup réfléchi* and decided it was better to end it between us right now. The reasons were obvious and insurmountable. She said she knew it was selfish on her part, but she knew in the bottom of her heart that one day she would leave and one day would be too late if we had children.

The kids were downstairs trying to eat out of each other's bowls. It had started playfully, but I could hear that it was degenerating quickly into a violent, messy battle.

Kids! Stop it!

I went back to the letter, an e-mail attachment a page long, single spaced, and found it elegant, truthful, and well reasoned. She wrote that she loved me but that she couldn't bear to live in the world I'd created with my ex-wife always underfoot.

Tu es fort et beau et intelligent, tu es un écrivain merveilleux et le bonheur va venir te chercher et t'emporter pour longtemps.

Prends soins de toi. —Laurianne

I couldn't stop staring at the words on the screen, trying to will them into reconfiguring into something less devastating. I hadn't been surfing in months, but one particular sensation I remembered vividly: being caught inside and the monster wave is sucking up all the water around you, rising up quickly, inexorably, to crush you with overwhelming force. I felt my sadness welling up just like that. It wasn't quite here yet, but I could feel it coming relentlessly fast and with a terrifying power.

Eew! Daddy! Chetty has a poop!

I have poop, said my little boy.

I hesitated only a beat, long enough to remember to breathe.

Come on up, Chetty.

I forced myself to sound relatively unemotional. He clopped up the stairs, I hoisted him on top of the dryer, laid him on his back, and unstrapped his Huggies. He smiled at me and I made myself smile back.

Hi.

Hi.

When I was done, I patted his ass and sent him back downstairs to his sister. Then I kicked the dryer and it clanged like a bell.

What's wrong, Daddy?

Nothing, Ava baby.

Lucia arrived to make lunches and drive Ava to school. I

faked small talk with her to get out of the house fast, and later when I was driving Chet, I was strangling the steering wheel, counting the minutes before I could crawl back into bed and sob. My own silence was maddening me so I turned on the radio and I swear to God the very first song I heard was the Beach Boys' "God Only Knows." I chuckled angrily, like a madman.

What, Daddy?

Nothing, sweet boy.

I dropped him off at school, smiling to the other parents. Amber wanted to plan a playdate but I ducked out without committing. I had to hurry home before the coming nervous breakdown rendered me incapable of operating a moving vehicle. Then I remembered that today was block-building day at Wildwood. The parents were supposed to meet their kids at ten and together we would construct some elaborate structure out of hundreds of wooden blocks. By now you probably realize that I get off on thinking of myself as a stoic martyr, so I felt absolutely, epically heroic swallowing my tears and driving across town to help my daughter build a sprawling Chinese restaurant out of tiny blocks and dowels.

I tried to stay there and breathe in the miracle of Ava's smile. As usual I was one of the only dads among all the moms, and she seemed especially proud. She wasn't just doing all right after her parents' divorce, she was thriving, like an exotic yet sturdy flowering plant.

Her father, however, was doing less well. This just could not be my life. She had said she couldn't imagine how Carmen could have ever left me. I rebounded from that devastation and fell into the happiest, most fulfilling period of my life. Of course I knew that our long-term prospects were suspect, but whose aren't? I flirted with the idea of calling Lucia, begging her to watch the kids, and flying to Paris that night. I knew, however, that was an act of madness even beyond the capabilities of my insanely immature heart. This was the only way that ours was ever going to end.

Now how was I going to end this book? The Bordelais wedding with the old guys playing the accordion and everyone dancing would have been so fucking uplifting. What now? If I killed myself, perhaps *Bedtime Stories* would become as famous as John Kennedy Toole's *A Confederacy of Dunces*. My kids would be ruined and would never again eat cooked food, but what if I won a posthumous Pulitzer out of pity?

It took me two days to be able to sit down with the kids. I picked a time after school, when none of us was particularly hurried.

Um, Ava. Chetty. I wanted to talk to you. Laurianne changed her mind and needs to stay in France. We're not going to get married but we'll all stay friends.

The kids nodded together.

Can we still go back to France? asked Ava. And can I have my birthday there again and can we swim in the sea and say good-bye to Lauri?

We sure can, my princess.

As soon as I read them their story and sang them their song, I picked up the phone and called Penelope. That was on a Wednesday, and she agreed to dinner with me that Friday night. I cackled, instantly again a winner. Before my friends could have time to pronounce their I-told-you-sos, before they could gather around and gawk at the romantic chainsaw juggler who had finally lopped off both of his forearms, I was determined to pull off the fastest heartbreak recuperation in recorded history.

The struggling French actress's loss is the famous and even more beautiful American actress's gain.

Thoughts of Penelope kept me alive throughout the week, although I wept daily and the check I wrote to Marta the housekeeper I first made out to Laurianne. I went surfing for the first time in months. I got washed and tumbled, didn't come close to standing in the choppy, wind-scarred slop, and yet I felt joy. I heard a laugh from somewhere and it took a beat to realize that it was coming from me.

Friday afternoon I read on the beach. I was to pick her up at eight but started getting ready at six. I prepared as carefully as if I were going to the Oscars—or my own execution. Mainly, I talked to myself:

If you fuck this up, Trey, I will strangle you with your own two hands. Do not mention what's her name, not once. All right, maybe once, because she knows that you had a French fiancée, and you need to make it absolutely clear that now you are free and clear. Your entire life has been leading up to this moment, as it does with every moment in the present, and your job is to learn from your vast encyclopedia of past mistakes. Try to be halfway cool, no matter how fucking difficult that is for you. Just keep your mouth shut and don't run on and on about nothing in particular. You know how childishly overexcited you get in the presence of beauty. And remember, absolutely no bursting into tears. If you feel you are about to cry, just coolly cover your face with a fake cough and excuse yourself to the men's room. She likes you. She has actually told you that she likes you. You have only yourself to get in the way. If you were a golfer, this would be the six-inch putt to win the Masters.

As always, I put the kids to bed at seven. They both like to whisper to me as I tuck them in. Ava fingered my shirt.

You're going out tonight?

Yes, baby.

Why do you have to go out?

Because I'm grown. You'll be asleep anyway. I love you.

I love you too.

• • •

WHEN THE FRONT DOOR OPENS on a first date it's like opening a door to an alternate and hopefully sunnier universe. Penelope looked so good I had to close one eye. I opened the door to my Mustang for her and we were both so sweetly shy. The seat belts are way back, no one can ever find them, so when a woman is in the car I delight in reaching around her waist and finding it for her. I know it's cheesy, like some swinging airline pilot from the seventies helping out the stewardess's golf stroke by wrapping his arms around her. I also find it irresistible.

That work often for you, fella? she asked.

Not often enough.

The drive to the restaurant was just ten minutes, but we complimented each other dozens of times. We were at a stoplight when she said this:

You have amazing hands.

Wow, I said. Thanks.

I spread them like stars on the steering wheel and wondered if just maybe my hands would be able to save my heart.

I am usually too cheap to valet, especially in Santa Monica, when I know a free spot is only a few feet away, but this was a first date, with Hollywood royalty no less.

The restaurant was loud, trendy, and new but our bubble was a vibrant peace. I held her hand to navigate the sea of singles at the bar while we waited for our table. Then, seated, we talked about real things: life, literature, relationships. With Laurianne, since it was all in French, I didn't care that we mainly talked about her career and the French reality show she was obsessed with, *Star Academy* (a cross between *American Idol* and *Big Brother*). Penelope was only four years younger than I, not fifteen. She had been educated at the best university in the nation, had been prelaw before deciding upon acting (against the wishes of her parents).

As we were talking, as I was looking at her and thinking that I would be staring at her even if she weren't directly across the table from me, as I was thinking to myself *I have never, ever been this close to someone so beautiful,* she rose from her bench, leaned across the city of glasses, cups, and plates between us, cradled my face with her hot hands, and kissed me deeply. Then she sat back down.

I finished whatever it was that I was saying at the time and then I said:

Excuse me? Did you just kiss me?

She smiled, nodded, and blushed at her plate. She was the lady, I was her tramp. Was I, Earth's unluckiest man, suddenly the luckiest? It seemed we could talk together, about everything. There didn't seem to be any aspects of myself that I felt I needed to hide for her to keep liking me. I asked her if she knew the Taoist tale about the old man of the steppes who finds a horse and she said she did not. I absolutely had to tell it to her right then.

THE OLD MAN OF THE STEPPES FINDS A HORSE

Traditional Taoist Tale

Once upon a time a wise old farmer who lived on the steppes awoke to find that his prize mare had broken out of the corral and run off. The neighbors cried, *Oh, what bad luck your best horse ran away!* The farmer, however, replied, *Who knows?* A few days later the mare returned and brought back with her a magnificent mustang stallion. The neighbors cried, *Oh, what good luck!* Again the farmer replied, *Who knows?* Then the farmer's son tried to ride the wild horse and was thrown and broke his leg. The neighbors shouted, *Oh, what bad luck!* and the farmer said, as always, *Who knows?* Then the local warlord raced into the village, conscripting all the able-bodied young men into battle. When he came upon the farmer's son and his broken leg he let him stay. His neighbors cheered, *Oh, what good luck that your son was spared!* The farmer could only answer as he had before, *Who knows?*

Penelope and I couldn't stop talking to each other. When I looked up it was two hours later and we were the absolute last couple in the restaurant. Back at her place we cuddled and kissed while her stereo randomly serenaded us. At a quarter to two she finally said she had to get some sleep. I offered to tuck her in but she declined.

It was really, really, really fun, Trey.

At her door we hugged. A long one. It was here that her demonic stereo decided to fill the room with "God only knows what I'd be without you."

Did you know that Brian Wilson wrote that song in seven minutes? At that precise moment it would not have been out of the question for me to have spontaneously combusted. Miraculously, however, I just laughed. Penelope frowned.

What? she asked.

It's just that I've had an amazing night.

I'm glad.

It wasn't until a full week later that I ruined it. She wasn't free again until the following Tuesday and then a big audition came up and she had to reschedule. I must have left one too many cloying, neurotic messages. She called back and said we should remain just friends.

Oh, how I howled at the injustice of the world. *Oh, what bad luck!* yelled the villagers.

I went right to the computer and looked at all of my pictures of Laurianne and cried so much that I probably became dangerously dehydrated. I cursed myself for not having insisted that she tattoo my name on her ass back when she'd wanted to.

I was making myself smile so much in front of the kids that I thought they would fear their dad had joined a cult.

As every parent knows, the bathroom is the only true sanctuary in any home. Unfortunately, kids also seem to understand that your taking a crap or talking on the phone is their cue to initiate a conversation with you.

Chetty knocked and knocked.

I'm in the bathroom.

He opened the door anyway and toddled right in. Though Ava was too big, he was still little enough that it not only didn't bother me, I actually wanted to model proper wiping so that he would very soon be inspired himself.

Why are you so sad? he asked. You miss Lauri?

Yes, I do. But I love you. I will always love you and I will be happy again soon. Do you ever get sad? I asked him.

Yes.

And then you get happy again later?

Yes.

It's just like that.

As soon as he left I vowed to get my shit together. Not only had I survived my mom's suicide, my wife leaving me, and the death of my best friend, my dad—I had thrived. I was just twenty-two when he died and I must say that I handled his leaving magnificently.

14

WHEN I RETURNED from Paris just two weeks after my dad had, he was noticeably thinner. We knew that was one of the signs of the progression of the disease. The whole world had seen the gray concavities of Rock Hudson's cheeks. My father, however, was not going to die. That was the only thing that I was sure of. Back in New York, every single morning I made him Cream of Wheat with a golf ball of butter and pure heavy cream. I served him in the bed that he now rarely left and scolded him mercilessly if he didn't finish it all. I held can after can of Ensure to his lips. I thought we were doing better, but his kidneys suddenly gave out due to a strep infection, said the stupid doctors. To clean his blood, they chose something that was new at the time, peritoneal dialysis, that you do at home four times a day for a half hour instead of the conventional hemodialysis at a renal center for three to five hours three times a week.

A catheter was inserted in his abdomen, and we had bags

and bags of dialysis solution that I ran through him. I carefully drained the waste bags into the sink. The doctors were pretty sure that the waste was so acidic that the virus could not survive in it.

My dad never would have come out to me if he hadn't gotten sick. I thought we told each other everything, but how could he have trusted the one big secret of his life to a kid who used the words *fag* and *faggot* dozens and dozens of times every day from 1971 to around 1977? However, after he confessed that night in Paris, I couldn't shut him up. While we were waiting for another bag to drain, he would talk and talk and talk. He started to tell me about some guy he had had a crush on while he was dating this woman who also liked that same guy.

I had to shut him up. Too much information.

I think he went into child psychiatry because he couldn't help it. He was so childish himself and loved every single little kid he ever met. He was not only my dad, but also the neighborhood dad, the dad to all my friends. For Thanksgivings after I got out of college, he always insisted on taking in all of my stray friends.

He was as vain as a movie star, inordinately proud of his freckles and hazel eyes. The first thing anyone ever said about him was how handsome he was. He often complained about how little money he got paid for being a shrink to poor black kids in Harlem. He said this to me more than once:

With my looks, I should've become a gynecologist.

After my mom died, I liked the image of my father as gigolo. When she was alive, I remember more than once catching him paging through *Playboy* at the Ridgeview pharmacy behind our house. I thought it was cool. I remember we were in Saint Thomas visiting my uncle. I was maybe twenty. An island beauty was mercilessly flirting with every man at the party. When it was my turn,

I thought that I actually had a chance. Then she flitted off to flirt with my dad. Afterward, sulking, I asked him what she'd said.

Oh, don't worry. I couldn't steal a girl from my boy.

As Christmas came, he got better, and my plan was for the cure to come sometime in the middle of the next year, say June of '88. In mid-January, when he went into the hospital with pneumocystis pneumonia, I refused to panic. The doctors had said that opportunistic infections were to be expected. Sitting up in his hospital bed, my silly dad found a nobility that I try to remember to borrow. He calmly explained that if the pneumonia didn't surrender to the antibiotics, he would have to be intubated and very likely would die. He told me that, at his memorial service, he wanted a childhood-friend-turned-opera-singer to sing an old spiritual, "There's a Man Going 'Round Taking Names," and he wanted to be cremated. I took notes just to humor him, but assured him that, as usual, he was just being a drama queen. Five days later, my godfather, who is also a physician, called me at three in the morning and told me to hurry back to the hospital. They'd backed off on the morphine my dad had needed for the pain of the breathing tube that was now down his throat, so for a few hours at most he would be coming back from that far-off place I'd seen in his wildly orbiting eyes earlier that evening.

When I got back to the hospital, his eyes were Caribbean clear, yet huge and eerily calm, though it was hard to see much of his face with all the white tape and corrugated plastic tubing. My fingers found his, and we just stared at each other as I cried.

I so wished he could still speak, because I was in no shape to say anything more than *I love you*. I'd turned twenty-three a few months before and needed him to know that I'd be fine. That he'd raised me just perfectly right.

I went home. A few hours later, he died. Four days short of fifty.

The bastards who arrived to pick up the dialysis works were dressed in hazmat suits. I wished for them painful, lingering deaths.

No one spoke about AIDS then. No one outside of a small circle knew for sure why he died. What's left of my family has pleaded with me not to tell the truth even now, twenty-two years later. But I want the entire world to wail at the tragedy that such a great man no longer roams the earth.

Seven years ago, I was diagnosed with focal segmental glomerulosclerosis of the collapsing variant (also known as collapsing glomerulopathy). It is the Cadillac of kidney diseases in that it is the most virulent, has the worst prognosis, and overwhelmingly afflicts black folks. The fact that I haven't yet required dialysis or a transplant (meaning that I don't yet have end-stage renal disease) is almost one for the history books. Early on, I told my wizard of a nephrologist with a wizard's name, Dr. Saleh Salehmoghaddam, about my dad's kidney failure from a bad case of strep made worse by ARC. He asked to see my dad's labs. My uncle dug up the old records, and I showed them to Saleh. Saleh showed me that my dad's T cells were fine until he went into the hospital for persistent anemia, an inevitable side effect of kidney disease. He received two blood transfusions, and almost immediately after the second, his T cells dwindled. He had contracted AIDS from that transfusion. The confusion was a blessing. If he had known, he probably would never have come out to me, and when he died, we would not have been so close.

15

I DON'T REMEMBER when it first happened, but I am pretty sure I first invited the kids back into my bed because I wanted to mope a little while longer before getting them ready for school. When Laurianne was around, I would hear their soft tapping on the door and sneak out of bed to let her sleep. Now they would burst in and again wrestle for the right to snuggle under a particular arm. If my vast bed was a sea upon which, with Lauri, I had the best adventures of my life, I would have been drowning in it now were it not for my two floaties.

Who needed a woman with such entertaining little ones around? Chet calls snowboarding *snore*-boarding. As soon as he hears a turn of a phrase, he uses it—almost always incorrectly.

You want a piece of me?!

He shouts this as he turns and presents a butt cheek.

Daddy, if I don't get a dessert, you bet your bottom dollar!

You know why I'm hugging your pillow, Daddy? Because it's got your germs on it.

I will never forget to forget to love you.

This last one he says right as I'm turning off the light.

The other morning, he woke up with a little hard-on and capered around the room.

My penis is so big! Daddy, look! My penis is so big!

Ava, always the skeptic, spun him around by the shoulders to have a look.

Bah! It's not *that* big.

Chetty, your penis is just right, I assured him. Now put it away and get ready for school.

So I was happy and busy with the kids and resolved that, even if the last half of my life did indeed proceed without a mate, I'd already had several greedy helpings of love. No longer would I be like Fellini's mad uncle in *Amarcord* who monkeys up to the top of a tree and screams, *Voglio una donna! (I want a woman!)* long into the night.

Then I happened to be at a small house party of a friend of a friend of a friend, and Pamela Anderson was also there, recently divorced, with her young son. I was changing Chet's diaper for just about the last time. We were on the carpet when she walked in on us.

Oh, I see you have your hands full, she said.

My brain rifled through its encyclopedic index of witty rejoinders to pick the very best one that would make her have to have sex with me.

Uh, yeah.

That's all I could come up with. And she was gone.

• • •

FOR TWENTY YEARS, MY RELATIONSHIP with Sally, the model/PhD, remained one of the great unresolved tragedies of my life. I had based a character in my second novel, *Home Repairs,* on her. We had once pornographically—but only verbally—flirted when Anna and I were dating but before we were married. Since then we had stayed in touch erratically, usually when I was heartbroken and wanted to see if I could coax her into talking dirty again. She would scold me and tell me that she was married and had two kids of her own. I published a precursor of this book in an anthology called *The Bastard on the Couch,* a sequel of sorts to the all-female anthology *The Bitch in the House.* I e-mailed her my essay because I still think about her, even after all these years, and even though we were only together a few weeks.

She responded, and this time our e-mails soon heated up. I was so damn excited! Not just because of the acts we talked about performing on each other's bodies, but because suddenly I'd found it! I had found the perfect, symmetrical ending for this very memoir. The very woman who had broken my heart and propelled me out of Manhattan and into the arms of Anna would return to me twenty years and four children later, and our new blended family would conquer the four corners of the known world.

Then one afternoon my cell phone shivered. I was in Paris, walking in front of Saint-Sulpice, deliciously melancholy remembering how Laurianne and I had rarely left her tiny bed in her tiny room in this very city. The sadness was fading fast now, becoming almost fun as the possibility of a new life with Sally bloomed in my brain. After all, it was here in Paris that I had been most in love with Sally (although she wasn't here at the time). My phone vibrated again, and although caller ID is erratic overseas, this call had Sally's Chicago area code but not her number.

I answered with an enthusiastic, Hello!

It was her husband. He asked me to never again speak with her and I never have.

· · ·

AND THERE WAS THE LOVELY, twentysomething yoga instructor. On our first dinner together, she told me that I would be only her third real boyfriend. Boyfriend? When did that happen? After our second dinner, she came over. The kids were asleep, and we made out a bit and she wanted to make love downstairs on the couch. I was hard and happy and ran upstairs to get the condom, but by the time I was downstairs again, a part of me had lost most of its enthusiasm. With Laurianne, we both got tested so I never used condoms. (I have to get blood tests once a month to check on my kidneys.) I tried to rekindle whatever magic we had had only moments before, but nothing worked. This woman was beautiful, my first redhead, with a long, sculpted body. But over dinner she had said phrases like, *When I meet your children,* and I knew that she never would. After Laurianne, I had tripled my resolve never to introduce women to my kids until after we'd dated for six months. With this woman, no matter how lovely, I knew we wouldn't make it past a week. I think all single people have their own internal Geiger counter that quickly estimates the half-life of a relationship with the current person they're dating.

I just didn't want to have sex with her badly enough to hurt her. She wasn't the only one. As with every new woman

that I spied at the farmer's market or checked out upside down
in yoga, when I looked at them, what I really saw was how they
were or were not like Laurianne.

Ornella fell in love and moved out. I advertised for a new
live-in babysitter on Craigslist, and almost a dozen applied.
There were two young Irish students who had already been au
pairs for several families, there was a Lithuanian girl with a
degree in early childhood education, there were others. I inter-
viewed them all and tried to divine how they would interact
with my household already crammed with women. With Laurianne gone, I allowed Carmen in the house more often, sometimes doing her wash here again when she was in between
apartments and living out of her car. And there was Lucia for an
hour in the mornings; Marta, the housekeeper; and of course
Ava, the child queen. I just wasn't sure how any of these new
girls would mix.

And then arrived Nora, twenty-four, who had looked
after a friend's baby a little. She is from New York, the place
where my heart still lives even after sixteen years in Los Angeles. She speaks flawless French, is achingly beautiful, and has
long, wavy dark hair.

I hired her immediately.

She was so happy and left to collect her stuff. I held my
head in my hands. Was I really that weak? Was I really capable
of inviting someone into my home to care for my two children
almost purely based on the fact that she reminded me of the last
great love of my life? I wanted to tell myself that even I was not
that nuts, to tell myself that I wasn't acting the romantic daredevil just to find the perfect ending to my goddamn book.

Carmen, understandably, insisted on meeting her. I

wasn't at home when they met. I was driving back from a promising meeting when she called me on my cell.

Trey, c'mon.

What?

Instantly I knew exactly what she was referring to, and my *what* was only my initial defense.

Look, she's cute and all, but c'mon.

She's taken care of a baby! I hollered. Our kids are big and just need someone kind who likes to play with them. At the interview, she played with them great.

I don't know who you're trying to fool.

A week passed. She actually was instantly at ease with the kids and delighted in taking them around the corner for gelato or up and down the boardwalk. After the kids went to bed, we would talk about contemporary art. I forced myself not to look too long into the depths of her eyes or else my balance would leave me. She had worked in galleries in Manhattan and had come out to Los Angeles to finish her degree. Like Linda, every morning she would leave her room in just a towel and skitter up the stairs to take a shower.

A week came and went, and I was so proud of myself that so far I had not yet tried to kiss her.

When Lucia met her, I was waiting for the torture, but she instantly loved her. Nora speaks Spanish much better than I do, thanks to a South American ex, and Lucia, Nora, and I would chatter and laugh in the mornings while we got the kids ready.

On the weekend, she showed the kids *The Sound of Music.* I vaguely knew the story, had heard most of the songs (Coltrane's "My Favorite Things" is one of my favorite songs, and I parodied it in *Platitudes*), but had never seen it. The three of them were hypnotized. I sat on the couch next to Chet. I pulled his thumb out of his mouth. I was trying to get him to stop, but he actually looks kind of distinguished with his thumb in his mouth, as if he is puffing away at a pipe. Ava was next to him and Nora was at the other end of the couch.

What a film! Romance, adventure, Nazis! Who knew?

Then Captain von Trapp waltzed with Maria, and I knew that this was *The King and I* with Linda all over again. What is it with Hollywood, single dads, and nannies? My body tightened. I slipped out of the room before Ava insisted that Nora and I marry.

Then one night Nora came home from a dinner with friends, her eyes sparkling. She'd met a boy. I was at once happy for her and jealous. She had met his father on their very first date, and he had asked about her father. I knew she had a complicated relationship with her own dad.

Maybe I could tell him you're my father, she announced.

I forced myself not to wince. I knew that it would be useless to explain that I would have had to have had her when I was eighteen.

I instantly thought about Ava, just seven, but how I so yearn for her to grow up to be as cool, put together, and kind-hearted as Nora is now. I would only be proud if someone confused me for the one who had raised her.

And just like that, I tucked Nora into a different compartment in my heart.

16

AND NOW, LADIES AND GENTLEMEN, for your reading pleasure, an article that I recently wrote for *Men's Health* magazine.

DATING OUT OF MY LEAGUE

By Trey Ellis

Growing up, I was an out-of-shape nerd with combination skin, a mouth full of metal, too shy to even *think* about talking to a real girl so instead conducted a string of intensely physical, serially monogamous relationships with the *Sports Illustrated* swimsuit issues and the scraps of pornography I happened upon by the train tracks down the road from my house. Little did I know that before my twelfth birthday the damage was already done. I had already cursed myself by having imprinted my neural pathways to only get fired up by women who were achingly—hopelessly—out of my league.

Not wanting to be a member of any club that would have me, I continued to retreat into fantasy. The result was that by the beginning of my sophomore year in college I was still a virgin. Driving across country to start the new school year and years beyond desperate to join the fraternity of the sexually active, I popped into the Mustang Ranch. Twenty minutes later I was back on Interstate 80, a hundred bucks poorer, but just as introverted and insecure as before.

Finally, however, the summer after my sophomore year, I was living in Atlanta during a summer internship. Friends of friends didn't know that I was about as experienced in relationships as the average fifteen-year-old so fixed me up with an older woman, twenty-something, who, when she wasn't a teller in a local bank, *was a cheerleader for the Atlanta Hawks.* Me? Dating a cheerleader? And not even a college amateur *but a highly trained professional.* In my (downright embarrassingly juvenile, superficial, stupid, sexist, you name it) book, that was one of those things that every real man must do before he dies— right up there with hang glide, own a Ferrari, and punch out your boss.

Our first real date was at the stadium for a jazz festival. I prepared for a week. I bought my first bottle of cologne (Drakar) from the department store, wore pants that weren't jeans for perhaps the twentieth time in my entire life, and was escorting the sexiest woman I had ever been in the same room with to our swanky box seats. I had made it. The nerd was dead. Long live Joe Cool!

Just as we were about to enter a shadow passed overhead. I had just stopped growing at six-two so was used to being about the tallest guy in the room so imagine my surprise when I looked up past her and saw some guy's head suspended somewhere around the stadium's ceiling.

"This your little brother?" he said in a voice so deep it shook the earth. Suddenly I felt about twelve and I could swear my braces had rematerialized in my mouth. The guy turned out to be a Hawks forward and our one date went rapidly downhill from there.

I am writing these words from my girlfriend's sprawling two-thousand-square-foot apartment in Milan. Rupa, the new, uniformed maid made us breakfast an hour ago and Cristina just told me that we've been invited to view the latest Gucci collection.

Ypsilanti, Michigan, this ain't.

Did I mention that my girlfriend is a countess?

We met almost a year ago because my career as a writer in the States was somewhere between the toilet and the storm drain. I had studied a year abroad in Florence and it has remained one of the happiest memories of my life so I seriously considered moving the kids and me back there. (Since the divorce they live with me.) Clay, my best friend back in college, had met an Italian girl and has stayed in Italy ever since. I e-mailed him and asked him to keep his eyes open for any interesting jobs. He immediately e-mailed me back that he knew this countess who was looking for a writer for her life story. When I heard the word "countess" I had visions of a fifty-ish Gabor sister with a tiara poked into a beehive of silver hair. I couldn't imagine wasting my time writing about some old broad's years fox hunting or smoking from pencil-thin cigarette holders or whatever it was that count-esses did in the twenty-first century so I blew her off. A week later Clay e-mailed me again saying she was a knockout and I had better get on it. Still, I wasn't con-vinced. I hadn't seen him in twenty years so had no idea of his taste in women. One man's Halle Berry is another man's Chloë Sevigny.

Besides, I was just recovering from a yearlong romance with a struggling Parisian actress/model and had promised myself to never, ever again have another long-distance relationship. I sent Cristina one formal e-mail introducing myself just so Clay would get off my back.

When Cris responded she sent back her picture so I would have "a face to go with the words."

Wow.

That's literally what I immediately wrote her back. For several weeks we e-mailed every day, then I called once, and then started calling every day (God bless cheap phone rates). In a few weeks Cris had decided to fly all the way to LA to visit me and I could think of nothing else.

Maria Cristina Margherita Savoldi d'Urcei

Bellavitis arrived dripping in diamonds and watches that I had only seen in magazines. I was an underemployed regular American guy and primary caregiver to a seven-year-old girl and a four-year-old boy. I booked the countess into the Best Western down the street. With both a continent and an ocean between us I was convinced (and my friends kept reminding me) not to expect anything more than a great story to tell about a wild week with minor royalty. She would go back to her castle and I would go back to hunting for a job.

I couldn't have been more wrong.

Since we had already spent a month getting to know each other before ever physically meeting, our relationship instantly took on more emotional depth than either of us had anticipated. Despite our differences in class, wealth, language, and geography, despite the fact that she is single and free while I'm a single dad, we discovered soul-deep connections so far strong enough to bridge even the vastest of gaps. By the end of the week I wanted her and was determined to find some way of keeping her.

"Cris" is not your father's countess. Though Fergie, the Duchess of York, has dined at her house and her cousin is a princess in Germany, she is a young, sexy, and elegant modern woman. Since that first week together, we have been together about two or three weeks, then apart a month, for over a year. Though everyone says that long-distance relationships can't last we're determined to beat the odds. We've both been married before so know what it's like to have another always underfoot. We miss each other terribly when we're apart but it is also so goddamn electric when we're together again.

Usually she flies to me, but this summer, while the kids were catching fireflies with their grandma on a lake in Georgia, I cashed in all my miles and flew to Cris and then we drove to Saint-Tropez. My Gap and Urban Outfitter wardrobe just wouldn't do so she bought me my first sport coat and pair of Gucci loafers. I felt like a black Bond escorting my blonde *contessa* to the terrace of the ultra-posh Byblos club to meet her friends just in from Monte Carlo. Though I tried to play it somewhat cool I couldn't help but gawk at a yacht in the harbor as large as my junior high school. Turns out Cris's friend Guido used to own it.

Cris is extraordinarily generous with me, the most generous woman I've ever known. She is also, however, nobody's sugar mama. She is used to dating men who drive Ferraris and Bentleys and who regale her with designer handbags that cost as much as I paid for my car (a '73 Mach I). So when her birthday came around I couldn't exactly pop into Macy's and pick up some perfume and a free gift bag (a twenty-dollar value!). Hey, did you know that while you're waiting for your charge to go through at Louis Vuitton the extremely courteous saleswoman will offer you a cappuccino, *free*?

One of the many magical things about women is that they're not as moronically superficial as we guys are. As long as we don't ever let them *know* that they're out of our league Julia Roberts will give a shot to Hugh Grant, the stuttering bookstore owner in *Notting Hill*—or real-life cameraman Danny Moder.

I learned this important lesson through pain. Very soon after that French actress I'd been seeing dumped me I had this fantastic first date with a beautiful working actress and daughter of Hollywood royalty. I *felt* out of my league even though the date was going amazingly well. In the next few days, instead of being halfway cool, I pestered her for another date until she stopped returning my calls. I felt like the kick-off returner watching the ball tumble out of the sky saying to himself, "Don't drop it! Don't drop it! Don't drop it!" then of course it falls right out of his hands and end-over-ends into his own end zone. I couldn't believe how stupidly I'd sabotaged myself. Then a few months later some friends fixed me up with a woman who, they said, had done some modeling. I was skeptical. What kind of modeling? Hand modeling? Cellulite modeling? When I opened the door to meet her my heart stopped. She wasn't just some model, she was an instantly recognizable supermodel. Years before I distinctly remember looking at her face on a billboard and thinking how unjust was this world that I would never get to go out with someone like her. Needless to say, after another great first date, I again pestered too hard and she lost my number.

With Cris I was determined not to fuck up again. I'm telling you, it was hard. Not only is she heart-stoppingly beautiful but she manages to be both extremely sexy and extremely elegant at the same time. In my more neurotic moments I wonder what could I possibly bring to this relationship that she couldn't get from the famous actors, athletes, and polo-playing captains of industry she was used to dating? Sure, I give great foot massages that have her purring like a kitten, but she has a professional masseur come to her palatial apartment once a week. Between yoga and the gym I think I'm in decent shape but her last boyfriend was an international soccer star, with, she once evilly mentioned, abs you can strike a match on.

In my most neurotic moments I feel like Porgy in *Porgy & Bess,* the poor, legless guy with this amazingly sexy woman. Everybody can see that it's only a matter of time before temptation gets the better of her and she runs off with Sportin' Life. Every time Cris introduces me to her guy friends with their Ferrari Maranellos ($292,730), their Bentley Continental GTs ($159,000), and their Rolex Daytonas ($10,000) I think about how much easier her life would be with one of them. She lusts after that sweet Bentley and I'm disappointed in myself that I cannot buy her one.

I know that there is nothing less sexy in a man than insecurity so I keep reminding myself that she chose me, the guy with the kids, the debt, and the New Age ex-wife who sometimes has to sleep on his couch. If Cris is crazy enough to put up with me, who am I to tell her she's wrong?

Ironically, I feel that it is this very unease that has actually helped our relationship. It has made us live for each moment because between the great distance and the great differences between us it seemed nuts to plan too far in the future. We talk openly and honestly and I admitted that I knew that if I didn't find some sort of great job soon we would no longer be able to stay together. If things didn't change I couldn't afford to be with anyone, let alone a countess in whose closets you'll find more fur than in a dog show.

Cris told me not to worry, that she brought good luck to the men in her life. I desperately wanted to believe her. I have been a novelist, screenwriter, and freelance journalist since my second year out of college. So many of my friends were all telling me that I'd had a good run of being my own boss, but now I had two small children to support. It was now time, they all said, to grow up and get a "real" job. They suggested I look into teaching or PR or law school. I knew they were wrong. I was just over the edge of forty, the new thirty, way too young to be forcibly retired. I knew that there was more in me to share with the world. Then I met Cris at the moment when I was least able to afford any girlfriend, let alone one on a first-name basis with most of the store clerks in most of the Hermès stores in Western Europe. Though what we had was so amazing and I had never felt so creative in my life, it was starting to look as if my choices were to retreat back to the Minor Leagues or work harder for this shot at the Majors with Cris, a place where I had always believed I belonged even when I was a kid having crab-apple fights back in the church parking lot in Ypsilanti. Dating out of my league brings out the best in me, makes me work that much harder and that much more determined to succeed.

Then, just last month, work started pouring in. I was asked to rewrite a movie and then out of the blue I got a commission to write an original play for Lincoln Center. There is still a continent and an ocean between us and two little ones in need of a stable home, so whether we can make this improbable relationship last or not, who knows. Yet the one thing I am certain of is that every day loving and being loved by this wonderful creature continues to raise my game.

Of course before meeting Cris, I had absolutely, positively forbidden myself to get into another long-distance relationship ever again. When I just mentioned the possibility, my friends offered to hook my nipples up to jumper cables in a desperate attempt at electroshock therapy. However, what is so much healthier about how this relationship began is that I had not yet seen her. You might have noticed by now that the compass of my heart is thrown off by outward beauty. My theory is that, as a writer, I view beauty metaphorically. Though the pictures she sent me were fine, for the most part, I still could not truly tell what she looked like. And of course I remembered the last time I had been seduced via the Internet and the future Mrs. Ellis had turned out to weigh more than your average left tackle.

Using written words to first get to know each other, for a writer, is a tremendous advantage. In some ways I could be more authentic because her live self was not in front of me making me react to her real-time reactions to my every phrase and inflection.

Also, since I didn't yet know her, both my heart and my libido were reasonably corralled.

I could also make the written me shape phrases for her from the persona of my inner Denzel Washington. W.W.T.C.G.S., What Would a Truly Cool Guy Say.[1]

In the beginning, we were still mainly discussing me ghost-writing her adventures and flirting only obliquely. She asked me what I thought our days would be like when she first arrived.

I wrote her that we would sit in my office in front of the computer most of the day, shaping the outline of her amazing diplomatic adventures in Libya. Then we would make love all night.

This exchange seemed to ignite a fire in both of us and for the rest of the month before she arrived in LA we wrote or talked very little of work.

Awaiting her arrival at LAX late in the evening, I felt like a pioneer awaiting his mail-order bride. I brought her not only roses but also a dozen Krispy Kreme glazed donuts because over the phone we talked often about her sweet tooth. Of course, I thought about the last time I stood in that airport with flowers, waiting for Laurianne to clear customs. I was much more excited than afraid, however. There is something so comfortable about repeating a journey, even one that ended in a fiery crash.

The first blonde woman who stepped out of customs made me gasp. Then I realized that she must have been at least sixty, and she hurried off. A guy with long hair again briefly triggered my sensors, and I made myself breathe.

When she finally stepped through the automatic doors, she was all eyes and a smile just for me. We hugged and told

---

[1]Derrida famously discusses the layers of authenticity between the written and the spoken self, contrasting his views with Rousseau's in Derrida's *Of Grammatology*.

each other innumerable times as we walked hand in hand to the car how weird this was; how we already knew so much about each other; how we already knew each other's voices so well, but our bodies not at all.

We went straight to her hotel room, took off our clothes, and almost silently made love. I think we needed to get it out of the way so our bodies could catch up with our hearts. Then we walked down Venice Beach to a late-night Chinese restaurant, returned to her hotel room, made love again, and nested until six, when I had to wake and rush home before the kids awoke.

Her second night in LA, she came over to my house after the kids had gone to bed and we closed ourselves in my room. Our hands kept playing with each other as I introduced her to *The Sopranos*. I said something that she hadn't understood and she purred, *Cosa*, baby? It was as if a naked Sophia Loren or Gina Lollobrigida had just asked, *What?* in Italian and then said *baby* in the sexiest Italian accent imaginable. My viscera liquefied. And yet she does not look like those actresses. She is my first blonde girlfriend ever, had short hair when we first met, and reminded me powerfully of Joey Heatherton.

That second night, now in my bed, I just couldn't believe that a few naughty e-mails could lead to such intense feelings. For a good hour that night, after again making love, I suspected that she was some sort of Sharon Stone in *Basic Instinct* psychopath or international con artist intent on emptying my bank accounts. I just couldn't get why she so wanted to get with me.

She had brought with her from Italy a gift for me, a kitsch pair of kissing wooden pigs glued to a heart that said *I Love You*. I thought it was suspiciously quick of her and again wondered if she were some sort of spy who had mistaken me for her latest assignment. And yet three days into her stay, while my countess was excitedly rifling through a bin of name-brand designer bras at Ross Dress for Less, I hugged her and whispered past a fat diamond earring and into her ear, *Io ti amo.*

She spun into my arms and her eyes shined.

Anch'io ti amo.

• • •

CRIS'S ENGLISH IS PERFECT, but for some reason we speak Italian together. Since the time I'd worked for Italian television in the eighties, I hadn't said much more than *What are the specials today?* in Italian to every Italian waiter who ever served me, and was amazed that she so effortlessly coaxed such a lovely language out of me again.

As the local expert on long-distance romancing, this time I was committed to correcting the errors I'd made with Laurianne. Although Cris met the kids early on, I didn't tell them she was my girlfriend. We didn't kiss or even hold hands in front of them for the first six months. During our probation, she always stayed at the Marina Pacific Best Western. Since she is much closer to my age, she actually understands how complicated successfully blending a family really is, and she was extremely cautious not to ever impose herself on my kids.

She did spoil us, however, with the best food I have ever eaten in my life. Although she's a countess by title, she's a regular Italian woman in her bones, and she stuffed us with lasagna made with fresh mozzarella from her family's series of farms and *cotelette alla Milanese* and our favorite, *moelleux aux chocolat,* better known in the States as hot chocolate lava cake. She's never once arrived in the States without some hand-prepared cheese or white truffle paste to make us some unforgettably wonderful meal.

Though she has never had children herself, she is a famous hostess in Milan, the Milanese Martha Stewart. On one trip when she saw that the preschool next door had thrown out a little bamboo hut, she begged me to restore it, and the four of us spent the day converting it into an island-themed lemonade stand.

The day some large boxes arrived from Amazon.com, she gathered the kids and told them they were going to build a rocket. I was in the back with the handyman trying to negotiate down the cost of the latest series of repairs. When I came in through the back, Ava and Chet were sitting patiently in their little wooden chairs inside the two cardboard boxes.

What are you doing, kids?

We're waiting to go to the moon.

Is it going to take a long time?

We're not sure.

Cris had so fired their imaginations that they actually believed that they were going to rocket into orbit. They were excited but unafraid.

Cris and I rarely talked about marriage, but we also knew that we could not forever continue being so far apart. As I mentioned in the article, we also talked honestly about how, if I did not find more and better-paying work, we could not continue together. She paid for most of her flights but not all, and though she's of noble birth, she still has to work to survive. She does many jobs, including public relations and event planning, but almost all of her contacts are in Milan.

For my part, I finally fired my agent. I thought he'd thank me, but he acted surprised and actually pissed off. Between the new agents and my own contacts, as I wrote in *Men's Health*, stimulating *and* paying assignments finally flowed my way again.

To celebrate our six-month anniversary, I sat the kids down and told them that this time and from now on Cris would be staying with us. They both seemed excited, not least of all, I suspect, because she always brought Ava a chic pair of boots and Chet a European soccer jersey when she came.

This time it was Chet, not Ava, who asked if they could still come in and cuddle in the mornings. I had to break it to him that I was kicking him out of my morning bed again, but they both took it well.

For the next year, Cris and I were pretty perfect. Sometimes we met halfway, in New York, and we would look for apartments. I had been threatening to return to Manhattan for a decade but had not yet figured out a way to convince Carmen to allow me. The more time I spent with Cris, the more I knew that I wanted to make a life with her, and moving to New York seemed the only way. The distance between us would be cut in half, and she could start spending a month with us and a week in Milan instead of vice versa.

When I mentioned the plan to Carmen, however, she assassinated me with her eyes.

You will not take my kids away from me.

She was cooking and teaching yoga for a friend's sister in exchange for room and board. With the threat of me forcing the issue of moving away, she agreed, finally, to take the kids overnight three nights a week. When Cris was in town, the freedom was fantastic. But usually she wasn't, and I just missed them.

For our first holidays together, I was flying to be with

Cris in Milan after having Christmas Day as usual in Social
Circle with the kids.

Here is what I wrote about it on my blog:

Christmas

On Christmas Eve I went to sleep with a big toe
that was bugging me, had I stubbed it very badly
but just didn't remember? Then, around three in the
morning I awoke to find my toe on fire. Odd, because
I couldn't actually see a blowtorch being held
against it but that's about how much it hurt. Was
it some sort of hairline fracture? How on earth
could something hurt so badly. I got to thinking
about Abu Ghraib and the limits of tolerability of
pain. In the movies they just pass out when the
pain gets bad enough. I was hoping for that. Didn't
come. I just looked out the window waiting for
dawn, wondering how bad it would have to get before
I should go to the hospital. Around five I decided
it was time. Walking, however, was a bitch. The
slightest pressure on that foot shot bolts of pain
through me that would have given a masochist
orgasms. I drove with my left foot the ten minutes
to the country hospital. I was here again in Social
Circle, Georgia. I just wanted to be seen quickly
and return home before the kids woke up to open
presents. There was no way in hell I'd wreck their
Christmas morning. The intake lady said gout. The
nurse said gout. The ER doc said bunion, gave me
a powerful opiate, and sent me home. We opened

presents with me on the nod, my foot up and iced. I left for Italy to see my girlfriend the next day, high, high, high and hobbling on a borrowed cane from my now-deceased ex-great grandfather. In Italy I called my own doctor back in LA and she said gout. Most definitely. It turns out that the pills I take for my kidney condition often cause uric acid to coalesce and it is the sharp edges of those crystals grinding against your bones that cause the unforgettable pain.

Oddly, I preferred having gout to a bunion. A bunion made me think of my grandmother's hammer toes, an affliction of the old and the poor. But gout? Gout was the disease of kings. Henry the Eighth had it. Thomas Jefferson and Alfred Lord Tennyson too. It was the price paid for a life of jolly excess. Cristina the Countess and I went to La Scala in Milan in a box seat, me still on crutches, and I imagined how many gout-ridden kings and princes had occupied that very same box over the centuries. The gout pills finally kicked in and by the time we were in Saint-Tropez I was fine. And a week later I was snowboarding in Saint Moritz. La dee da.

When I got back to Los Angeles, I was determined to move to New York with Cris. I had to definitively fix my life, and I knew that New York was the answer. I refused to allow my ex to shackle me to this vast, sunny, and rudderless suburb, a city that I have forever visited but never loved. Carmen, née

Anna, broke my heart once. I'd be goddamned if she would break it again. I could not wait for my fantasy guru to astrally summon her to Goa, Pondicherry, or Jaipur. However, I also refused to call in the lawyers. I would never put my kids in the middle of something so ugly. Whenever I bored my friends with my fantasy of moving back to Manhattan, they inevitably just shook their heads and said Carmen would never allow it.

It turns out, however, that it wasn't the astral plane but cyberspace that was going to make the impossible possible. A friend forwarded me an e-mail from a friend of his. The film division of Columbia University's Graduate School of the Arts was looking for an assistant professor. I had already loved teaching screenwriting at Sundance in Brazil, in Lake Tahoe, and in France (where I had met Laurianne). And I had always planned on one day returning to the university life that had formed me. Growing up around first the University of Michigan, then Yale, and finally Columbia was magical for me, and I needed that for my kids. If, somehow, I could convince Columbia that I was the right person for the appointment, then the central organizing principal of my life—that everything is possible with love—would finally and unassailably be proven. All of my life others have tried to convince me to corral my heart, and all of my life I have argued that true love makes you leap with such an intensity that you don't have time to look. Yes, she's a countess who's never had kids and lives six thousand miles away. Yes, I'm raising two kids, mainly by myself, and my income stream is as unreliable as life itself. And your point is?

Cris's hopes were as inflated as mine. She met me in New York for my first interview. I decided not to say anything to

Carmen. If I was lucky enough to get the job, then I would strategize later about how to convince her.

When they finally offered me the position in the spring, I sat Carmen down and explained that this would be a great adventure for the kids that she should not deny them. Her current boyfriend was a German meditation teacher, and a few months earlier she had suggested that we all move to Europe since both of our lovers already lived there. I reminded her that New York was as close to Germany as it was to LA. She could live in Germany or she could live in or around New York.

She said she'd think about it.

The next day, she agreed. She said she was tired of struggling in Los Angeles herself, had only stayed around so long to be close to the kids.

Wow. My plan actually worked. Now I had to actually go through with it. Now I had to break it to the kids.

It was over our traditional dinner of organic macaroni and cheese from a box and microwaved frozen broccoli that I told the kids that we were moving to New York City.

Ava howled and that made Chet howl.

No, she said firmly. No. No. No.

I'm sorry, baby, I told her. We're going. You're going to love it. I promise. It's the most exciting place in the world, and it's not so very far from here, but it's already halfway to France, which you love. All your best friends have parents that come to New York often, so I'm sure they'll bring them to visit once in a while.

No! No! No!

Over the next few weeks she calmed down, and I heard from Carmen, Nora, and Lucia, and her mother's friends that she was asking everyone she knew questions about Manhattan.

When Lucia told me that Ava had finally told her that she was scared but also excited about the move, I breathed.

For Chet it was going to be easier. Starting kindergarten is the most natural of breaks.

For me, the best news was that I finally had an ending for this book. Happily ever after. Cris, the kids, and I would start our new life together in Manhattan in the fall.

My countess is nothing like the duchess in *The Sound of Music*. She loves children, although she has never had any herself and has never really taken care of any. The plan in the summer was two romantic weeks for just the two of us in France (like the summer before, which had been another honeymoon, as wonderful as Sonoma with Laurianne, as wonderful as Fukushima or Santorini with Anna). While Cris and I enjoyed our freedom, Carmen would be taking care of the kids, showing them the wonders of the Rhine with her boyfriend. Then our big two-week test in Saint-Tropez *en famille*.

Carmen refused to take the kids for two weeks. She insisted that she and her boyfriend were working on a *project* that needed their undivided *attention*.

I argued. I railed. I lost.

I was almost two hundred pages into this very book, and it was due at the end of the summer. I was graciously offered an extension, but I would still have to write every day to finish by the end of the year.

Ava's favorite memories in her young life were her summers in France. The only time Chet had been there, he had been inside his mother's belly. They were as excited as bees to have me all day, every day, all to themselves. So was Cris. So was my laptop.

I was quite literally sick to my stomach most of the

month, satisfying none of them. The fight between Cris and me
began the day we arrived and continued like a river through
every day of the month. Throughout our relationship, we had
rarely fought. Though the distance was hard, I was beginning to
realize that, in other profound ways, the distance was also ideal.
When we saw each other, we were usually as intensely thrilled
to be together as that first day she had arrived at the airport.
Since she was gone most of the time, it allowed me to prioritize
parenting without Cris feeling slighted. This time, at the climax
of one of our worst fights, while the kids were downstairs sleeping, she spat out this: *I see why Carmen left you.*

Even just writing those words now has made me take my
hands off the keyboard and cradle my complaining belly.

At month's end, I flew with the kids back to Los Angeles,
and a few days later they flew by themselves for the very first
time from LA to Atlanta to stay with Carmen's mother, giving
me four weeks to pack up, rent out our house, find them a new
school, and resettle us in Manhattan before Labor Day, the day
after which the kids and I would both be starting school. I was
petrified to have them fly by themselves but didn't have a choice.
I bought them a portable DVD player to anesthetize them during the flight. I drilled little Ava in assembling and disassem-
bling the player's battery pack the way a marine learns to break
down and put back together his assault rifle.

Cris still planned on coming to New York for a week after
we got settled. I was pretty sure that that was not what I wanted
anymore. I loved her so much, and when it was just the two of us,
I enjoyed some of the most romantic and sexy, thrilling and wonderful experiences of my life. Yet in New York it would rarely be
just the two of us, and Saint-Tropez this summer proved to both

of us that in four we were not very good at all. If I was forced to make a choice, I didn't have any choice at all.

Columbia helped me find an apartment to rent. Manhattan housing is as scarce as white truffles, so without seeing it, I accepted the first place they offered. They also helped me navigate the school system, and I enrolled the kids in a sought-after public school that my various guidebooks told me was run like the progressive private school I was ripping Ava out of.

While the kids were away, I oversaw the prepping of our house for rental: the painting, the demolishing and resurfacing of the front courtyard with a full skip of pea gravel, the resealing of all the skylights and the roof, and the tenting of the whole thing for termites. I borrowed a friend's F-150 truck and drove away from Home Depot with hundreds of pounds of topsoil and more than a dozen ten-gallon containers of purple fountain grass. I had to pimp out my house so the rent I could charge would cover my terrifying mortgage. I was finally converting our large, architecturally significant but disheveled house into one of those groovy, cement, loftlike homes you see in *Dwell*. Too bad I was never again going to live in it.

I had been a furniture mover for Nice Jewish Boy with Truck in college and still consider myself something of an amateur expert. This would be my second move in the four years since Anna left. I had thought that I had traveled light to this new house, but I spent ten days just throwing away and giving away and Craigslisting almost everything I owned. The rest I packed myself, books mainly and the kids' stuff that I thought meant so much to them they would actually remember they had it (and would shriek if they knew I had thrown it away).

Emotionally, this was a much easier move than the one

out of our Santa Monica palace. I had been married in the other place and had sprinkled some of my dad's ashes on the hillside overlooking the Pacific. I remember trying to pack up the photo albums during that first move but found myself lingering over every picture, running my fingers over the extra wedding invitations that we'd saved.

This time I threw them in a box and sealed it with one noisy pass of the tape gun.

I was forced out of that home, but this home I was leaving freely. It was always just a way station for me.

I had called myself a single father since the night she'd left, but I had never truly been one. Carmen was around, and Lucia and the nannies, and at various times I had enlisted all my friends. In New York, however, it would just be the three of us. They are eight and five now. They dress themselves. They put away their own dishes. Sometimes. Chet was eight months old when our grand adventure began, and now he is growing into the most charming movie star of a little boy. He's like a miniature hybrid of Bill Clinton and Denzel Washington.

Ava has been a little lady since birth. She is sensitive and sensitive about her beauty. I am sensitive about it too. I flew back to Georgia for the three days around Chet's birthday, and we shopped for school clothes for Ava at the Limited Too at a mall in Georgia. I had been obsessing on the least painful way to integrate her into her new school, so I had become fixated on the perfect outfit she should wear that very first day. When I saw the glittering *High School Musical* T-shirt, I knew that I had found what I was looking for. Every tween in America had become obsessed with the Disney Channel hit, and her wearing that T-shirt her first day would prove to the hardened, gum-smacking, New York public school third-graders that she wasn't some sort of California weirdo.

There, in the Limited Too, I also realized that I have only another year before they stop making skorts in her size and she will insist on wearing full-fledged miniskirts. And next year might also bring those terrifying T-shirts with those built-in bralike things.

My friend Helen suggested that in a few years I should order a book put out by the American Girl cult that my daughter is enrolled in, *The Care and Keeping of You*. She said it would explain to Ava the changes she should expect at puberty.

Instead of waiting, I ordered it immediately from Amazon and it arrived two days later.

I opened it at random and found myself face to face with a two-page spread of a cartoon vagina.

I closed the book, and I don't think it made the voyage across the country. I realized that, unless I convert us all to Islam, my little beauty is going to make me suffer.

I put it off for weeks, but I knew that Cris and I had to talk. I still loved her so much. We still talked, texted, and e-mailed several times a day. However, we both knew that we no longer had a future as a couple. We both needed to be free to find better fits. I reasoned that since, like me, she's been married before, she also must realize that we live several lives before we die, and if we're very, very lucky that includes more than one love of our life. If it were not for Cris and the promise of her love, I wouldn't have fought so hard for my position at Columbia. For that, among a million other things, I will forever be grateful to her.

Much of me is still romantic, dopily, hopelessly so. I cling to my delusions because they warm me, not because I still believe

that they are real. I could spend the rest of my life watching
Annie Hall on a continuous loop.

I need the eggs.

• • •

I LANDED IN NEW YORK a week before the kids flew
up from Georgia. When I arrived at the apartment, brown paper
was still blue-taped to the floor and several squads of workers
were fussing over every room. I was staying with friends for
three days because I had been promised that in just three days
all the work would definitely be done. Unless this was another
Manhattan project, I doubted it. I pictured the kids going to
school powder-coated in construction dust.

I had rented out the house in Venice furnished. In New
York, I wanted to start new with new things. That super NASA-
certified memory foam mattress absolutely could not come with
me this time. Every day before the kids arrived was a race to buy
beds—bunk for them, king for me—dressers, a couch, and a
chair on Craigslist; getting cable and gas service; going to Bed
Bath & Beyond at least three times a day, plus Staples and Cir-
cuit City; taking the free bus to Ikea in New Jersey; scheduling
the delivery of the thirty boxes from LA; and going to Columbia
to actually start preparing for my classes.

Riding the number-one subway up and down Seventh
Avenue, I had forgotten about the homeless men who enter every
car and dramatically spiel or sing for change. The singers, especially, are almost always excellent. I had also forgotten how
many women there are in the subway who have the capability of
stopping my heart. Suddenly, a thought came to me that made

me laugh aloud like a loon. The old Greek guy next to me scooted away. I imagined myself entering the subway car from the one behind it and performing:

Ladies and gentlemen, excuse the disturbance, but I would like to regale you all with this simple song:

When I fall in love it will be forever
Or I'll never fall in love
In a restless world like this is
Love is ended before it's begun
And too many moonlight kisses
Seem to cool in the warmth of the sun

When I give my heart it will be completely
Or I'll never give my heart
And the moment I can feel that you feel that way too
Is when I fall in love with you.

I know the song is a lie. I have lived that lie. It is my favorite song.

· · ·

THE QUESTION THAT ROTTED me for weeks was whether I should send Cris a letter attached to an e-mail, as Laurianne had done. Should I call her on the phone? I loved her and have never had a relationship so honest and adult, but since we now knew that we couldn't live together, at least not until Chet went away to college, it wasn't fair to either of us to tie each other down.

I called and we talked. She was surprised, but she did not cry. Instead, in Italian, she said this:

Do you hear yourself? Do you hear how adult you sound? When we first met, you were terrified of losing me like you lost Carmen, like you lost the French girl, so you clung to fantasy after fantasy. You lived in your head and ignored what was real and in front of you.

I guess, maybe, I grew up, I told her.

Si. Adesso sei un uomo. Cento percento.[2]

---

[2]*Yes. Now you're a man. 100 percent.*